Emerald Labyrinth

A Scientist's Adventures in the Jungles of the Congo

ELI GREENBAUM

Emerald Labyrinth

FOREEDGE

ForeEdge
An imprint of University Press of New England
www.upne.com

© 2018 Eli Greenbaum

Manufactured in the United States of America
Designed by Rich Hendel
Typeset in Quadraat by Copperline Book Services

For permission to reproduce any of the material
in this book, contact Permissions, University Press
of New England, One Court Street, Suite 250,
Lebanon NH 03766; or visit www.upne.com

Library of Congress Cataloging-in-Publication
Data available upon request

Paperback ISBN: 978-1-5126-0097-1
Ebook ISBN: 978-1-5126-0120-6

5 4 3 2 1

To Wendy
for countless sacrifices
in support of my work,
and my African and
American students —
past, present, and future

CONTENTS

Color images can be found following page 174

PREFACE

At least one author has remarked that those who drink from the Nile are destined to return to Africa forever. In my case, the spell was cast in 2001 by the Niger—Africa's second-largest river—during my first jaunt into West Africa. The circuitous and unexpected path that first muddied my boots with African soil near that great river had a lasting effect on me, and time would prove that my professional focus would be centered, literally, in Africa. As I have discovered how much remains to be learned in my field, and how relatively few scientists are working in Africa, my career focus has progressed into a dedicated passion for scientific discovery in one of the most biologically diverse but unknown places on Earth. The urgency of this work is crucial, because explosive human population growth is driving deforestation, climate change, and other negative impacts to hasten the disappearance of the very biodiversity I am trying to discover and understand.

Many have mistaken this passion for a psychotic sense of adventure. "You're going to come back from Congo in a box," or some variant of this comment, has been suggested to me repeatedly by friends, family, and colleagues, especially before my first jaunt into Central Africa. Who can blame these well-meaning people?—the Democratic Republic of Congo remains a mysterious "heart of darkness" to many outsiders, even 118 years after Joseph Conrad's famous novella was published. Perhaps they have a point. As I will explain in more detail later, Africa's World War (a conflict centered in Congo at the beginning of the twenty-first century) left approximately 5 million Congolese dead, several dangerous militias linger in eastern Congo's jungles, and a sprinkling of landmines and unexploded ordnance persist in some areas that saw heavy fighting. Add to that a smorgasbord of crippling and deadly diseases, dangerously poor infrastructure, and at least three dozen species of venomous snakes, with of course no antivenom in the hospitals, and one begins to wonder if an expedition to Congo is indeed a suicide mission. Thankfully, several people and organizations either ignored the danger, were blissfully ignorant, or funded me to see what would happen, and I am eternally grateful to all of them, especially the ones who supported my first foray into Congo in 2007 (see the acknowledgments).

The primary focus of this book is the popular science of biodiversity exploration, and communicating this work to the general public. In 2012, I was awarded a grant (DEB-1145459) from the US National Science Foundation (along with colleague Kate Jackson) to continue my research on the amphibians and reptiles of the Congo Basin, and some of the results I present in this book are a result of that grant. As part of my responsibility for using American taxpayers' money for this research, I am required to engage and educate the general public about what I am doing with their funds, and in 2016, I started this process with a YouTube video to explain my work in laypersons' terms.[1] As aptly explained by the greatest scientific communicator of our time, Dr. Neil deGrasse Tyson of the American Museum of Natural History, "If you get tax money to do your research as we do in astrophysics . . . NASA and the National Science Foundation, then . . . it is not only your duty, it's an *obligation* to share the fruits of your research with the public. If the public does not embrace science, then not only does science go out of business—so does the public."[2] A corollary of this statement with relation to my own work might state that if the public does not understand biodiversity science, then continuing mass extinction, including the human species, is inevitable. This book is one aspect of that goal, but aside from the obligation, I truly enjoy sharing my passion with people. The personal narrative you are about to read is true, but because I wish to continue working as a professor in Africa for as long as my health and luck allow, some minor details (e.g., names of people) of the story have been modified.

Eli Greenbaum
July 2017

LIST OF ABBREVIATIONS

Alliance of Democratic Forces for the Liberation of Congo: AFDL

Amphibian Survival Alliance: ASA

Avtomat Kalashnikov assault rifle: AK-47

Centre de Recherche en Sciences Naturelles: CRSN

Forces Armées Rwandaises: FAR

Forces Armées Zairoises: FAZ

Institut Congolais pour la Conservation de la Nature: ICCN

Institute for Scientific Research in Central Africa: IRSAC

International Union for the Conservation of Nature: IUCN

Lord's Resistance Army: LRA

National Science Foundation (USA): NSF

Nongovernmental organization: NGO

Rassemblement Congolais pour la Démocratie: RCD

Rocket-propelled grenade: RPG

Rwandan Patriotic Front: RPF

United Nations: UN

United Nations Educational, Scientific and Cultural Organization: UNESCO

United States Agency for International Development: USAID

Wildlife Conservation Society: WCS

A NOTE REGARDING PROVINCES

In 2015, the government of Congo redrew the map of the country to modify its provinces and create several new ones. Because this story takes place in 2008–2009, long before these changes came into effect, I use the province names and boundaries that were in place at that time.

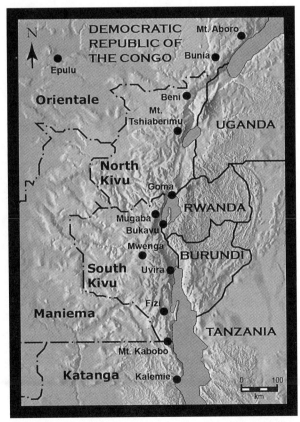

Map of the author's travels in Democratic Republic of the Congo in 2008–2009.

Emerald Labyrinth

NO JOY IN THE BRILLIANCE OF SUNSHINE

1 On a beautiful spring morning in May 2008, I was recovering from jet lag in the comfortable living room of an old Belgian house in Lwiro, Democratic Republic of the Congo (Congo for short). From my perspective as a herpetologist and evolutionary biologist, Congo represented the holy grail of unknown biodiversity in Africa, and I felt a strange intermingling of nervous excitement and weariness. My tired eyes lazily scanned the wall of large glass windows facing the front yard, when I suddenly focused on a perfectly round hole in the middle of one of them — it was a bullet hole — probably from one of the AK-47 assault rifles that are ubiquitous in eastern Congo. Although I had heard stories about very nasty militia in the area, I did not know the details, and I decided that it would be interesting and wise to interview the house's ancient caretaker Lyadunga about the history of Lwiro. Just as my exhaustion was starting to make me think better of this idea, a flash of vibrant color caught my eye on the side of the windows and I heard a loud *thwack*.

Too curious to ignore it, I stepped outside to the front of the house to see if I could figure out the source of the noise. When I did not see anyone nearby, I searched the flowerbed in front of the windows and discovered one of the most beautiful animals I have ever seen. Not seeing the glass clearly, a bird about the size of a baseball had flown into the window, and, stunned, it was now lying in the flowers. I gently picked up the bird so that I could snap off some photos, and after a few seconds, it had recovered enough to perch on my finger. The bird had a sharply pointed reddish beak, orange feet, a white and

orange-brown breast, and a gorgeous pattern of malachite blue and purple flecks on its head and wings. It was an African pygmy kingfisher,
Ispidina picta.

This particular species of kingfisher migrates within sub-Saharan Africa[1] and is a solitary hunter in relatively dry habitats, or if it is near forests it prefers clearings, which is why I happened to come across it in the
deforested area surrounding Lwiro. They like to feed on insects, aquatic
invertebrates, and frogs, and they usually breed during the rainy season,
constructing their nests at the end of a small tunnel 1–2 feet (30–60 cm)
long in the side of stream banks, erosion gullies and pits, aardvark lairs,
or even termite mounds. They lay two to six eggs, and both parents care
for the young.[2] Because the species has a large distribution, it is not considered threatened.[3]

As the delicate and resplendent creature regarded me with its large
black eyes, I knew I was experiencing an once-in-a-lifetime connection
with one of Congo's feathered gems. The unlikely chance of this type of
tantalizing glimpse into wild Africa had lured me here in the first place,
and repeated experiences similar to this one would continue to draw me
back. I reveled in the unpredictability of Africa and knew that at any time
of the day, a surprise could come whirling around the corner that would
fascinate, terrify, or assault the senses in some marvelous or horrific way
that could not be imagined before it had become an actuality. Whether
such occurrences would leave me feeling thrilled or literally on my back
was the fluctuating reality I would soon come to accept as the labyrinth
of Congo. I watched the fairy-like apparition of shimmering color recover and fly away, leaving a fleeting pocket of warmth on my finger,
a tingling of adrenaline in my legs, and an adventurous sense of hope
and imagination about the deepest parts of the jungle that would soon
engulf me.

For centuries, Central Africa has been a paradoxical combination of mystery, danger, and exotic allure. Before the first Europeans set foot on soil
that is now Congo in the late fifteenth century, imaginative European
bestiaries spread rumors about fantastic and mythical creatures, including giant roc birds that could snatch elephants, ants the size of small

dogs, and even one-eyed or three-headed humans, sometimes with the heads of lions. If these nightmarish creatures were not enough to dissuade intrepid adventurers, the Seas of Darkness and Obscurity along West Africa's coast were said to contain fire that rained from the sky, boiling oceans, serpent rocks, ogre islands, gigantic waves, and whirlpools with a one-way ticket to Satan himself. On the flip side, thanks to a forged, widely circulated letter, supposedly from a long-lost Christian king named Prester John to the pope around 1165, Europeans were led to believe that the king ruled over scores of African kings, centaurs, and giants from a palace with amazing riches, including the legendary fountain of youth.[4]

Eventually, greed and curiosity trumped the rumors of certain death, and in 1482 a Portuguese captain named Diogo Cão[5] sailed farther south than any of his predecessors. During this voyage, he was lured to the African coast by water that was dark brown, full of vegetation—including large trees, some even standing upright—and with a current that stayed strong far from shore. Cão had discovered the mighty Congo, the world's deepest and second-largest (by discharge) river, known to the local Bakongo people as Nzere (later translated as Zaïre), the river that swallows all others.[6]

Joseph Conrad famously described the Congo in his novella *Heart of Darkness*, which was based on his jaunt as a pilot of the steamboat *Roi de Belges* (*King of the Belgians*) in 1890:[7] "Going up that river was like traveling back to the earliest beginnings of the world, when vegetation rioted on the earth and the big trees were kings. An empty stream, a great silence, an impenetrable forest. The air was warm, thick, heavy, sluggish. There was no joy in the brilliance of sunshine."[8]

Although the rains fluctuate with the seasons in Central Africa, the Congo snakes across the equator twice, allowing its waters to be constantly fed by tributaries flowing from both hemispheres. As a result, the great river never suffers from major floods or low water, and has a strong current throughout the year, with an estimated one-sixth of the world's hydroelectric potential.[9] The river is 2,980 miles (4,800 km) long, 9 miles (15 km) wide in places, and originates in the highland savannas of Katanga province in southeastern Congo. The river contains gorges and cataracts that prevent navigation in several places, including Portes d'Enfer (Gates of Hell), Kisangani (formerly Stanleyville), and the Crystal Mountains to Matadi. The cataracts at Matadi were the main obstacle to exploration of the Congo's interior for four centuries after the European discovery of the river by Cão.[10]

Shortly after arriving at the mouth of the great river, Cão initiated the first interaction with the local Bakongo tribe, which eventually led to an increased number of Portuguese visitors, initially including many priests and, later, slave traders who were eager to profit from the growing demand for labor in Portugal and its newly established colony at Brazil.[11] As time went on, about one in four slaves sent to America's southern tobacco and cotton plantations originated from the Atlantic side of equatorial Africa, including the Bakongo kingdom.[12] Millions of slaves were sent from Congo and other areas of western Equatorial Africa between the arrival of the Portuguese and 1900, and the death toll from the slave trade was catastrophic, because roughly half of the slaves who were captured ended up dying before they could be "exported."[13]

Nearly three centuries after Cão's arrival, the Bakongo kingdom had been all but destroyed by corruption and warfare with the Portuguese. Intrigued by preliminary reconnaissance of the Congo River and its impressive cataracts, the British government financed an expedition to map the river and record the natural history, culture, business prospects, and slave trade in 1815. Led by Royal Navy captain James Kingston Tuckey, the expedition collected the first specimens of amphibians and reptiles from the Congo, some of which would be included in the first major work on Angolan and Congolese herpetofauna eighty years later.[14]

Tuckey and his team were offered slaves everywhere they went, and were often met with suspicion when they declined to barter for them. He explained that "domestic" slavery would probably not disappear if the Europeans abolished slavery, but the Africans he spoke to all agreed that if white men did not come for slaves, the common practice of kidnapping would vanish, and wars would become less frequent. In a fate that would befall countless subsequent European visitors to the Congo, Tuckey and seventeen of his companions, including all of the scientists, died within the three-month duration of their exploration of the river.

Four of these men were killed during an attack on one of the expedition's boats, but the rest seem to have perished from yellow fever.[15]

By 1840, the British Royal Navy was trying, with mixed success, to clamp down on the transatlantic slave trade south of the equator. Within four more decades, the British had an extensive operation on the Congo River, trading in ivory, copper, and palm oil to the tune of £2 million per year. The British seem to have treated the Congolese relatively fairly in their business dealings, but the slave trade with other Europeans continued. An increasing number of European and American missionaries became active at this time as well. Although some exploration of the Congo River continued by intrepid explorers, including the self-described "amateur barbarian" Sir Richard Burton,[16] few Westerners were able to explore beyond the Matadi cataracts, and the vast majority of the Congo remained a blank, unexplored spot on the map of Africa for decades.[17] None of them could have imagined that in the following century and beyond, people would *fly* to Africa at astonishing speeds.

——————

Shortly before my encounter with the kingfisher, I had spent about two days on planes originating in New York City and a restless night's layover in Kigali (the capital of Rwanda) before descending from the customs office of the small airport at Cyangugu, Rwanda, on the border with Congo. I had not slept much during the draining journey to Africa, but I was energized by the prospect of spending ten weeks in the most remote and beautiful parts of the country to look for rare and new species of animals and unlock the secrets of their evolutionary history. As I emerged from the small building next to the airstrip with my luggage, I was hit by a blast of hot and humid air, piercing sunlight, and the quintessentially African smell of burning wood. Two smiling men met me outside. Chifundera Kusamba, my colleague and logistics leader, shook my hand and greeted me enthusiastically. Incredibly fit for a man approaching sixty, his youthful appearance and boundless energy made me guess he was at least fifteen years younger when I had first met him in Congo the year before. Mwenebatu Aristote, a stocky and charismatic man in his late twenties, fluent in five languages, also bid me welcome. We had all worked together the previous year in Kahuzi-Biega National Park, where I had made a preliminary survey of the amphibians and reptiles (herpetofauna) only a few hours north of the regional capital of Bukavu, which is located on Lake Kivu's southwestern shore just across the border from Cyangugu.

"You are so fat! What are you eating in America?" teased Aristote.

"I am working too much in America," I explained. "I sit at a lab bench all day, eat too much bad food, and so now I am fat." Physically, I was the epitome of the typical American, and certainly fat by Congolese standards.

"Do not worry. Soon you will eat good Congolese food, and we will walk to Itombwe, and then you cannot be fat." I could not foresee then how right he would be about that latter point. Aristote was a member of the Babembe[18] tribe in the Itombwe Plateau, a rugged group of mountains west of Lake Tanganyika. He was also an undergraduate student in biology, an ex-commander of the Mai-Mai militia during the recent war, and an incorrigible flirt with every attractive young lady who ran into our expedition.

We piled into a taxi for the short drive to the border via a winding road adjacent to the shimmering blue water of Lake Kivu, the last of Africa's great lakes to be discovered by Westerners in 1894. The ruins of several colonial-era hotels, businesses, and houses could be seen nestled into the hillside adjacent to the lake, but some newer buildings and poorly constructed shacks were all along the waterfront. Here and there I noticed beautiful trees that seemed out of place, lonely remnants of the forest that once flanked the lake long ago. The majority of the natural lakeside vegetation is now replaced by an ugly combination of cassava or banana crops, spindly Australian eucalyptus trees, or grass with patches of natural reeds at the shore. Sprinkled near the ruins of the colonial houses were overgrown flowers of all kinds — lantana, bougainvillea, cannas, and other colorful calling cards of European colonists that had survived decades of the African climate when most of the buildings had not. After ten minutes we arrived at the border of Congo, and following the requisite form and exit passport stamp from the Rwandans, I was walking on a rickety wood-and-metal bridge over the Ruzizi River, which connects Lakes Kivu and Tanganyika. There was a light rain, and my boots were covered with light brown mud by the time I approached the Congolese customs building about half a mile (1 km) away.

I was only a few hundred feet away from Rwanda, but already I could feel the difference between the countries. The potholes in the decaying pavement were much worse, and there was trash everywhere on the sides of the road. The poverty was viscerally obvious. I looked at the weathered and resigned faces of the women selling bananas and vegetables on the side of the road. Drenched from the rain, they half-heartedly raised their commodities and shouted out inflated prices to me, and as I politely refused, the asking prices quickly degenerated to almost nothing. Men with legs crippled by polio used their arms on converted bicycle parts to pedal themselves on makeshift wooden carts with small loads of goods or luggage, often with a young boy helping to push them along. Barefoot elderly women carried enormous loads of vegetables, firewood, or bamboo and were hunched over so much from the weight that their bodies approached a right angle as they slowly shuffled along the gentle incline of the road. Children with cheap flip-flops in tattered rags followed in the wake of their families, carrying smaller loads either dangling by thin straps on their backs or balanced on their heads.

"Muzungu, ange!" (White man, take care!), shouted a man in Swahili as I wandered too close to his wheelbarrow. *Muzungu* was a word that I had heard many times before and would hear countless times again during my time in Congo. It was a constant reminder that I was an outsider, and depending on the viewpoint of the people shouting it, this word could denote amusement, friendly curiosity, an expectation of a handout, suspicion, or fear.

As I approached the border and customs building with Chifundera, Aristote, and a couple of porters with my luggage expertly balanced on their heads, a woman in a white doctor's jacket approached me and asked for my yellow fever card, a document as essential as a passport to enter tropical African countries. Without a word she took the card and ducked into a small building to register my information. Currently endemic to Africa and Latin America (the disease was introduced from its source in Africa to the New World via the slave trade hundreds of years ago), yellow fever is a mosquito-borne virus that causes hemorrhagic fever and is almost always fatal in unvaccinated travelers from temperate regions. Early symptoms and mild cases include fever, head and body aches, and chills. After a few days this can progress to the deadly toxic phase of the disease, including severe abdominal pain; kidney and liver failure; bleeding from the mouth, eyes, and nose; stomach bleeding with severe vomiting; meningitis; and jaundice—a yellowish pigmentation of the skin and eyes, which gives yellow fever its name. Death follows the final stages of shock, delirium, stupor, and coma.[19]

While I waited on the side of the road for the woman to reappear with my vaccination card, the rain stopped and I noticed all the pass-ersby staring at me. There were plenty of non-African people in eastern Congo—about twenty thousand United Nations (UN) troops had been there to keep the fragile peace since the official end of the war in 2003—but perhaps I stood out because I was on foot and not in an expensive vehicle, I was not wearing a uniform, and I had a large brimmed hat to prevent my fair skin from burning to a crisp. My pants were tucked inside large brown canvas and leather snake-proof jungle boots, which came up to my knees to prevent ants and other biting pests from accessing my legs and to make it easier to remove the mud that would invariably ap-pear in heavy amounts whenever it rained in Congo. Although the rain-forest at Bukavu was destroyed long ago, the streets oozed with mud whenever the smallest bit of rain fell, and this would mix with the ubiq-uitous trash to create a slippery sludge. After a heavy rain, one's senses could be assaulted by a combination of the earthy water-soaked African soil, open sewage, rotting food, and other noisome trash. There was also a constant and permeating smell of burning charcoal or wood, used for cooking and heating by nearly every household. Sometimes large heaps of trash would be seen burning on the side of the road in an effort to eliminate the accumulation of waste.

My vaccination card was handed back to me, and I was motioned to the larger adjacent building for immigration and customs. The old Bel-gian buildings were easy to spot: all of them had arched entryways and metal-framed doors with glass windows. Chifundera guided me inside and translated as the requisite questions were asked by a dour immigra-tion official in a sharp Armani-like suit, who slouched behind an old wooden desk.

"Nyoka!" he exclaimed as Chifundera told him my business. This is the Swahili word for snake, and like almost any place in the world, snakes often elicit gesticulations of horror. The official launched into a story about some particularly nasty experience he had suffered at the figurative hands of a snake, and then he expressed concern that I would be killed if I were to continue with my plans to look for them. His eyes widened with shock as Chifundera assured him that he could handle snakes without harm and that he would look out for the crazy muzungu next to him. Somehow (likely at my expense) after a few jokes and several more minutes of talking, Chif and the official were laughing like old friends, and my passport was stamped to allow me on my way.

We stepped out of the building into the now blinding sun and steam bath of humidity, and I could see the porters impatiently waiting for us as Aristote held the hand of a girl while attempting to woo her. Chif shouted orders at everyone with an annoyed gesture, and then after crossing the final barrier to the city of Bukavu (a rusty old road gate), I was accosted by a small army of vendors, money exchangers, taxi drivers, and beggars looking for a quick buck. Wanting to be polite, but feeling overwhelmed, I mumbled, "Non, merci" (no, thank you) as I tried to wave everyone off to get to the taxi that Chif had selected for our transport to his house. The smell of vendor's fruit, putrid fish, and human bodies that had not bathed for days lingered in my nostrils as I muscled my way through the crowd to a small car with a suspiciously head-shaped crack in the windshield. I could barely hear the greeting of the driver as I deposited myself in the passenger seat next to him, because of his radio, which was blaring out Congo's popular rumba music through blown speakers.

Aristote appeared at the opposite window long enough to ask the driver to pop the trunk for my luggage. A sharp tapping noise at my window startled me, and I turned to see somebody smearing some kind of juicy tropical fruit against the glass and shouting out prices in French. Several people were jockeying for my attention, but it was the sickly and crippled beggars that caught my eye and tugged at my heartstrings. I lowered my window long enough to hand out a few dollars, and then I started hearing shouting coming from the back of the car. The porters had apparently changed their mind about the salary that had been negotiated when they were hired in Rwanda only fifteen minutes ago, and I could see Chif wagging his finger at them with disapproval. Aristote was throwing in his two cents in between the shouting, and then as quickly as the dispute started, all the yelling stopped, Chif waved his hand at them with a dismissive gesture as they were paid, and we sped away from the border.

The city we entered had been a village ruled by noblemen of the Bushi kingdom when the first Arab slavers and Europeans arrived in the second half of the nineteenth century. In the following century, the Belgians named the place Costermansville for Paul Costermans, a prominent government inspector and one of the original architects of the Congo Free State,[20] but the name reverted back to Bukavu in 1953. Known then as the "Switzerland of Central Africa," the city was powered by a hydroelectric dam at Ruzizi Falls, and it still has scores of beautiful Belgian mansions with lush gardens that lie on five peninsulas near the southern shore of Lake Kivu—the peninsulas have been likened to a verdant hand dipped in the lake.[21] At 4,921 feet (1,500 m) elevation, Bukavu often has spring-like weather, and a tourist guide from 1956 boasted, "During the rainy season the vegetation is luxuriant, the hills are green, the air is clear, the light intense, and visibility extends to the volcanoes in the north of the Kivu."[22] The city was a major trading center in the colonial era until it was overtaken commercially by Goma on the northern shore of Lake Kivu in the 1970s.[23] Bukavu currently has more people—according to some estimates, around 1 million.[24]

Because the roads of the city, and most of the country for that matter, have not been repaired in decades, I saw enormous potholes and cracks everywhere as our car drove along. At times the driver would swerve around them, narrowly missing other beeping, oncoming vehicles that were also zigzagging among the pitfalls, and at other times, he would hit the brakes so that the car could gently dip into particularly large and deep furrows in the road. At roundabouts, police with prominent yellow helmets blew their whistles and gesticulated at the traffic, pulling hapless drivers to the side of the road to ensure their paperwork was in order. Enormous and overloaded lorries and smaller pickup trucks with scores of people on them hobbled along the roads while belching out huge clouds of black smoke from crippled engines. Dozens of mo-

A glimpse of Bukavu at Lake Kivu near the Congo/Rwanda border, with one of the five peninsulas composing the city's "verdant hand."

torcycle taxis carried two or three helmetless passengers at a time as they honked their horns and weaved among traffic. Pickup trucks and large lorries full of soldiers in army uniforms with AK-47 assault rifles strapped over their shoulders could be seen here and there in the blur of movement. We passed by a UN building with a high wall and razor wire around its periphery, with a bored Pakistani soldier manning a machine gun in a guard tower. The UN soldiers sprinkled throughout the city were conspicuous in their blue helmets or berets and camouflage fatigues and their shiny new white trucks, "UN" painted on the doors in large black letters.

In the chaotic traffic, people attempted to dash across the road on foot, sometimes with babies strapped to their backs, or with enormous loads balanced on their heads. After skirting through a roundabout with peddlers selling fruit, cigarettes, sodas, and stale cookies at its periphery, we reached the city prison, an imposing edifice of rock and steel that had been built by the Belgian colonizers.

I gestured to the prison and said, "Aristote, do you need to stop at your house to greet your friends?" Chifundera grinned at the joke.

"Noooooooooo, that is not my house!" Aristote retorted. "Maybe if the muzungu is bad on this trip, that can be *your* house!"

As the car slowly climbed the steep road, we passed people shuffling along both sides of the road. Some men were wearing suits, usually a size or two too big, with the bottom of their pants and shoes covered in mud. Schoolchildren wore blue pants or skirts with crisp white shirts. Affluent women wore colorful kitenge (the African version of a sarong) with matching elaborate head wraps, sometimes with a baby wrapped in cloth around their midsection and straddling their hips from the back. The poorest people shuffled along barefoot in faded and torn rags, often with T-shirts that had obviously been discarded from the United States. We were on the street that led to Chif's house, where he lived with his wife and five teenage children.

"Chif, so how is the truck?" I asked. Several weeks before, I had wired a small fortune to him to repair a Toyota 4×4 that we were going to use for our ambitious field season. I had assumed it would be ready now.

"Ahhh, well the mechanic is working on the truck now," Chif said. Bad sign, I thought. "Maybe it can be ready tomorrow," he continued, "but I think now we can get another taxi to go to Lwiro, and then I can return to fetch the truck when it is ready tomorrow . . . or the next day."

Lwiro is a small town about a two-hour drive north of Bukavu on the curvy road that skirts along the western edge of Lake Kivu. Just after the end of World War II the Belgians built an enormous scientific research center at Lwiro that was the headquarters of the Institute for Scientific Research in Central Africa (IRSAC). In the 1950s, the center had state-of-the-art research facilities for biology, zoology, botany, tropical disease, geophysics, cartography, and nutrition, and some of the Belgian scientists trained Congolese students. There was a large guest house for visiting scientists, weekly movies and social events, numerous houses where the Belgians could live with their families, a well-stocked library with beautiful mahogany woodwork that rivaled the finest in Europe, modern hospital, school, large machine shop for mechanical repairs, tennis court, and even a kidney-shaped swimming pool fed by warm water from an underground hot spring. At the nearby site of Tshibati, there was an "experimental zoology farm" with captive-breeding programs for buffalo, eland (a large antelope species), and primates, including one of the earliest successful efforts to breed the mountain gorilla in captivity.[25] The Belgians fled during the violent aftermath of independence in the 1960s, and the infrastructure of the center slowly started to deteriorate as it was starved of funding and attention. Subsequent raids by militia during the war made things worse, but much of the place has survived reasonably intact, almost frozen in time from the 1950s.

After the colonial era, it was renamed the Centre de Recherche en Sciences Naturelles (CRSN), and Congolese scientists continued the scientific work of their predecessors with funds from international grants and collaborators whenever possible; until recently the Congolese government had provided little financial support. Chifundera was the only herpetologist on duty there, and he had one of the old Belgian houses at his disposal. Few foreign biologists traveled to Congo to establish collaborations after colonialism ended, and Chifundera had been very excited to find a herpetologist to work with him when we first exchanged emails. I had been just as eager to work with him, and I had stayed at his house in Lwiro during my initial expedition the previous year. I assumed I would be staying at the same place when I returned this year.

I told Chif that I was concerned we were losing time waiting for the truck to be repaired but that it was okay to go to Lwiro straight away so that I could start doing some work. Preliminary analyses of the specimens and DNA samples I had analyzed from the woodland/agricultural landscape at Lwiro and the nearby secondary montane forest at Tshibati the previous year suggested that some new species of spiny reed frogs were present in the area, and with additional specimens and data, it would be possible to describe them in future scientific publications. I knew I would be jet-lagged for a few days, so perhaps it was just as well that I would be forced to rest on a reasonably comfortable bed until my body could catch up to my present African reality.

When we arrived at the impressive gates to CRSN in the early afternoon, Chifundera confidently gestured to the gatekeeper, and we were waved through along a road of loose rocks and potholes past the large guest house and main research center to a little driveway. It was next to a beautiful tree that had spindly vines tussled around its trunk. When I commented that I did not recognize the place, Chif informed me that the administration had deemed my continued interest in CRSN to be important enough to warrant new accommodations at the former director's house. Aristote would watch over me, and I would meet a new cook that Chif had hired to keep the team fed for the rest of the expedition.

The house, located in the middle of a small clearing on a hill and surrounded by beautiful flowers and trees, was impressive. Two stories tall, it had three large bedrooms, a white brick facade with three large windows, and a 2-foot-tall (0.6 m) stone trim at its base; and the old clay roof tile, typical of all colonial-era Belgian buildings, had been replaced with a sharp-looking red metal roof. There was an enormous covered garage adjacent to the main entrance to the house, which had an equally impressive wooden door that was at least 4 feet (1.2 m) wide and 8 feet (2.4 m) tall. The house had an attractive stone-like tile floor with mahogany woodwork throughout, and each of the three bedrooms had its own sink (no mirror), toilet (without a seat), and bathtub, all of which are rare luxuries in Congo. Although the upholstery on the furniture was torn or faded in some places, the decorations and furnishings of the house seemed to be untouched from the way they had been in the late 1950s. The original light fixtures on large black iron candelabras were still working, and a spacious fireplace in the living room suggested the house had been a nice place to socialize during the chilly evenings in Lwiro, which sits at a relatively high elevation (ca. 5,500 feet, 1,700 m) in the Mitumba Mountains. The caretaker of the house was a diminutive, barefoot old man named Lyadunga who looked to be in his eighties, and he politely showed me into one of the bedrooms so that I could rest after my long journey. Exhausted, I spread out on the bed and dozed off.

I awoke with a start at dusk to the sound of heavy rain on the metal roof and flashes of lightning flickering through the windows. For a few moments I stared at the pattern of cracked paint, mold, water stains, and spiderwebs on the neglected walls of the room and struggled to shake off the weariness of my travels. I emerged from the bedroom to find Aristote and Chifundera eating a meal of cassava, goat meat, and tomato sauce by candlelight, and they invited me to join them. Eaten alone, cassava has the consistency and taste of what I would expect from cardboard, and its modest caloric content burns away quickly. But together with goat meat and a decent tomato and onion sauce, it can be a delicious meal. Acknowledging my addiction to soda, the men had left a semi-cool bottle of Coke for my meal, which energized me so much I was ready to start working when we were finished. Flashes of lightning sent flickering strobes of illumination on the lawn and trees around the house, but I could see the rain was diminishing—perfect conditions for nocturnal frogs.

Because Interahamwe militia, major perpetrators of the Rwandan Genocide, and petty thieves were still active in the area from time to time, we set off just after dusk accompanied by a soldier armed with an AK-47. Like all well-equipped herpetologists who work with nocturnal species, we had headlamps strapped to our heads so that our hands would be free to catch animals. As we passed the research center, Aristote and I spotted several geckos scurrying across the walls. Commonly called tropical house geckos, *Hemidactylus mabouia* are common in and near human habitations throughout much of sub-Saharan Africa. Like many other species of geckos, the 6-inch-long (15 cm) *Hemidactylus* we observed have lamellar toe pads adapted for clinging to vertical surfaces, which even allow the lizards to run across ceilings upside down.

As we descended from the hill of the research center, we followed a small footpath that weaved among several huts made of bamboo and mud. Small cultivated areas were sprinkled among the huts, but remnants of some natural woodland/savanna mosaic vegetation could be seen here and there, including a few trees. On one of these, I spotted a sleeping chameleon, *Trioceros ellioti*. Occurring in and near the Albertine Rift, the mountainous western branch of Africa's Great Rift Valley, from the eastern border of Congo to Burundi, this species reaches about 7.5 inches (19 cm) in total length and does quite well in areas that have been heavily disturbed by human activity.[26] Along with house geckos, such animals are often called "trash species," because they are common in places where man has destroyed the natural environment. As I gently separated the chameleon from its nighttime perch, its pincer-like feet grasped my fingers, pinching them slightly with the claws. Originating in the late Cretaceous about 80 million years ago when dinosaurs still ruled Earth, chameleons evolved zygodactyl feet with fused digits that are perfectly adapted for an arboreal life in trees, and many species have distinctive coiled tails that are prehensile. Chameleons famously rely on camouflage to avoid predators and sneak up on prey, and they utilize turret-like eyes and projectile tongues to snatch insects that are often more than a body length away.[27]

"Hapa chini!" (Down here!), yelled Chif. I looked over to see him and Aristote stooped over a large puddle formed from the rain and knew that they had spotted a frog. Aristote slowly rocked his body forward as his light blinded his target, and with a rapid swipe of his hand I heard a splash and then his telltale "mmm hmmm" that signaled a successful capture. I walked over to see a medium-sized frog with a pointy snout, a lime-green stripe on its back, and very long legs sandwiched between Aristote's fingers. It was a *Ptychadena*, commonly called the rocket frog, for its ability to jump several feet in a single bound. If Aristote had missed on the first attempt to catch it, it would have been long gone by now. We continued for a few hours, finding sleeping lizards, various trash species of frogs, and even a large fruit bat resting upside down on a small tree near a hut. By the time we returned to the house, it was very late. As I fell asleep, I wondered what it must have been like to be one of the scientists who worked in Lwiro during the colonial era. In some ways, Lwiro must have been a scientific paradise, but were the Belgians kind to their Congolese neighbors?

As the Industrial Revolution burgeoned in the 1850s, advances in technology for transportation, medicine, and communication allowed the United States and Europe to extend their influence (and colonization) to all corners of the globe. Most of the planet was no longer a mystery, at least in terms of rudimentary knowledge about geography, natural history, and culture, and perhaps this is why the Western world became so enamored with the sometimes romantic and always adventurous lives of the African explorer, who boldly delved into the depths of the dangerous heart of the unknown continent. Explorers like John Speke, Richard Burton, David Livingstone, Henry Morton Stanley, and husband-and-wife team Samuel and Florence Baker filled in thousands of square miles of unknown territory on the maps of the time, and after writing sometimes embellished books about their adventures, they became internationally famous. But in addition to filling in the basic gaps of knowledge for the sake of curiosity, the discoveries of the explorers were touted and celebrated, because in a very real way, these acts conveyed a sense of ownership of the new territory to their European fans. One cannot help but think of an analogy to a three-year-old: I found it, so it belongs to me, and I'm not going to share. Of course they did not find it, because the Africans had been there all along. But this sense of entitlement, as well as arguments for bringing Christianity and "civilization to the natives," prompted many European nations to expand their colonies. Yet even well into the second half of the nineteenth century, the majority of Congo remained unexplored and, as a result, unclaimed by European powers.[28] However, a Welsh orphan and the calculating, arrogant king of a country smaller than Maryland would soon change all that.

Leopold Louis Philippe Marie Victor was born on April 9, 1835, to parents Louise Marie and King Leopold I of Belgium, a country that had come into existence only five years earlier after a revolt against Holland.[29] At school young Leopold showed interest in maps, geography, and little else, and as time passed, the king noted that his son had become "subtle and sly," but others who did not know him so well remarked about the prince's obnoxious behavior, clumsy demeanor, lanky appearance, and enormous nose. After the prince was forced into a marriage of mutual revulsion with the Austrian Archduchess Marie Henriette, the naive newlyweds had to be taught the facts of life by Leopold's cousin, Queen Victoria of England, and her husband Prince Albert. Eventually the couple would have several children together, but in 1869, at the age of nine, Leopold's only son and heir to the throne caught pneumonia and died. After that, Leopold wanted nothing to do with his wife, spent little time with his daughters, and promptly shut his sister Charlotte away from public view when she suddenly went mad.[30]

Although the Duke of Brabant, as Leopold was known before assuming the throne, spoke French, German, and English, he did not bother to learn Flemish, spoken by half of his countrymen. When he considered the throne of Belgium that would become his in 1865, he complained, "Petit pays, petit gens" (Small country, small people).[31] Bored and wanting to escape his tiny country temporarily, Leopold traveled widely in Eurasia and Egypt, where he indulged his interest in geography, and developed a new interest in business. During a month-long trip to Spain, and during his research into the profits of the Spanish and other European colonizers, he learned that the key ingredient to their gratuitous financial success was forced labor. In 1861, the duke made a speech to the Belgian senate in which he tried to convince his countrymen that Belgium should have a colony by noting that, "reduced to itself alone, [Britain] is only a nation of twenty-eight million inhabitants, but with its colonies it counts more than two hundred millions, and everywhere on the globe finds itself at home."[32]

Eventually, Leopold turned a greedy eye to Africa, where about 80 percent of the land remained under the control of native rulers. In 1876, he spared no expense to organize a geographical conference at his Royal Palace in Brussels, which ended with the establishment of the International African Association, to be chaired by Leopold, an organization that would ostensibly set up a series of bases in Central Africa for practical training of the locals, scientific laboratories, and supplies for continued exploration. When the gullible conference participants returned home and lionized the seemingly altruistic king's new association, donations poured in from across Europe. The association met only once the following year, when it designed a new flag featuring a gold star on a blue background to symbolize hope in the "darkness" of Congo.[33]

Meanwhile in the summer of 1877, Henry Morton Stanley, a famous explorer who had disappeared in East Africa two and a half years before, emerged half-starved near Boma, a small town near the mouth of the Congo River. Many Africans had died as a result of Stanley's penchant to shoot first and ask questions later during the expedition, but he had successfully followed the river from its source at Lake Tanganyika nearly 3,000 miles (4,828 km) to the mouth, taking innumerable measurements and observations along the way, thus documenting the entire course of the river for the first time, and setting the stage for future colonization. Many objective observers agreed that it was the greatest feat of exploration of the nineteenth century.[34]

Stanley claimed to be American—he actually fought on both sides of the Civil War—but he was really the illegitimate son of a Welsh housemaid. During the expedition, he had carried the American flag and Union Jack, and although both countries congratulated him during his triumphant return from Africa, neither one expressed any interest in Stanley's emphatic pleas to colonize Equatorial Africa. But Leopold was delighted by this news, and he rolled out the red carpet for Stanley and convinced him to launch another expedition to the Congo River. But this time his purpose would be for business—he would oversee the construction of a road around the Matadi cataracts (eventually this would be made into a railroad), and then use steamboats to establish trading posts along the navigable extent of the river. Depending on the audience, anyone who asked questions about this ambitious endeavor was told by Leopold that the work was either for scientific exploration, abolition of the Arab slave trade, or a humanitarian society similar to the Red Cross.[35]

Stanley set sail for Africa once again in early 1879, and the better part of the first two years of his tenure was spent building the difficult road around the Matadi cataracts, which he accomplished with a Congolese, Zanzibari, Belgian, British, French, and American work crew. When he used sledgehammers and dynamite to remove enormous rocks during this process, the awestruck Africans called him Bula Matari (Breaker of Rocks), a moniker that would eventually include all white officers of the Congo Free State. After a near-fatal bout of malaria and a brief return to Europe to recuperate in 1882, Stanley was urged by Leopold to return to Africa again, and with bribes of cloth and alcohol, Stanley easily convinced hundreds of illiterate Congolese chiefs to sign treaties conceding their land and a trading monopoly to the king. The treaties also included the important stipulation of labor to the state, which would prove to be devastating, and soon the gold-and-blue flag was flying all along the Congo River. However, Europe was now involved in the "Great Scramble for Africa," and it seemed unlikely that any competitor would recognize Leopold's claim to the territory Stanley had "developed" for him.[36]

Luckily for Leopold and unfortunately for the people of Congo, there was one other major power in the world that could recognize his claim. Among Leopold's loyal aides was a former American ambassador to Belgium named Henry Sanford, who was sent to America with a carefully crafted letter to Republican president Chester A. Arthur. The president was convinced by Sanford's arguments that the king was interested in antislavery and humanitarian efforts in Congo, and that Americans would be welcome to buy land and trade freely in the new colony if they should see fit to recognize it. Less than a week later when the president addressed Congress, he spoke highly of Leopold and the work he was doing in Congo. Sanford's lucky streak continued when Senator John Morgan, a former Confederate brigadier general and racist chairman of the Senate Foreign Relations Committee, embraced the idea of the Congo colony as a potential way to funnel freed blacks back to Africa, where they would pose no threat to white women, or perhaps worse, entertain obviously troubling ideas about equal rights. It was a foregone conclusion when the secretary of state declared the United States recognized King Leopold's claim to the Congo on April 22, 1884. France soon followed suit, and it was then only a matter of time for other European countries to do the same.[37]

All that remained was to draw up the borders of the colony, and give it a name. Starting on November 15, 1884, Chancellor Otto von Bismarck of the growing German empire hosted a conference in Berlin, where powerful men from several European countries gathered to discuss the future of Africa in a way that would presumably prevent competitive warfare. Leopold was not present, but he had several well-paid representatives in his place, including Sanford and Stanley, who officially served as technical adviser to an incompetent ambassador from the United States. In 1885 at the age of fifty, Leopold's evil and brilliant campaign reached its pinnacle when the king, and not his defunct International African Association, became the sole governing entity of the new colony, now recognized as the Congo Free State.[38]

In the years that followed, some money began to flow back to Belgium, thanks to the high demand for ivory, which was easy for Belgian officers to obtain either by shooting elephants, or indirectly from villagers by stealing it at gunpoint, or through various deceitful practices. The Belgians' disregard for the Congolese people led to damning reports of various horrific abuses, including slavery. George Washington Williams, a famous American black writer who visited the Congo in 1890, wrote widely circulated letters to the king and US president Benjamin Harrison to complain, among other things, that the Belgians would sometimes shoot Africans for sport. Williams coined a phrase that would be repeated many times in later centuries—crimes against humanity. Belgian officers routinely kidnapped women to become their concubines, beat Africans (including children) with a hippo-hide whip called the *chicotte*, took whatever resources they wanted from destitute villages, and worked chained men like beasts of burden until they died from exhaustion, disease, or starvation. One Belgian captain named Léon Rom—a possible model for Mr. Kurtz in Conrad's *Heart of Darkness*—became infamous when he decorated his garden with the heads of twenty-one Africans killed during a raid to quell a rebellion near Stanley Falls.[39] But the worst was yet to come, and the effects would reverberate into the twenty-first century.

I slowly awoke to the sound of at least a dozen birds singing in the gardens surrounding the house, which I am sure had changed little in fifty years. When I emerged from the bedroom, still weary and now very hungry, I was greeted by a short man with a worn baseball cap, a prominent mustache, and a happy twinkle in his eye.

"Bonjour, Chief!" (Good day!) he said as he lifted his cap deferentially. "I am Marcel, zeh cook," he said with a thick accent as he shook my hand enthusiastically. His charisma immediately charmed me. I peeked into the kitchen to see multiple cabinets, very large workspaces with two sinks, and a square footprint with an electrical outlet where a sizable refrigerator must have stood long ago. The kitchen had a back door leading to a large courtyard behind the house with space for firewood, a stone oven, and areas for washing laundry. I imagined the former owners of the house must have had a small army of servants. I mumbled enough French to convey the idea that I wanted breakfast.

Marcel's talents as a cook would not win him a James Beard Foundation Award, but in his defense, the resources he had at his command were modest at best. I was soon presented with a little bread and half-rotten butter, some tea, and a tomato-and-onion omelet slathered and fried in liberal quantities of the orange-brown cooking oil that can be found everywhere in Congo. Somehow I managed to eat the worst breakfast I had ever had with a smile, to the delight of Marcel. Aristote and I spent the morning photographing the animals we had captured the previous evening, and then I saw four men approaching the house.

The two oldest men, Wandege Muninga and Maurice Luhumyo, had been on the field team the previous year when we worked at Kahuzi-Biega National Park. Both of them worked with snakes as "technicians" in the CRSN herpetology laboratory under the supervision of Chifundera. Wandege, a tall and thin man in his forties with a gentle and somewhat goofy disposition, was often the brunt of teasing jokes by everyone. He seemed to have a sixth sense about snakes and was very good at finding them. Maurice was Wandege's mentor with snake wrangling, and he was also thin, but much shorter and elderly. He spoke with a gravelly voice, always referred to me as the muzungu, and rarely found any animals on his own accord, but tribal obligations made Chifundera insist that he be a paid member of the team. John and Felix Akuku were brothers with chiseled facial features and bright eyes in their twenties — Chif wanted to include them on the team this year because we would need strong, trustworthy men during the difficult journey to the more remote areas we wanted to visit, including Itombwe, where John, Felix, and Aristote were born. All of them removed their hats and shook my hand to welcome me back to Lwiro, and then greeted the ever-popular Aristote with equal enthusiasm, launching into an animated conversation in Swahili about family, health, and women.

When I had finished the hours-long work involved with processing the previous night's specimens and associated DNA samples, I took a seat in one of the comfortable chairs of the living room that faced the windows at the front of the house. I looked through them to the beautiful gardens that the caretaker continued to nurture, and marveled at the amazing diversity of birds that danced among the branches of the trees as they sang. The place was very soothing and peaceful, a welcome feeling after the tiring days that were now behind me. I knew from previous experience in Africa that nobody is ever in a rush when it comes to mundane business, and I would have to be very patient before the truck would become available for the fieldwork. To pass the time, I asked Aristote to translate a conversation I wanted to have with the caretaker Lyadunga.

I learned that the old man was in Lwiro even before the Belgians settled the area after World War II, and that the great difficulty at that time was warfare between neighboring tribes and danger from animals. Apparently, people would occasionally be killed by a lion or leopard or the odd elephant charge. Once the Belgians arrived, they destroyed the natural vegetation and the animals with it, forever altering the way the Africans would live off the land. Lyadunga was nostalgic as he described the salary he used to receive under the Belgians, and the end of tribal warfare that colonialism precipitated. He told me about the kind director that used to live in the house with his family, and how he was never mistreated by them. After independence, Lyadunga's steady salary evaporated, and some of the old, violent tribal rivalries returned. As Aristote continued translating, I noticed a resigned sadness in his eyes, as though he had heard tragic tales like this many times. When the war came to Lwiro in the late 1990s, Interahamwe militia from Rwanda killed Lyadunga's wife and many of his friends with machetes. I felt awful for bringing all of this up, and shocked by the harsh reality, I did not want to hear any more. Lyadunga ended his narrative by telling Aristote and me that even now, after everything that had happened, he wanted his old salary back so that he could have a good life again. Aristote told me that the man was very old and that the Congolese could never accept colonialism again. Stunned by what I had heard, I returned to my seat in the old Belgian living room and stared at the bullet hole in the glass.

In the late nineteenth century, ivory and palm oil were barely beginning to repay the substantial debts Leopold had made to finance his colony,

The caretaker Lyadunga, around eighty years old, stands on the patio next to the Belgian house that was built just after World War II in Lwiro. The well-trimmed grass is maintained by machete.

including much of his personal fortune and an enormous loan from the Belgian government. Export duties were implemented to raise desperately needed income, and at a conference held in Brussels in 1889, the king used antislavery efforts as an excuse to collect import duties, thus beginning to erode his charade of free trade in the state. Leopold made good on the antislavery promise, however, and in a series of horrific, bloody battles against Arab African slave traders in eastern Congo in 1892–1893, the better-armed Belgian forces killed an estimated seventy thousand men and eventually ejected the slavers. In one of these battles, Belgian Captain Francis Dhanis joined forces with fifteen hundred Africans led by a former slave named Ngongo Lutete, who had defected from the Arabs. Dhanis remarked that Lutete's warriors, "were a considerable help in fighting, but were somewhat embarrassing allies since after each combat they rushed to eat the slain."[40] In fact, Congolese on both sides routinely cooked and ate the dead and wounded.[41, 42]

By the early 1890s, bicycles, automobiles, telephone components, electric wiring, and other technological advancements made world demand for rubber skyrocket. Large quantities of synthetic rubber would not become available until World War II, and it would take nearly twenty years for rubber plantations in Asia and Latin America to reach full production. Thus in the late nineteenth century, natural rubber vines and trees in the tropics were the only source of latex, the key component used for rubber products. The profits from rubber were so large (exceeding 700 percent) that the Congo soon became the most lucrative colony in Africa, and Leopold urged his Belgian officers to use any means necessary to increase production. To meet that goal, the Force Publique, an army of African mercenaries and slaves with European (and sometimes American) commanders, ballooned to nineteen thousand men and consumed half of the state's budget by the late 1890s.[43]

Because it would not be feasible to chain men together and watch over them deep in the swampy jungles as they climbed dozens of feet into the canopy to reach the rubber vines, other measures had to be devised to coax them into collecting the rubber without supervision. Enterprising Force Publique officers (including Léon Rom) figured out, to deadly effect, that they could kidnap village elders, women, and children and hold them for ransom until the men in the village brought in the demanded quotas of rubber. Men who refused to comply saw their families killed on the spot; women were raped, and the stockades built for the starving hostages were so unsanitary that many died anyway. But many of the soldiers of the Force Publique were victims themselves: they had been transported in chains to regions too far away from home to contemplate escape and were severely abused by their white officers.[44]

The Congolese rubber streamed into European markets via Belgium, and as enormous profits poured into Leopold's coffers, he became known as the "builder king," because he used the money to construct lavish palaces, museums, parks, monuments, and a golf course. At the turn of the century, Leopold fell in love with a beautiful girl named Caroline; she was sixteen and he was now sixty-five. What Leopold did not yet know was that she often worked as a prostitute, and her pimp was a former French officer named Durrieux. One can only imagine how the affair progressed between two people separated in age by half a century (perhaps Hugh Hefner can provide insight), but in short order the king was showering her with expensive gifts and money. Caroline funneled a large portion of this money back to Durrieux in what is likely to be the single greatest act of pimping in history.[45]

For the last few years of the nineteenth century, Leopold's well-oiled PR machine squashed reports about the Force Publique atrocities in Congo, but the flow of negative information was relentless. In 1906, Mark Twain penned a short work entitled *King Leopold's Soliloquy*, which highlighted some of the worst horrors of Congo and cast Leopold as a despicable villain. He wrote, "The train of revilers of missionary testimony, whose roseate pictures of conditions under the king's rule have beguiled the uninformed, hurries out at the wings and Leopold is left to hold the stage, with the skeleton that refuses longer to stay hidden in his Congo closet."[46] In the 1970 edition of Twain's *Soliloquy*, the editor Stefan Heym noted that American newspapers ignored many reports of atrocities because of Leopold's decision in 1906 to allow J. P. Morgan, John D. Rockefeller, Thomas Fortune Ryan, and Daniel Guggenheim to invest in Congo, and he added, "Their money has been in the Congo business ever since."[47]

This war of public perception continued for years, and meanwhile thousands were dying in Congo and Leopold continued to get rich. But then a flamboyant lawyer named Henry Kowalsky, who had been receiving an enormous salary from Leopold to lobby the king's Congo agenda, had a change of heart when his contract was not renewed, and he leaked the shady arrangement to a popular magazine—the scandal included substantial bribes to a member of the Senate Foreign Relations Committee. Americans were outraged, and soon the government was joining Britain's calls to end Leopold's rule of Congo.[48] Damning testimony from several investigations convinced the Belgian people too—an influential Jesuit priest and law professor named Arthur Vermeersch remarked, "Our honour and the good name of Belgium are at stake."[49] Two weeks after learning about some of this testimony, acting governor general Paul Costermans, the man for whom Costermansville (i.e., Bukavu) would be named, grew depressed from the horrific truth about the colony he had helped to build, and slit his throat with a razor.[50] The king managed to delay Belgian annexation of Congo for two more years, until November 1908, when he *sold* the Congo to Belgium for tens of millions of francs, even after millions in Leopold's unpaid debt had been forgiven.[51]

Belgium, now in control of the renamed Belgian Congo, maintained much of the existing legislation and officials from the state, and for at least four more years, many of the atrocities that had outraged the world continued.[52] Between outright murder, disease, starvation, and other horrific consequences, about 50 percent of Congo's human population disappeared between 1880 and 1920.[53] Millions more would die at the turn of the twenty-first century, and in June 2008 I walked into the messy aftermath of this crushing era of human misery.

Why have I spent the last decade collecting scientific specimens from this dangerous heart of Africa? What do I hope to learn? What is the benefit to Congo and the world? Why should you care? We are just beginning to understand Congo's impressive biodiversity, but human activities are simultaneously wiping it out. There is a limited window of opportunity

A weathered monument to King Leopold II stands to this day in a courtyard at the Royal Museum for Central Africa in Tervuren, Belgium. The museum was one of many extravagant and enormous buildings constructed on the king's orders around the turn of the twentieth century.

to identify and protect threatened species before their habitats are completely destroyed. As I will explain, humanity has much to gain from this biodiversity science.

——————

Shortly after my return from my expedition to Congo in August 2008, I was unpacking specimens and their associated tissue samples (i.e., small samples of muscle in vials of ethanol) for DNA analyses in my new evolutionary genetics laboratory at the University of Texas at El Paso. It had been very exciting to find the animals in remote corners of Congo, but in most of the cases I had only a vague idea of what I had collected. With few exceptions, I could identify which genus each specimen belonged to, but beyond that, the herpetofauna of Central Africa is so poorly known that I could not easily figure out the species. *Contributions to the Herpetology of the Belgian Congo*, the most current synthesis of the amphibians and reptiles of Congo, is nearly a century old, and most of the region's species were described in the mid-twentieth century by Belgian herpetologists Gaston-François de Witte and Raymond Laurent, often based on brief descriptions in French, and without illustrations. Some of the older descriptions from the nineteenth century were even worse, and because all of the men who had seen these animals alive when they were described were now dead, there was nobody to consult for help with identifications. Luckily for me and our understanding of Congo's biodiversity in general, these scientists and countless others like them left behind one permanent source of information to help future scientists identify species correctly—preserved specimens that are available to the international scientific community in museum natural history collections. As the name implies, these collections are permanent repositories of the three-dimensional history of life on our planet, and they are absolutely essential to help scientists identify poorly known species like the ones in Congo, make morphological comparisons to provide evidence that a new species is really new and not actually something that was described and forgotten long ago, and to describe new species in the modern era. Specimens in an internationally recognized museum collection, including the quintessential holotype that represents the new species, must be referenced in competent species descriptions so that future scientists can track them down and confirm that the morphological features (e.g., size, color pattern, shape, scale patterns, and other observable and quantifiable structures) provided in the original publication are actually present on the specimens. Many scientists have made mistakes that are only caught later, sometimes centuries later, from re-examination of their specimens.

The challenging and time-consuming work that goes into the taxonomic study of any group of organisms is not considered cutting-edge science by the greater scientific community, and scientific papers describing new species are not valued as much as "big science" papers that are testing large-scale hypotheses related to biodiversity changes over time, evolution, biogeography, ecological modeling, conservation assessments, and climate-change predictions. I completely agree that in the modern age of supercomputers, bioinformatics, genome-scale datasets, and improved technology in the laboratory, "big science" questions are important to twenty-first-century biology, and their prioritization by the scientific community is understandable. But what is the source for much of the data that are being used for these mega-analyses? Many modeling analyses rely on datasets that originated from locality records of museum specimens, and thanks to digitization grants from the US National Science Foundation (NSF), tens of millions of specimen records are now available to the global scientific community via online databases like VertNet and iDigBio. The model studies capture these data along with multiple sources of information about temperature, rainfall, and other quantifiable factors of climate and environment (sometimes from satellites) to understand where a given species has occurred historically, and where it might occur in the future under different scenarios of climate change.

Similar analyses, again based on museum specimen data, have also been used by scientists to predict the spread of invasive species (e.g., imported red fire ants, zebra mussels), which threaten native species and cost billions of dollars in damage to the US economy every year.[54] Evolutionary genetics and genomics studies that are trying to understand major patterns of evolutionary relationships rely on genetic data from previously published studies and tissue samples from increasingly rare expeditions, most of which are stored in museum collections near their associated voucher specimens (the specimen from which the tissue sample was taken in the field). That way, if the results of a genetic analysis are suspect, one can check the voucher specimen to ensure the taxonomic identification is correct. Once any kind of genetic data is published in a scientific publication, it is almost always uploaded to the National Institute of Health–funded database GenBank, where anyone can search for the DNA of any organism from the planet. Unprecedented access to all of these data is allowing researchers from around the world to produce many exciting studies, but these users are often relying on the accuracy of the original collectors, museum curators (lead researchers and head stewards of the collections), collection managers, students, and volunteers who entered untold millions of these records into the museum databases in the first place.

When grabbing a bunch of data from VertNet or GenBank to look at a given species' geographic distribution, for example, one must be very careful that all the records are referable to the same species. Mistakes can happen — it is common for museum curators to make a best guess at the identification of a specimen that is brought to the collection, enter the record into a database, and perhaps years later when a taxonomic expert examines the specimen, the identification is corrected. Thus taxonomic expertise is absolutely essential to determine whether a species is distinct and valid, conduct quality control measures on questionable database records, and synthesize scientific literature to provide an overall picture for a given species. In the case of conservation assessments by the International Union for the Conservation of Nature (IUCN), which produces a "Red List" of threatened species of plants and animals that is recognized internationally, data from museum specimens are relied upon to understand a given species' geographic distribution, habitat preference, life history (e.g., longevity), reproductive biology, and, most importantly, its validity as a species. Such assessments are extremely important for national park wardens, governments, stakeholders, conservation organizations, and the international community to implement conservation measures for species that are threatened with extinction. If it is clear that the geographic distribution is relatively small, or that a significant portion of the species' habitat has been destroyed, or any number of other negative trends are obvious, then the IUCN applies specific criteria to determine the level of threat, ranging from Least Concern (the species is abundant and widespread) to Critically Endangered (on the verge of extinction).

For example, the Montane Reed Frog (*Hyperolius castaneus*) is a colorful, medium-sized frog that is common in marshes and forest edges throughout the Albertine Rift Mountains. Before I spent several years studying the detailed morphology and genetics of the isolated populations of this frog, the IUCN had used a rough estimate of its geographic distribution, based on museum records and data published in the twentieth century, to determine that the species should be classified as Vulnerable (i.e., vulnerable to extinction). As I started sampling populations throughout eastern Congo and western Burundi and Uganda, I noticed that there was a great deal of morphological variation attributable to color pattern (see color plate). Looking at this variation without the benefit of genetic data, it was impossible to say whether the reed frog was really just a single highly variable species, whether the variation was attributable to gender or to sexual maturity, or whether a morphologically cryptic species might be hiding in this variation. Because I had access to multiple specimens of males, females, subadults, and tadpoles from many different areas of the Albertine Rift where colleagues and I had worked, I was able to combine a careful study of the specimens' measurements with a detailed genetic analysis to determine that populations in the Itombwe and Kabobo Plateaus of eastern Congo were one "elevated" species (*Hyperolius constellatus*, formerly only a subspecies), and populations elsewhere in the Rift were another one (*Hyperolius castaneus*).[55] With this new information, the geographic distribution of *Hyperolius castaneus* was expanded to about 73,000 square kilometers, including several national parks in the Rift, and it is no longer considered threatened by the IUCN. However, the newly recognized *Hyperolius constellatus* occurs in less than 9,000 square kilometers in areas that have weak conservation protection, and it is classified as Vulnerable.[56] Thus, without the benefit of museum specimens and taxonomic expertise, scarce conservation resources for this particular frog species would have been spread throughout the Albertine Rift instead of focusing on the Itombwe and Kabobo Plateaus, where such efforts are needed most.

Over the years, as I have explained this work to the hundreds of undergraduate students I have taught in my genetics course every semester, I sometimes get a question about how harmful collecting might be to these species, and this is a fair question, because we certainly do not want to wipe a species out in our endeavors to understand it better. Nobody would condone the collecting of rhinos, eastern gorillas, sea turtles, or other endangered species that have a conservation program in place and have been intensively studied by biologists for decades. But some scientists have argued that we should not collect specimens of any kind anymore, citing the example of the Great Auk (*Pinguinus impennis*), a bird that was wiped out by greedy collectors in the nineteenth century after its population declined from overhunting. To ensure that possibly small populations like the auk are not affected, these scientists advocate the use of photos with a smartphone to document rare species.[57] I hope my previous example of *Hyperolius castaneus* color pattern variation demonstrates the absurdity of this idea. One hundred twenty-three prominent members of the scientific community, including champions of taxonomy and conservation biology like E. O. Wilson, quickly lined up to pan the smartphone idea. The examples of overcollecting leading to extinction are rare and involve either recreational or commercial interests, not scientific ones. Moreover, the dubious overcollecting argument distracts from the demonstrably more important threats of habitat loss, overharvesting, pollution, climate change, and invasive species.[58] A separate response dubbed the photo-only perspective "taxonomic malpractice," because many published taxonomy studies that lacked vouchered museum specimens cannot be independently verified and have been thrown out as unreliable.[59] Two years later, proponents of photography-based taxonomy tried to make their case again in a provocative piece published by the journal *Nature*, but nearly five hundred taxonomists from around the world, including myself, quickly responded to reject their counterproductive arguments.[60]

What other benefits do whole, preserved specimens from expeditions offer to science and the greater public good? The Missouri Botanical

Garden sends thousands of plant samples (collected during expeditions) from their herbarium collections to labs that are developing new drugs. A new species of Cameroonian vine identified from their collections contained a compound that has shown promise to prevent the transfer of HIV from mother to child.[61] Animal specimens can be examined for their internal anatomy, providing crucial information about their ecology (e.g., what they eat), reproductive biology (e.g., whether they lay eggs or give live birth, time of sexual maturity), parasites and diseases, pollution exposure, brain chemistry, cytoarchitecture and anatomy, and many other aspects that cannot be researched with a photograph. For example, while taking X-rays of specimens of the West African skink *Chalcides pulchellus* during my time in graduate school, I noticed a strange string of vertebrae in the stomach of one specimen from Mali. When I was granted permission to dissect it, I was shocked to find that the lizard had eaten the tail of a much larger tree snake in the genus *Dipsadoboa*.[62] Another striking example should serve as a warning about the danger of climate change to all of us. Thanks to large series of *Plethodon* salamander specimens collected over many decades in the Appalachian Mountains of the eastern United States, scientists were able to document a long-term trend of decreasing body size in nearly half of the species, which they attributed to global climate change. The hotter and drier climate increases metabolism in the amphibians, and they must either eat more or decrease their size to compensate—and apparently natural selection forced many of them into the latter strategy.[63] In fact, similar studies have documented body size declines in many other groups of animals from all over the world, suggesting that size decline might be one of three universal responses to global climate change, along with altered phenology (seasonal timing such as emergence from hibernation and migration) and shifting geographic distributions away from habitats that are now unsuitably hot or dry.[64] None of these important findings would be possible without careful comparisons of collections dating from the present to many decades into the past, and this example highlights how collectors in the 1950s could not anticipate the questions that would be answered through their specimens in the future. I am certain that the specimens I collected recently in Congo will help to answer important and unforeseen questions in future decades as well.

Because specimens represent a snapshot of the environment in a given time and space, questions about those environments can be answered long after they have disappeared. For example, in 2011 my Congolese colleagues and I collected a single specimen of the Makese Banana Frog (*Afrixalus leucostictus*), the only one we have ever found in Central Africa, from a beautiful rainforest stream near Kalundu village in the western foothills of the Itombwe Plateau. Only a year later, the team returned to the site to look for more, but the entire forest had been cut down to make way for crops. Thus this single specimen record is the only evidence that this forest-adapted spiny reed frog species ever occurred at this site. Millions of similar examples to this one are known from across the world. My colleague John Simmons recalled his early fieldwork efforts in the Amazonian rainforest of Ecuador, where he collected an impressive diversity of amphibians and reptiles over the course of a year in the early 1970s. Thank goodness he did, because when he returned to the area in 1984, he found that miles of forest had been destroyed to make way for human settlements and shops, and nearly all of the species he recorded from his earlier expedition can no longer survive there.[65] But sometimes when combined with conservation strategies, biodiversity inventories can actually prevent deforestation. Amazingly, since 1999, inventories by curators and collaborators of Chicago's Field Museum of Natural History have established protection for 26.6 million acres of wilderness in the Amazon, one of the most biodiverse regions in the world.[66]

As technology gets better, many specimens that have been sitting around for decades on dusty shelves suddenly have new secrets that can be uncovered. Stable isotope analyses have been used to understand food webs and trophic level positioning (i.e., an organism's place in the food chain) for plants and animals living in ecosystems that have changed over time.[67] Although formaldehyde preservation, the most commonly used method for preserving fish, amphibians, and reptiles, often fragments or destroys DNA in specimens (this is why tissue samples are usually preserved separately in vials of ethanol), recently developed methods

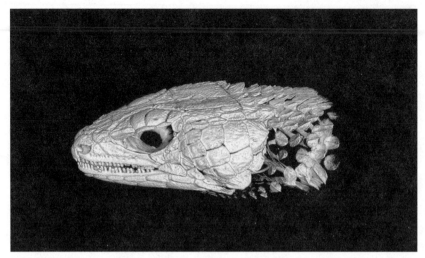

High Resolution X-ray Computer Tomography (CT) scan of a *Cordylus marunguensis* skull with osteoderms. Image courtesy of Edward L. Stanley.

have allowed scientists to obtain large genomic datasets from formalin-fixed specimens collected decades ago.[68] Another exciting innovation is High Resolution X-ray Computer Tomography (commonly called CT scans), which can be used to make three-dimensional reconstructions of bones, osteoderms (bony deposits that form scales and other dermal structures), and even cartilage from intact specimens. These CT scans have allowed scientists to make extremely detailed comparisons among different groups of animals that would have been unimaginable in the twentieth century, when skeletons were prepared in a time-consuming and often damaging process of skin and flesh removal. Osteological images from CT scans were used by my colleague Edward Stanley and me to describe a new species of girdled lizard that, against my better advice, Chifundera and Wandege collected from the edge of a minefield in Katanga, Congo, in 2010.[69]

In the case of amphibians, molecular testing of specimens, both in the field and from historical collections, has allowed scientists to understand the devastating spread of the aquatic chytrid fungus, an emerging disease that has been directly linked to the decline and extinction of at least two hundred species of frogs and salamanders over the last thirty years, especially in Australia and the Neotropics. The disease has been called the "greatest disease-caused loss of biodiversity in recorded history."[70] Although there seems to be a link between global climate change and chytridiomycosis, the disease caused by chytrid infections, most evidence supports the novel-pathogen hypothesis, which postulates that the fungus spread to areas (almost certainly via global trade of frogs for the pet trade and biomedical research) that had not harbored the disease before, including pristine ones in Central America. The naive immune systems of many native amphibian species succumbed when they were exposed for the first time, leading to widespread "die-offs," with hundreds of dead frogs lying about in the forest. Zoospores from the fungus infect keratin (the same protein in your fingernails) in skin cells, disrupting osmotic regulation, leading to cardiac arrest and death.[71] The exact origins of the chytrid fungus remain unknown, but a study from 2014 found two distinct genetic strains of the fungus in specimens collected as early as 1894 in the Atlantic Forest of Brazil, strongly suggesting that chytrid originated there and spread worldwide in the twentieth century. However, chytrid has also been widespread in Asia and Africa for decades, and as with Brazil, there have not been many reports of massive die-offs like the ones in Central America. Yet another study found chytrid in Illinois in 1888. New genetic strains of chytrid should be sought worldwide before scientists can be sure of chytrid's origins.[72]

Before the Illinois study, the earliest-known chytrid infections were from a questionable record of a Japanese giant salamander in 1902 and several African frogs collected in the 1930s. An Out-of-Africa hypothesis suggested that chytrid originated in Africa and spread through the global trade in clawed frogs (*Xenopus laevis*), which can tolerate chytridiomycosis without dying, and were shipped around the world in the twentieth century for use in human pregnancy tests, biomedical research, and the pet trade. Because escaped or released populations of the frogs have established themselves in California, Arizona, Mexico, Chile, France, United Kingdom, Italy, Japan, and Indonesia, it is likely that they have helped to spread chytrid around the world. But the only African amphibian species that seems to have disappeared from chytrid, the Tanzanian Kihansi Spray Toad (*Nectophrynoides asperginis*), became extinct in the wild after the government used millions of dollars in loans from the World Bank to install a hydroelectric dam (cutting off 90 percent of the water) at the only waterfall where the species occurred. It is not clear if the water alteration, chytrid, pesticides, or a synergistic effect of all three doomed the species, but the dam remains the prime suspect.[73] The good news is that eleventh-hour US captive-breeding programs were successful, and in 2012, two thousand toads were reintroduced to their native habitat, and more reintroductions were planned for 2014.[74] Jennifer Pramuk, animal curator at the Woodland Park Zoo in Seattle, who was involved in the effort to save the toad, noted a recent population estimate of about 589 wild frogs, an encouraging number for the reintroduction efforts.[75]

The picture of chytridiomycosis in continental Africa remains a paradox, but studies based on natural history specimens are continuing to provide insights. A 2013 study noted the complete absence of the fungus in West Africa, but warned that it can be easily transported from infected to noninfected areas.[76] Some studies in western Central Africa have not detected the fungus, but more recent ones have, including the first record of the fungus in caecilians, the eel-like, fossorial cousins of frogs and salamanders.[77] In Congo, chytrid was first detected in two reed frog species that we found in lowland rainforest near Kahuzi-Biega National Park and montane forest near Lwiro in 2007.[78] Subsequent studies of specimens from my team's fieldwork, including many places described in this book, detected chytrid among a wide array of frogs from multiple sites in the Albertine Rift.[79] Another study expanded the known cases of chytrid in the Rift, and tests of historical collections of Congo frogs at the Royal Museum for Central Africa (Tervuren, Belgium) found the presence of chytrid in a specimen of the Itombwe River Frog (*Phrynobatrachus asper*), collected by Laurent in 1950.[80] Many unanswered questions about chytrid remain, and it is clear that testing of wild populations and specimens should continue.

Although our first priority should be for conservation efforts to save living species from extinction in their natural environments, many additional extinctions are inevitable, and in fact they are happening as you read these words—the respected website Mongabay.com estimates 137 tropical rainforest species are lost every day. Thanks in large part to chytrid, amphibians are disappearing more rapidly than any other major group of vertebrates, at least a third of amphibian species are threatened with extinction, and this is likely an underestimate. This trend is likely to get worse, because many amphibians have small geographic distributions, which are more susceptible to damaging climate change and complete annihilation as the pace of habitat destruction increases across the globe.[81] In general, species with small range sizes, and concomitant small population sizes, have the highest probability of extinction risk. Insidiously, many studies have shown that habitat destruction is most severe in places where these small-ranged species are concentrated, including those in Africa. A recent conservation assessment noted that only 2.2 percent of the world's area contains the entire known ranges of 50 percent of the world's amphibians, and these areas have the added benefit of including at least a portion of the range for a substantial number of the remaining amphibian species on the planet. Unfortunately, most of these areas are not currently protected, and they are likely to disappear unless drastic action is taken immediately.[82] Because many amphibians have a so-called biphasic life history, with tadpoles and salamander larvae spending the first part of their lives in water before metamorphosis transmogrifies their bodies for a life on land, some have argued that when amphibians go extinct it is like losing two species—one in the water and another on land.[83] And when amphibians disappear, predators that rely on them for food (e.g., fish, snakes, birds) decline too, causing a negative domino effect that damages the entire ecosystem.

If captive-breeding programs are not feasible or successful, natural history collections will be a last-ditch insurance policy to bring some extinct species back from annihilation so that they can be reintroduced to restored habitats in the future, assuming that the majority of the ecosystem remains intact. But of course to bring a species back, we must first know that it exists, and in many cases, the only evidence for this is represented by a preserved specimen in a museum's natural history collection. Indeed, I have collected specimens during expeditions to Congo that are likely to be the only representatives of several new species, and I can only hope that they will not be driven to extinction before I can find the time to describe them. These specimens and their associated tissues might provide a genetic and morphological blueprint for resurrecting species from extinction in the future, and, indeed, ethical considerations and guidelines for "de-extinction" are well under way.[84] This might sound like *Jurassic Park* science fiction, but cloning technology gets better every year — we have come a long way since Dolly the sheep was cloned in 1996 — and the first step to cloning something is to piece together its entire genetic profile, known as the genome. In recent years, scientists did that by sequencing the entire genomes of several long-extinct mammals, including a horse that was at least half a million years old.[85] If genomes can be obtained from these ancient specimens, it will be presumably even easier to obtain the genome of recently extinct species from DNA left behind in museum specimens or "frozen zoo" initiatives, which freeze tissues of critically endangered animals for future cloning, just in case captive-breeding efforts fail.[86]

Collection-based expeditions must continue and be expanded immediately because we are only just beginning to understand the biodiversity of our planet, but the extinction crisis is allowing it to wither away rapidly. Despite 250 years of taxonomic study and about 2 million described species, a 2011 study estimated that approximately 86 percent of the species living on land and 91 percent of species in the ocean (mostly microscopic ones) remain unknown. With these estimates, it will take 1,200 years, over 300,000 taxonomists, and $364 billion to discover and describe all these unknown species.[87] But in recent years, advances in high-throughput DNA sequencing technology has uncovered unprecedented numbers of new microbial species, and in 2016, a study estimated that the planet actually contains about 1 trillion species of microscopic bacteria, archaea, and fungi (of which 99.999 percent are undiscovered), blowing previous estimates out of the water.[88] Taxonomists do not have the luxury of hundreds of years or more to complete this work, because it is painfully clear that humans have been pushing many known and unknown species to extinction for centuries, and as the pace increases while human populations explode in the tropics where most of the planet's biodiversity is concentrated (see chapter 4), we are losing the race to discover species before they are wiped out. In her book *The Sixth Extinction*, journalist Elizabeth Kolbert acknowledged this dichotomy by trying "to convey both sides: the excitement of what's being learned as well as the horror of it."[89]

It is true that extinctions have happened throughout Earth's history, a "background" rate of extinction that occurs from natural forces has been happening since the beginning of life itself (the average species lifespan is roughly a million years), and there have been five catastrophic mass extinctions, including one that killed off the dinosaurs 65 million years ago.[90] But current extinction rates are about a thousand times higher than the prehuman baseline, these rates are increasing, and there is no doubt that we are to blame for what many are calling the sixth mass extinction in the human-dominated "Anthropocene" epoch.[91] Although estimates vary based on possible future scenarios, several of the world's most respected conservation biologists fear that between one-half and two-thirds of all plant and animal species will be extinct by the end of this century.[92] If that happens, we are next, because the human species depends on biodiversity for our existence—we cannot live without the sustenance, air, water, and materials that a diverse number of species provide to us. In the case of people living in developing countries near tropical forests, bees, flies, moths, butterflies, bats, and other animals are absolutely essential to pollinate crops they rely on for survival. In fact, biodiversity is tied to food production worldwide, and one widely used estimate claims that one in three bites of food is linked to pollinators.[93]

Because we have only a rudimentary understanding of the species on Earth (especially in Congo), and recognizing the existence of a species by giving it a name is a necessary prerequisite to understanding how it is linked to the global ecosystem, nobody knows for certain how much biodiversity the planet can lose before an irreversible and catastrophic tipping point is crossed. But it is clear that as extinctions increase, ecosystem function declines.[94] Yet we know next to nothing about the inner workings of many individual ecosystems, let alone the global ecosystem. Indeed, many have suggested that the human brain is the most complex system in the universe, but this is not correct. Emeritus Harvard biologist E. O. Wilson, often called the father of biodiversity, stated, "The most complex is the individual natural ecosystem, and the collectivity of ecosystems comprising Earth's species-level biodiversity."[95] Paul Ehrlich, president of Stanford University's Center for Conservation Biology, used a widely cited analogy to explain this situation. Imagine you are a passenger walking along the tarmac to board your flight, and you notice that a mechanic is busy removing rivets from the wing. Don't worry, he says, he's been removing a handful of rivets every day for a while, but with thousands of rivets in the wing, removing a few isn't a big deal. But at what point is the removal of one rivet too many for the wing to stay on? Obviously, from your viewpoint the removal of just one is insane. Would you get on that plane? Ehrlich states, "An ecologist can no more predict the consequences of the extinction of a given species than an airline passenger can assess the loss of a single rivet."[96] Even more worrying, a 2016 study from the journal *Science* suggested that more than half of the planet's land surface has already lost an unsafe level of biodiversity, which could have dire consequences for humanity in the near future.[97]

Given the magnitude of the problem, the United States should be leading the world by creating a major scientific initiative to discover and describe every species on Earth, an enormous global undertaking akin to the Human Genome Project or NASA's goal to colonize Mars. In the interest of our own future, and while there is still time, we should be spending billions of dollars on expeditions to document the remaining biodiversity of the planet, train and hire a new generation of taxonomists (including biodiverse countries like Congo), bolster the natural history museums and universities that care for and study specimens, redouble our efforts to conserve the remaining natural areas that sustain this biodiversity, expand captive-breeding programs to try to increase population sizes of species that are plummeting in the wild, and educate the public about the importance of biodiversity to our continued presence on Earth. But what are we doing instead? In the case of natural history museums, which have been the hub for international scientific expeditions, studies of taxonomy, and biodiversity education for the public for centuries, funding and interest has been declining for decades. In 2016, NSF temporarily suspended funding for the Collections in Support of Biological Research Program, and many museums around the country have faced draconian budget cuts. In an effort to increase revenue from

visitors, some museums have ditched their research collections and curators to focus on Disneyesque entertainment, and others will not include exhibits on evolution because they do not want to risk offending
their conservative religious visitors. In taking this approach, these institutions fail to teach the public a crucial lesson about "how our own
species fits amid millions of others."[98]

Like whole-organismal biology in general, the study of taxonomy is
in trouble, because many powerful people have the mistaken view that
the field has limited scientific value beyond simple identification that can
be accomplished with a photograph, some measurements, and perhaps
a little bit of DNA data. In reality, taxonomic definitions of a group of
organisms (i.e., circumscriptions) are scientific hypotheses that must be
tested with multiple sources of painstakingly obtained data, including
DNA data when possible, and even though much of evolutionary biology, ecology, and conservation biology rely on these hypotheses, they
are often underappreciated. The vast majority of biology jobs, including
those in academia, do not require any knowledge of taxonomy, and top
journals in biology will not accept species descriptions unless they are
part of a broader study, if at all. As a result, students are spending less
time learning how to identify and describe new species, and more time
learning how to do the "big science" that will result in publications in
top journals and a path to increasingly competitive jobs. Centuries of
taxonomic expertise, passed down through generations of scientists,
is eroding as older taxonomists retire with no equivalent replacement.
NSF has sponsored programs that funded traditional taxonomists and
trained many new ones, but many of these enthusiastic students could
not find jobs as taxonomists, and the scientific community is failing to
reverse the trend.[99] Modern taxonomists certainly need to embrace new
interdisciplinary methods and internet platforms to ensure that their research is relevant and fundable in the twenty-first century, but habitat
destruction and disease have already wiped out many species all over the
planet, the coming years will certainly be the last opportunity for scientists to sample many other species before they disappear, and it is in
our best interest for our priorities to match the harsh reality ahead. The

bottom line is that species cannot be protected unless the world knows of their existence. As a major extinction crisis gains steam across the globe and the opportunities to expand protected area networks draws to a close, I imagine future generations will question our priorities at this critical moment.

KING KONG OF KAHUZI VOLCANO

2

Twenty-four centuries before the establishment of the Congo Free State, a Carthaginian admiral named Hanno was ordered to sail down the western coast of Africa to establish colonies. He followed his orders loyally, and at one point during the voyage he entered a bay near a "fiery mountain," perhaps an active volcano. On a nearby island, the explorer encountered savage hairy "people," and the Carthaginians managed to capture three of them. The explorers tried and failed to tame their prisoners, and then killed and skinned them as souvenirs before returning home to the Mediterranean. The account of the voyage was written in Greek (not the Carthaginian language of Punic) and must have been written centuries after the voyage took place. The details of exactly where the sailors explored and what kind of ape the savage hairy "people" actually were remains a debatable mystery, but the word that the Greek translators used to describe the apes has endured for centuries: *gorilla*.[1, 2]

Gorillas are distinguished by their socially complex behavior, close evolutionary relationship to humans, and nearly vegetarian diet, with the occasional insect for variety. The great apes only occur in the forests of Central Africa, two national parks in Congo were created to protect them (Virunga and Kahuzi-Biega), and these critically endangered primates represent the quintessential embodiment of poorly known and threatened wildlife in Congo. The complicated history of the gorilla's discovery, taxonomy, and challenges for conservation in Congo, as well as surprising connections to the United States, are shared by other rare species in the country.

Thus it is instructive to explore these interconnected themes with goril-las to understand Congo's vanishing biodiversity as a whole.

The mention of gorillas conjures up fantastic images of enormous, fierce apes, including the twentieth-century inventions of Mighty Joe Young and King Kong, who kidnapped a beautiful woman and battled dinosaurs in a mysterious land before time. These ideas originated much earlier in the nineteenth century, when the first reports of wild gorilla be-havior started to emerge from an intrepid explorer named Paul Belloni du Chaillu, who was a keen observer himself but had a penchant for repeat-ing exaggerated stories overheard from Africans. In 1848 as a teenager, Paul followed his father, a French businessman, from New Orleans to the coast of Gabon, where one of the first trading posts was established for ivory, rubber, and indigo. During his four years there, du Chaillu learned some of the local languages and heard amazing stories about the inte-rior by talking with native traders. He returned to the United States in 1852 long enough to study biology, obtain grants from two geographical societies to finance his exploration, including the Academy of Natural Sciences in Philadelphia, and become a naturalized American citizen. He returned to Gabon in 1856 and spent four long and difficult years exploring the interior, accompanied only by Africans. Because he was a polyglot, du Chaillu made friends with numerous tribes easily.[3]

Once while half starved, du Chaillu ran ahead of his African com-panions in pursuit of a monkey to shoot, when he stumbled upon three members of the infamous cannibal Fang tribe. They were so horrified by the white man that they dropped their possessions and froze wide-eyed to stare at him, convinced that he was an evil spirit. This happened again when the explorer entered the land of the Ashira tribe: the shocked chief instructed his people, "Be silent; do not trouble the spirit [du Chaillu]; do not speak lest you awake him. Our forefathers nor ourselves ever saw such a wonder as this."[4] During his travels, the dense jungle ripped the explorer's clothes to shreds and destroyed his shoes, but he contin-ued barefoot and nearly naked, supposedly traveling over 7,450 miles (12,000 km) on foot. He withstood over fifty attacks of malaria (thanks to copious doses of quinine), countless other tropical diseases, painful swarms of army ants, an outbreak of smallpox that killed several of his men, and a nasty wound from a poison arrow. He also survived deliberate arsenic poisoning from his own cook and remarked in passing that the near-death experience cured a lingering fever. As a trained biologist, he collected hundreds of natural history specimens of birds, mammals, amphibians, and reptiles, scores of which (especially birds) proved to be new species. But his largest claim to fame was arguably his description of the wild gorilla, which he likened to the devil.[5] In the mid-nineteenth century, gorillas were known only from a handful of skeletons and skins, and no Westerner had ever observed them in the wild.

In 1861, du Chaillu published a book titled *Explorations and Adventures in Equatorial Africa*. The book was a best seller for its time — ten thousand copies sold within a two-year period — but it was derided as fiction by some prominent critics.[6] The first time du Chaillu picked up the trail of gorillas in the wild, he was terrified, because the Africans had told him stories of gorillas that carried off women to be raped, grabbed men with their feet to be strangled in trees, and were actually evil spirits of men who had disappeared in the forest. But once the gorillas sensed him coming, they shrieked in alarm and retreated into the jungle. In subsequent encounters with wild gorillas, du Chaillu hesitated to shoot when he observed human-like, tender moments between females and their offspring. But when he snuck up on lone silverbacks he saw another side of gorilla nature. "I could see plainly the ferocious face of the monstrous ape. It was working with rage . . . and gave a truly devilish expression to the hideous face . . . he gave out a roar which seemed to shake the woods like thunder, and, looking us in the eyes and beating his breast, advanced."[7] On one ill-fated gorilla hunt, du Chaillu found one of his men lying in a pool of his own blood with his intestines hanging out of his belly, and the African's gun had been bent and flattened. Before the man died, he told the explorer that an enormous male gorilla had attacked him and destroyed the gun with its powerful jaws. The incident led to a famous illustration in the book, which showed the enraged gorilla standing upright on two legs above the mortally wounded African and bending the gun in half with its hands. Yet when du Chaillu killed a gorilla, he remarked, "It was as though I had killed some monstrous creation, which yet had something of humanity in it."[8]

The territory du Chaillu traversed from the coast of Gabon was an enormous feat of exploration for its day, especially since colonialism had not yet established a framework to facilitate travel for white men in Central Africa. By comparison, the volcanic mountains of the Belgian Congo, Rwanda, and Uganda were vastly more remote in the mid-nineteenth century, and as a result, it would be half a century before specimens of a second species of gorilla would be shot there. In 1902, a captain and railway construction engineer in the German East African Imperial Army named von Beringe shot two gorillas on Mt. Sabinio at the convergence of modern-day Congo, Rwanda, and Uganda, and he is credited with the discovery of the mountain gorilla.[9]

A more ambitious explorer was Rudolph Grauer, an accomplished Austrian mountaineer and zoologist who was the son of a prominent Jewish family from Troppau (Opava in modern-day Czech Republic). Rudolph had military training at an academy at Wiener Neustad, and he studied law at Vienna and agronomy at Halle. He participated in an excursion to North Africa, and once African adventure had a grip on him, he went on two game-hunting trips to Uganda, where he collected scientific specimens and climbed the Ruwenzori Mountains to a height of 15,750 feet (4,800 m). In 1907, Duke Adolf Friedrich of Mecklenberg, who would go on to perform incredible feats of exploration himself, asked Grauer to explore the volcanic highlands of Rwanda. After successfully accomplishing this, Grauer returned to Africa to collect natural history specimens at Lakes Kivu and Tanganyika, and Burundi. With funding from a fellow Austrian big-game hunter, Grauer returned a final time for a marathon expedition from Lake Victoria to Lake Tanganyika, and then north along the border of Belgian Congo all the way to Beni and the nearby forests west of Lake Albert. During these expeditions, Grauer collected thousands of natural history specimens of amphibians, reptiles, birds, and mammals, including rarities like the okapi and gorilla. In the rugged mountains west of Lake Tanganyika that are now known as the Itombwe Plateau, Grauer shot sixteen gorillas in 1908 and 1910. To the great detriment of history and science, Grauer did not write any books about his travels, and after settling in Austria, he suffered from tropical diseases he had acquired in Africa; he died at the relatively young age of fifty-seven at a hospital in Vienna.[10] However, many new species described from Grauer's collections, including amphibians and reptiles, were named in honor of the explorer.

The skins and skulls of gorillas shot by du Chaillu, von Beringe, Grauer, and other collectors eventually ended up in American and European museums, where they were examined by mammalogists, some of whom were more competent scientists than others. The gorilla was first described as *Troglodytes gorilla* in 1847 from some bones brought to a reverend named Savage at a mission house in Gabon. The original description was published in the minutes of a meeting of the Boston Society of Natural History by Savage's biologist colleague Dr. Jeffries Wyman. The two friends published a more detailed paper about the discovery later that year, and they explained that the idea for the species name originated from the account of Hanno's voyage. Only a year later, a British biologist named Owen described a second species (T. *savagei*) in honor of the reverend, who supplied London's Natural History Museum with additional specimens. In a second publication later that year, Owen admitted that T. *gorilla* was the name that had priority—in zoology, the oldest published name for a species is the one that is upheld for it, and all subsequently published names for the same species are considered invalid synonyms. Four years later, a French biologist named Isidore Geoffroy St. Hilaire published a paper in which he argued the valid species of gorilla should belong to its own new genus, *Gorilla*, an action that continues to be recognized today.[11]

Based on aberrant skulls, skins with some reddish hair, and unusually large or small specimens, Hilaire and several other authors named a handful of additional species of gorillas from western Central Africa, but in time they all proved to be minor variants of the same original species described in Boston. However, this profligate naming of invalid species was nothing compared to "Professor" Paul Matschie, an eccentric, anti-evolution curator of mammals at the Berlin Museum. According to his obituary, Matschie took some university classes at Halle and Berlin, but never passed any exams or earned a degree. After taking a volunteer position with the museum in 1886, he worked his way up to curator of mammals in 1895, and was bestowed with the title of professor in 1902.[12]

The poorly trained zoologist wanted to make his mark, and he strived to find minor differences in scores of mammal specimens collected from different sides of rivers in order to describe them as new species. More than once he even described two species from the right and left sides of a single specimen! His logic was that the animal was collected from a watershed and must represent a hybrid of two unknown species, an argument correctly dismissed as absurd by many of his contemporaries. In this way, Matschie and his copycats inflated the number of invalid gorilla species to ridiculous proportions. It was only by accident that the gorillas shot by von Beringe in the Virunga Volcanoes and named as a new species (*Gorilla beringei*) by Matschie actually represented a bonafide new species. He also named the Cross River Gorilla (*G. diehli*) from western Cameroon (now considered a valid *subspecies* of *G. gorilla*), and Grauer's Gorilla (*G. graueri*, now considered a valid subspecies of *G. beringei*) from a specimen shot by Grauer at the Itombwe Plateau. It would take many decades to sort out the taxonomic mess created by Matschie's misguided actions, and arguments about gorilla taxonomy have continued into the twenty-first century.[13]

The shooting of gorillas for trophies and museum specimens continued well into the twentieth century, but one of the more colorful scientific collectors of this time eventually realized that the gorilla population in eastern Belgian Congo was vulnerable and needed to be protected. In the latter half of the nineteenth century, an amazingly talented taxidermist named Carl Akeley grew up in Clarendon, New York (about an hour east of Buffalo), where his family briefly considered committing him to an insane asylum for being obsessed with dead animals as a boy. With an unwavering passion for his profession, Carl eked out an existence on the edge of poverty while he worked as a sort of freelance taxidermist: at one point he preserved Jumbo, the famous, gigantic elephant of P. T. Barnum's circus that met an untimely end when he was hit by a train in Canada. The care with which Carl brought animals back to "life" became widely known, and when he passed through Chicago to see one of his stuffed broncos on display at the Field Museum, he was shocked when Daniel Elliot, the curator of zoology, offered to hire him on the spot as chief taxidermist. In almost the same breath, and assuming his offer would be accepted, Elliot asked Akeley if he would like to join him on an expedition to Africa.[14] How could he say no?

Several weeks after a hasty departure by ship from America and vomiting a worrying portion of his weight into the sea, the seasick Akeley was informed by Elliot that they would collect rare mammals in the inferno of southeastern Ethiopia and Somalia. After nearly dying of thirst on the poorly planned expedition, Akeley had a run-in with a leopard that almost ended his life again.[15] As President Theodore Roosevelt described it several years later in his book *African Game Trails*,

> My friend, Carl Akeley, of Chicago, actually killed bare-handed a
> leopard which sprang on him. He had already wounded the beast
> twice [via wild shots into the bush] . . . whereupon it charged,
> followed him as he tried to dodge the charge, and struck him full
> just as he turned. It bit him in one arm, biting again and again as
> it worked up the arm from the wrist to the elbow; but Akeley threw
> it, holding its throat with the other hand, and flinging its body to
> one side. It luckily fell on its side and with its two wounded legs
> uppermost, so that it could not tear him.[16]

Akeley won the death brawl, but concerned that the leopard had been feeding on a decomposing hyena carcass, he demanded that massive amounts of antiseptic be injected into his extensive wounds when he stumbled back to camp, and remarked "during the process I nearly regretted that the leopard had not won."[17]

Akeley would bear the grisly scars of the leopard attack for the rest of his life, but this was not his last brush with death in the African bush. After switching employers again, Akeley's new boss Henry Fairfield Osborn, director of the American Museum of Natural History in New York City, sent Akeley back to Africa in 1909 to collect elephants for an exhibit planned for the museum. Akeley took his first wife, Mickey, on the trip, and they rendezvoused with Roosevelt near Mt. Elgon on the western border of modern-day Kenya, where the former president was immersed in an enormous hunting expedition with his son Kermit. The group soon killed four elephants, but they were cows and calves, and Akeley was really focused on getting a spectacular bull or two. Because every white man with a gun in Africa wished to shoot a bull elephant at the turn of the century, large tuskers, bulls with impressive tusks, had become quite rare. Carl and Mickey roamed East Africa for seven disease-ridden and punishing months in search of the perfect bull for the museum. Carl finally came upon one on Mt. Kenya, but the bull found him first, and the taxidermist was brutally beaten by the enraged pachyderm. The attack left Carl unable to walk because of several broken bones, and his face had been shredded to the point that brandy leaked out of gashes in his cheeks when he tried to numb the pain. When his guides rushed down the mountain and informed Mickey of the attack, she mounted a midnight rescue in the freezing rain and found Carl unconscious in his tent under a swarming mass of ants busily picking away his exposed flesh. Carl looked like a one-eyed mummy after Mickey bandaged his face together, but while he was recovering, he started to have visions of a museum exhibit that would be far more ambitious than the elephant one—he would create an enormous hall of all African mammals. He thought he would need a million dollars, an enormous sum of money for the time.[18]

When Carl returned to New York, Osborn quickly got on board with Akeley's African Mammal Hall vision, but estrangement from Mickey, who was increasingly reclusive, and World War I delayed the taxidermist's plans for several years.[19] During the downtime, Carl tinkered with his invention of a new motion picture camera that would be more versatile in the field and allow him to make movies of wild animals in Africa.[20] Perhaps because he had movies on the mind, he came up with a clever idea to help fund the African Hall. A Kansas husband-and-wife team named Martin and Osa Johnson had made a fortune traveling to exotic places in the South Pacific to make movies about cannibals. Akeley suggested to Osborn that the museum could help finance the Johnsons on an expedition to Africa to film wild animals with Akeley's camera, and in return, some of the movie proceeds could help fund the hall. After Osborn and Johnson agreed, Carl convinced Osborn to provide him with ten thousand dollars to shoot specimens of mountain gorillas in 1921, with the idea that mounted specimens of these exotic creatures would generate interest and funding for the ambitious hall.[21]

Although Carl was now approaching sixty, his trip to the Belgian Congo was a success, and he shot several gorilla specimens in the Virunga Mountains and even got some footage of the stunning scenery with his new camera. But somewhere along the way, he became concerned about the gorillas, because he noticed they were not as common as some people claimed (local European priests erroneously said there were thousands), and perhaps their human-like expressions, especially after witnessing their relatives being shot, resonated with him. Carl wrote that as the silverback gorilla he shot "lay at the base of the tree, it took all one's scientific ardor to keep from feeling like a murderer. . . . He was a magnificent creature with the face of an amiable giant, who would do no harm except in self-defense or in defense of his friends. Of the two, I was the savage and the aggressor."[22]

Before leaving the Congo on his 1921 trip, he wrote to the local Belgian officials about the need to preserve the gorillas before trophy hunters shot them all. When he returned to the United States, influential friends helped him push his proposal for a gorilla sanctuary in Congo through the offices of American and Belgian politicians and ambassadors until it landed on the desk of King Albert I of Belgium, the successor to Leopold II. Albert was sympathetic to Akeley's idea because the king had visited Yosemite and the Grand Canyon during a trip to the United States in 1919, and he had been impressed with the idea of national parks. Most of Belgium's natural areas had been destroyed long ago, but now he had an opportunity to create the first protected area of its kind on the African continent. In March 1925, the king issued a decree that would protect 93 square miles (24,000 hectares) of mountain gorilla habitat in Congo, and even more territory in the lowlands for a game reserve, which would henceforth be known as Parc National Albert.[23] Four years later, the boundaries of the park were enlarged to include the entire volcanic chain of mountains in Virunga, and the Parc de Volcans was established on the Rwandan side of the border.[24] Not to be outdone, the British established the Kigezi Gorilla Sanctuary on the Ugandan side of the mountains in 1930.[25] Although these actions were great for the gorillas, repercussions for indigenous Batwa pygmies were devastating—they suddenly lost access to the forests that had sustained their ancestors since time immemorial. Because the Batwa were the least influential of the African tribes in eastern Congo and had the disadvantage of relatively poor health and widespread illiteracy, they were powerless to protest these actions.[26]

Meanwhile, the Johnson team had a box office success with their 1923 movie *Trailing African Wild Animals*, which generated handsome profits for the African Hall. Akeley brought his second wife, Mary Jobe Akeley, and landscape artists from New York on another trip to Africa in 1926 so that they could collect more specimens and get drawings of the beautiful spot at Kabara where he had shot the silverback gorilla on his last trip. Carl said fairies danced there—the site looked down from the icy montane meadows to the active volcano of Nyiragongo and the shimmering blue water of Lake Kivu.[27] When Carl died near this spot from blood hemorrhaging (most likely from altitude sickness) a day after reaching it, his grieving widow, friends, and colleagues (African, American, and European) constructed a tomb of mahogany and concrete for him, and there he remained until Congolese poachers inexplicably dug it up and carried away his bones in 1979.[28] Although it would take several more years after Akeley's death and a lot more money to reach completion, the Akeley Hall of African Mammals opened to the public at the American Museum on May 20, 1936. Glimpses of the vanished African wilderness of Akeley's era remain frozen in time to this day, including a large diorama featuring the silverback gorilla Akeley shot at Kabara.[29] Perhaps in the late 1920s there were about two thousand mountain gorillas in the Virungas, but even with the putative protection of the parks, their numbers soon nose-dived.[30]

For decades, rudimentary knowledge about the behavior, ecology, and accurate population estimates of the mountain gorillas remained vague at best. A few studies of gorillas in Uganda were published in the 1950s, but deeper, extended observations were lacking.[31] Finally, in 1959, an American biologist named George Schaller decided to move to Congo with his wife Kay to begin a long-term study of the gorilla. After deciding to focus on the mountain gorillas in the Virungas, he established a base at a modest shack-like building that had been built at Kabara near Akeley's grave. With few interruptions over the course of a year, Schaller made daily contact with the gorillas, and in the early 1960s he published a series of scientific papers and a landmark book called The Mountain Gorilla: Ecology and Behavior,[32] which would solidify his career as an eminent field biologist and champion of wildlife conservation. One piece of data stands out from his study: the total estimated population of mountain gorillas in the Virungas had dropped to about five hundred.[33] In his book The Year of the Gorilla, Schaller warned, "History has shown that animals as rare as the mountain gorilla are highly vulnerable, and constant vigilance must be maintained to prevent the scales from tipping from security to extinction."[34] Political turmoil in the aftermath of Congo's independence in 1960 forced Schaller to terminate his gorilla study early, but he went on to make enormous contributions to the biology of other endangered mammals across the world.[35]

Schaller's unlikely successor was also American, but that is where the similarities end. Dian Fossey was born in San Francisco in 1932 to an insurance agent father with a penchant for drinking, which resulted in divorce from Dian's mother when the girl was only six. Her religious mother Kitty remarried soon afterward, but Dian's stepfather was a cold disciplinarian who prevented her from taking meals with her parents until she was ten. Throughout her life, she suffered from severe allergies, asthma, and frequent pneumonia. She had a lifelong love of animals, but poor grades in chemistry and physics stymied her aspirations for a degree in veterinary medicine. She switched to occupational therapy, graduated in 1954, and accepted a job working with disabled children at a hospital in Louisville. After crossing paths with a Rhodesian (present-day Zimbabwe) suitor who waxed poetic about the untouched wildlife of Africa, Dian decided to take out an enormous loan to see for herself. While on safari with a hired guide in northern Tanzania in 1963, she stopped at Olduvai Gorge in the remote hope of meeting her hero Louis Leakey. The famous paleoanthropologist had uncovered hominid fossils that essentially proved man evolved in Africa, and he believed that studying great ape behavior would lead to insights about human origins. Perhaps because the eminent scientist found the six-foot-tall Dian attractive, he greeted his unexpected intruder enthusiastically, and when he asked her what she was doing in Africa, she replied that she wanted to live and work there, perhaps with gorillas. Intrigued, Leakey invited her to see a fossilized giraffe he had just discovered. When Dian twisted her ankle as she was trying to get a photo of it, the pain induced her to vomit all over the ancient artifact. Undeterred by Dian's unsavory accident, Leakey bandaged her ankle, encouraged her to persevere through the pain to visit the gorillas, and keep in touch.[36]

Several days later Dian climbed Mt. Mikeno with some British filmmakers who happened to be at Virunga to film gorillas, and she had her first exciting glimpse of the apes in the wild. Needless to say, she was spellbound. After returning to the United States, she considered a marriage proposal from the *brother* of her Rhodesian suitor, who had met her on the trip to Africa and then enrolled at Notre Dame. But in 1966, Leakey happened to come to Louisville to give a lecture, and when Dian approached him, he immediately recognized her. The next day they met at his hotel, where Leakey explained that he thought she might be the right person to start a long-term study of gorillas if she would agree to have her appendix removed! His logic was that she would avoid a potentially deadly health crisis in the isolated Virungas. Dian was so excited by the prospect that she agreed immediately. After feigning abdominal pains, sometimes on the wrong side, she successfully convinced a surgeon to remove the appendix. She soon quit her hospital job and declined the marriage offer so that she could follow her dreams.[37]

A few days after Dian's thirty-fifth birthday, her camp at Kabara was established, and she was joined by a Congolese gorilla tracker named Sanweke who had worked for Akeley and Schaller. Within six months, Dian was making impressive progress observing the gorillas, but she was having an increasing amount of difficulty asserting her authority over her employees. Because she was literally in her own little mountain world, war came to eastern Belgian Congo without warning, and she was ordered to leave immediately or face certain death. Shortly after fleeing to neighboring Rwanda, she began enlisting the help of white expatriates to establish a new gorilla research base on the Rwandan side of the volcanoes. In September 1967, Karisoke research camp was established in the high saddle between Visoke, Karisimbi, and Mikeno Mountains in Parc de Volcans. Dian immersed herself in the work of studying the gorillas and driving away destructive cattle and poachers, sometimes at gunpoint. For years, Leakey secured funding and assistants for her, but after a brief affair with her in Kenya, he died of a heart attack in 1972. Because Dian was working on her PhD in England and was becoming famous from prominent stories in *National Geographic* (one of her main sponsors), she soon obtained an impressive level of international prestige, and with it she was able to obtain a great deal of funding for Karisoke independently.[38]

Over the following years at Karisoke, Dian engaged in a few failed affairs with married or otherwise committed men, and she wrestled with occasional bouts of drinking and depression. But she always seemed to find solace in the company of the gorillas, which she continued to study in collaboration with numerous foreign students, including many Americans, who came and went. As chronicled in her book *Gorillas in the Mist*, and the movie of the same title starring Sigourney Weaver, she waged a veritable war against poachers and cattle ranchers, and several times she had to rehabilitate baby gorillas who had been snatched from the wild for zoos in Europe. This war took a devastating turn when poachers reduced the estimated mountain gorilla population to about two hundred animals in 1978, killing Dian's most beloved gorilla Digit in the process. Psychologically, Dian would never be the same, and she wrote to the president of Rwanda, the National Geographic Society, and numerous international conservation agencies to demand that poaching in the Virungas should be punished with harsh prison sentences or even death. She also set up the Digit Fund to channel international donation money into antipoaching efforts that the Rwandan park officials were unwilling or unable to engage in themselves. When more gorillas were killed in apparent reprisals for Dian's unorthodox antipoaching approach, she resorted to using vibrating Halloween masks, rubber snakes, and other bogus *sumu* (witchcraft) to get captured poachers talking, and her methods were very effective. Given the thousands of destroyed traps and scores of poacher arrests that occurred from her efforts, it is conceivable that she actually prevented the extinction of mountains gorillas. However, her "active conservation" approach also resulted in numerous enemies, including African poachers, Rwandan park officials, European ex-pats, international conservation agencies, and disapproving scientists from many countries. And then one evening the sumu was turned against her when someone left a carving of a puff adder on her doorstep. Dian knew it was a death curse, but she kept it a secret from everyone except her journal, whose final entry read, "When you realize the value of all life, you dwell less on what is past and concentrate more on the preservation of the future."[39]

On the morning of December 27, 1985, Dian Fossey's body was found with a fatal machete wound to the head. She had managed to grab her revolver during the struggle with her killer, but the scattered bullets next to her body were of the wrong caliber to fit the gun. The Rwandan police charged two men with the murder. One was a Rwandan tracker named Rwelekana who had been fired by Dian years before, and he reportedly hanged himself while in prison. The second person was an American student named Wayne McGuire who had been working at Karisoke during Dian's murder. He was encouraged to flee by the American embassy and was convicted of the murder in absentia by a Rwandan tribunal. The case against McGuire is doubtful, because he had no apparent motive and the evidence in his trial has been heavily criticized.[40] The controversy over Dian's death remains to this day, but she would have been pleased to know that her martyrdom ensured the survival of the gorillas she loved in life.

Although Dian was shocked to learn that gorillas were dying because of parasites picked up from humans during poorly supervised tourist activities, she understood that the Rwandan government and its people would benefit from gorilla tourism. Within a short amount of time after Dian's murder, gorilla tourism was generating millions of dollars of income for Rwanda, a country with few natural resources, and education programs fostered the idea that gorillas are part of Rwanda's natural heritage. Amazingly, some of the Rwandan staff of Karisoke continued to look out for the gorillas during most of the dark days of civil war and genocide in the 1990s, and despite the use of the Virungas as an escape route for fleeing refugees, only four gorillas disappeared during this time.[41] In recent years when I have traveled to Congo via Kigali, the capital of Rwanda, I have seen scores of European and American tourists preparing to visit the gorillas, and a prominent billboard in the airport's parking lot once showcased the birth of baby gorillas. Scientific research of the gorillas and other rare animals continues at Karisoke, and the future is encouraging. But despite the recent good news, the mountain gorillas of Virunga are just one catastrophe away from extinction, and as Schaller emphasized, our vigilance must never relent if we hope to see them thrive in the future.

The first time I violated the rules of gorilla etiquette, I was quite ignorant about proper protocol when dealing with one of my species' close relatives, especially the variety that outweighs us by 200 pounds (91 kg). It was the late 1980s, and I was volunteering in the Reptile House of the Buffalo Zoo. The gorilla exhibit at that time was one of the more recent renovations at the zoo, and I enjoyed a quiet sojourn in the cave-like tunnels every morning before starting work. It was soothing to look through the brightly lit glass windows into the otherworldly enclosure, and the slow walk was also an opportunity to warm up from the bitterly cold Buffalo winters.

Usually the gorillas were off exhibit at that time of day, or if they had been liberated, they were typically lying around in a corner eating their breakfast. Under no circumstances did they ever glance in my direction or seem to notice me, and most mornings I gave them a quick glance and moved on. But one particular morning I noticed the silverback sitting with his back against the glass window. I could not resist taking a closer look, and I quietly walked to the window to see the pale gray luster of the fur on his back, and the oddly shaped and massive head only inches from me. I doubt he could have heard me through inches of glass, but somehow his sixth sense alerted him that something was amiss, and he turned his head in my direction. At the time I didn't understand that direct eye contact is interpreted as a challenge by dominant silverbacks, and I looked at his brown eyes for only a moment before he stood up on both legs, seemingly towering above me, and commenced beating on the glass with a sudden fury that gave me one of the great shocks of my life. Convinced the glass would break momentarily, I ran and did not look back.

In October 2010 a baby gorilla was born at the Buffalo Zoo to a mother who had also been born there, a promising track record for the captive-breeding program of the species. Most of the gorillas in captivity, including those in Buffalo, are Western Lowland Gorillas (*Gorilla gorilla gorilla*), which is the smallest of the four *subspecies* that occur in Central Africa. Because of habitat destruction, poaching, and even an outbreak of Ebola that slowly oozed through Gabon and neighboring countries in the mid-2000s (killing as many as 95 percent of infected animals), western gorilla populations have been declining rapidly in recent decades. Poaching has become especially problematic since the late twentieth century, as weaponry improved and a wealthy urban elite emerged in Africa's cities. These elites have more cash to spend on wild animal meat, collectively called "bushmeat," including large primates like chimpanzees and gorillas. As ape conservationist Peter D. Walsh explained, bushmeat is more expensive than fish or meat from domestic animals, but "urban consumers view ape meat and other types of bushmeat not as a vital protein source, but as a sentimental link to their rural heritage: something akin to the Thanksgiving turkey or Christmas goose."[42]

As recently as 2007, estimates of western gorilla populations hovered around 50,000, down by 50 percent from estimates in the 1970s. However, a survey published by the New York–based Wildlife Conservation Society in 2008 increased the population estimate by at least 125,000 animals, because previous work had missed an enormous population of gorillas in a remote and inaccessible swamp in northern People's Republic of Congo (aka Congo-Brazzaville, bordering Congo to the west of the Congo River).[43] Despite the good news, the western gorilla is still officially listed as critically endangered because the factors leading to outbreaks of Ebola remain a mystery, and the human-based threats increase every year as more people occupy our crowded planet.

The other subspecies of gorillas have not fared as well. The Cross River Gorilla (*Gorilla g. diehli*), downgraded to a subspecies after it was named by Matschie, lives in the isolated montane jungles between Nigeria and Cameroon and is distinguished from the Western Lowland Gorilla by a smaller skull and distinct dental proportions. Cross River Gorillas became isolated from Western Lowland Gorillas during climatic oscillations and resulting vegetation shifts in the Pleistocene about 17,800 years ago, but limited gene flow (movement and mating of individuals between populations) continued until about 420 years ago, when mankind started to have an impact. A century later, as firearms were introduced to Africa, hunting pressure caused a sixty-fold decrease in the Cross River Gorilla numbers, and the most recent estimates of the critically endangered sub-species' population range from only two hundred to three hundred. With such a dwindling number of animals, the future prospects for the sub-species are dim, and it certainly does not help that the illegal bushmeat trade continues to be a major problem in West Africa.[44]

The black, hairy, and massive-jawed Eastern Mountain Gorillas (*Gorilla beringei beringei*) of the Albertine Rift have actually increased in numbers in recent years, but their total count still hovers around a paltry 880.[45] Occurring in the forested Virunga Volcanoes at the confluence of Congo, Rwanda, and Uganda, these gorillas have benefited immensely from ecotourism programs at Mgahinga and Bwindi Impenetrable National Parks in Uganda, and especially Parc National des Volcans, where tourism accounted for $214 million of Rwanda's revenue in 2008. Ecotourism is extremely curtailed in Congo's Virunga National Park because of ongoing militia activity. For example, three park rangers and five soldiers were killed in January 2011 by Interahamwe militia, who destroyed the victims' vehicle with a rocket-propelled grenade (RPG). In fact, 152 Virunga rangers have been killed since 1996,[46] mostly as a result of the money at stake for the illegal charcoal trade, which devastated at least 25 percent of the southern half of Virunga's forests and was estimated to be a $30 million/year industry in 2008.[47] Charcoal is made by the militias from Virunga's trees in mud ovens, and then smuggled to nearby Goma, where almost every household uses it for cooking and heating. In 2007, the world was outraged by Brent Stirton's award-winning photos of a family of mountain gorillas that had been shot at point-blank range in the park, and investigations eventually led to the arrest of Honore Mashagiro, the corrupt warden of the southern sector of Virunga, who allegedly ordered the gorilla killings as a warning to the dedicated and fearless rangers. The militias have diversified into the business of *bangi* (marijuana), which they seed in areas that have been destroyed for the charcoal business.[48] Most recently, a 2016 report by the Enough Project suggested the charcoal industry is destroying more of Virunga than ever, thanks to a mafia-like organized crime syndicate between the Interahamwe, Congolese police, military, politicians, and businessmen.[49]

The largest subspecies of gorilla, Gorilla beringei graueri, commonly known as the Eastern Lowland Gorilla, actually occurs from the mountains of Mt. Tshiaberimu[50] in the northern sector of Virunga through Kahuzi-Biega and Maiko National Parks to the Itombwe Plateau, but all of these gorilla populations are now isolated from each other, which might lead to potentially deadly genetic problems from inbreeding depression — mating between closely related individuals and resulting loss of genetic diversity in the population that can lead to increased mortality rates and decreased reproductive success. Because of the remoteness of eastern Congo's jungles, population estimates for this subspecies were anecdotal for most of the twentieth century, but in 1998 researchers estimated about seventeen thousand gorillas; 86 percent of these individuals occur in the lowlands of Kahuzi-Biega National Park and nearby Kasese. Even in areas of low human population density, gorillas are commonly considered pests, and the apes are killed for meat or as retaliation for crop raids.[51] In recent years, many of these gorilla populations were killed off completely or became fragmented and isolated — the fragile group on Mt. Tshiaberimu currently numbers only six individuals,[52] and the site is almost completely surrounded by deforested agricultural and urban areas. Because gorilla family groups tend to stick together when the silverback confronts intruders, poachers can kill several individuals at once, which has contributed to the catastrophic decline. The most recent estimate in 2015 suggested that about 3,800 Grauer's gorillas remain in Congo (a 77 percent drop since the late 1990s), and as a result, they are now critically endangered, the most serious category of threat. Because there are currently no viable captive-breeding programs, the Grauer's gorilla will certainly slip into extinction within a decade if conservation of the remaining wild populations fails.[53]

The current taxonomy of gorillas recognizes two species, each with two subspecies. I am going to sidestep the detailed and controversial philosophical arguments regarding the definition and validity of a subspecies, which I fear will not prevent evolutionary biologists from attacking my condensed explanation below, but one could easily write a book about this subject, and indeed some have already.[54] Although I have some European colleagues that disagree, most modern biologists no longer name subspecies, because in many cases they have proven to be meaningless in terms of evolutionary biology. Many subspecies of vertebrates were named in the twentieth century to acknowledge slightly aberrant, peripheral populations of widespread species that had unique color patterns. But starting in the 1990s, when scientists examined many of these putatively distinct populations with DNA sequence data, they often found that the populations were not genetically distinct from other populations of their species and that the aberrant color patterns could be explained by minor genetic variation within species — analogous to different populations of humans having blue or brown eyes. On the other hand, some subspecies that have been examined with modern methods have proven to be genetically distinct, sometimes to the point that they are not even the closest relative to other populations of the same species, and when that happens, scientists "elevate" the subspecies name to full species status (recall the example of *Hyperolius constellatus* above), and the subspecies name replaces the old species name.

So why do people still recognize subspecies of gorillas? Some biologists now think of the subspecies category as a group of animals that have diverged genetically and morphologically to a *relatively limited degree* — they are no longer exactly the same as other populations of the same species, but they have not been on their own evolutionary path long enough to warrant recognition as a distinct species. Allopatric speciation, in which populations of the same species become geographically isolated and begin to diverge, is the most common mechanism by which new animal species have formed in time and space and is likely the way that gorilla lineages evolved. Initially there was only one species of gorilla, but somehow long ago, this ancestral group of gorillas split in two because some kind of physical barrier prevented the two groups from interbreeding. Over many thousands of years or more, each of the two isolated populations of gorillas experienced their own unique random genetic changes (i.e., genetic drift) and natural selection, which in turn led to morphological changes in jaw shape, hair color, body size, and other observable and quantifiable features. After enough time had passed, the two iso-lated groups of gorillas had changed to such a degree that they became two different species. But the exact point in time when this happened is an arbitrary construct of human beings, and those who argue for the subspecies classification contend that some populations of gorillas have not been isolated long enough to be morphologically and genetically dis-tinct species and are thus in the subjective gray area in between. This is certainly the case for the Cross River Gorillas, which have been isolated from the Western Lowland Gorillas for about eighteen thousand years (fewer than one thousand generations), hardly enough time for substan-tial genetic changes to have occurred. Often, hundreds of thousands of years or more need to pass before isolated vertebrate populations diverge enough to be considered distinct species.

Populations of the Western Lowland Gorilla, currently considered to be one subspecies (G. g. gorilla), have relatively marked genetic differ-ences resulting from isolation on different sides of major rivers. Dra-matic worldwide climate changes that occurred between the Miocene (23–5.3 million years ago) and Pleistocene (2.6 million–12,000 years ago) probably separated the eastern (G. beringei) and western (G. gorilla) species (i.e., allopatric speciation) by causing the Congo Basin forests to recede, with expansion of large areas of intervening savanna habi-tats, which the gorillas hesitated to enter. This change forced Eastern Lowland Gorillas into small, isolated patches of forest called refugia. After the climate changed again and the forests expanded to their current widespread state, the Eastern Lowland Gorilla populations expanded rapidly through much of eastern Congo and the Albertine Rift, but they never crossed back into western Central Africa, perhaps because of bar-riers from major rivers, including the Congo.[55] Although the genetic dif-ferences between gorilla subspecies are relatively modest, I agree with most conservation biologists that every effort should be made to protect each and every isolated gorilla population from annihilation. We have much to learn about our own evolutionary history by doing so.

At the conclusion of my team's first herpetological survey in Kahuzi-Biega National Park in 2007, the amiable warden invited me to visit one of the habituated groups of Grauer's gorillas at Tshivanga, near the park head-quarters. The park was established in 1970 to protect the gorillas, but also boasted sizable populations of chimpanzees and elephants, other large mammals, rare birds, and various other species of endemic wild-life. I was surprised to find a gift shop there with souvenirs and books for sale, and being a lifelong bibliophile, I eagerly purchased one of the last copies of a pamphlet about the park and its flora and fauna. Dated from 1995, the pamphlet and the gift shop were remnants of better days at the park before the war. The photos showed happy European tourists trek-king through the forests to photograph gorillas, and in 1990 there were up to 284 gorillas in the highlands of the park. Tourists were advised to book their visits with one of the four habituated gorilla groups in advance during peak tourist seasons in the summer, Christmas, and Easter.[56]

After meeting with park rangers who monitor some of the habituated gorillas daily, I learned that a census during a lull in the war's fighting in 2000 showed that gorilla numbers in the highlands of the park had plummeted to 132 and that some of the habituated groups had been completely annihilated because they were easier targets.[57] As the fight-ing during the war continued, more gorillas were poached and the ele-phant population plummeted to almost nothing. Gangs of Interahamwe militia continued to pop up from time to time to ambush and kill park rangers, but the intrepid rangers were still committed to protecting the park and its wildlife, especially the gorillas.

The rangers gave me a brief rundown about basic gorilla biology and told me that they had seen a gorilla group led by a silverback named Chimanuka not far from Tshivanga the previous day. Armed with AK-47s and machetes, a small group of rangers, Aristote, and I walked away from the gift shop across a small field of cassava plants. After a few more minutes we entered the edge of the forest, and we soon found pieces of vegetation that had been chewed by gorillas. Only a few minutes later we entered more pristine forest, and I started to smell the musky scent of the animals that I recalled so well from my time at the Buffalo Zoo. I felt a surge of adrenaline course through my legs as the lead ranger paused and pointed to a female nonchalantly sitting in the middle of some trees just 30 feet (9 m) away from us. Suddenly I could see several shaggy black forms lying on the ground around her, and a young gorilla was swinging on a vine right next to her.

My hands shaking, I grabbed my camera and started taking pictures. I now understood why some of the most seasoned African travelers claim that encounters with gorillas are among the most exciting wildlife experiences on the continent. There is an inexplicable rush to seeing such a powerful, rare, and human-like wild animal in its native environment. One cannot help but think about the common ancestor humans shared with gorillas about 9 million years ago and how our lineage may have been living exactly like this in a time and place erased from all collective memory, but perhaps still sentient in our souls. The rustling of leaves at our feet started rousing the other animals, because one by one I heard loud sighs, snorts, and grunts as the animals became aware of our presence and slowly sat up. The adult females seemed to ignore us, but the youngsters regarded us with a searching expression in their small brown eyes that seemed to fluctuate between curiosity and wonder.

Suddenly I heard a deep groan and a snort that was louder and more powerful than the others, and I spotted the distinctive silvery gray hair of the dominant male, Chimanuka, as he turned his body around in his nest and opened his eyes. For several moments he just lay there looking up at the trees above him, sluggishly contemplating whether he should get up, as I often find myself doing in the morning. The first female I had spotted as we approached was sitting next to him, and she tenderly caressed his arm as the youngster continued to swing on a vine behind them. I heard something in the trees above us and noticed a small gorilla climbing through some vegetation to regard us from a vantage point about 10 feet (3 m) off the ground. The silverback pivoted his body to the side to look in our general direction, and then he yawned, revealing enormous and fearsome canines.

Seemingly disturbed by our presence, several of the females started to wander off away from us, rustling leaves and cracking branches as they shuffled through the desiccated vegetation on the forest floor. Chimanuka decided it was time to get up, and he slowly shifted his body up to a sitting position and stared off into the forest, but he seemed to be keeping an eye on us with his peripheral vision. His head was massive and elongated, with a cone-like skull; a huge potbelly accentuated the lower half of his torso, and a distinctive red patch of hair framed his sharp brow ridges. Small clouds of black flies swarmed around his head and body, and the youngster who had been swinging on the vine continued to stare at us curiously as he walked toward his father.

Now somewhat awake and hungry, the enormous male started wandering off in the direction of the group, pausing to snap off large pieces of bamboo and other vegetation for feeding. The youngster seemed to mimic the erect and confident stride of his father as he followed him through the path of discarded shoots and stripped vines. We also followed cautiously and slowly, whispering excitedly as we spotted more and more of the family. One of the rangers pointed to a dense clump of trees, and with my telephoto lens I managed to photograph a shy mother with her newborn baby as she spied at us through a narrow window of vegetation while cradling the youngster against her breast. Several of the juvenile gorillas were playing, snorting, and screeching as they ran and pushed into each other, sometimes with such force that they rolled away from their playmates in rapid somersaults. Occasionally Chimanuka paused from his eating to grunt or bark in the direction of the chaotic playing, but after a few moments of concerned glaring, he reached up to the trees to pull down more vegetation for his breakfast.

It was during one of these bouts of gorging that the massive silverback sat down facing us as he munched away on several shoots. Seeing a magnificent opportunity for a close-up of his head, I steadied my telephoto lens from a crouching position only 20 feet (6 m) away and stared at his eyes as I maneuvered the lens toward him. That was a mistake. In my excitement to be sharing the same space with such a magnificent creature, I had completely forgotten one of the golden rules I learned at the Buffalo Zoo about dealing with a silverback—never stare at his eyes, because this can be perceived as a threat to his dominance. After clicking off a shot that I would see later was perfectly focused on two glaring, angry eyes, Chimanuka emitted a sharp bark and charged at us. Thinking I was about to die by dismemberment, I hit the deck in the fetal position to look as nonthreatening as possible, a defensive maneuver I recalled from Sigourney Weaver in *Gorillas in the Mist*.

But the rangers that worked with him every day knew better than I that this was just a bluff. Without moving, they simply held up their hands to block Chimanuka from mischief as he thundered by, and he quickly came to rest a few feet away from us as he sat down to start eating again. Visibly shaking, I looked up to see Aristote's amused face. The rangers looked down at me and started laughing.

"Were you scared you might die?" asked Aristote with a grin.

Not amused, and thinking about the enormous size of the silverback, I replied, "Yes!"

Everybody apparently spoke enough English to understand my reply, and they all broke into heavier fits of animated laughter.

Aristote helped me to my feet, shook his finger at me like I was a child and said, "Do not worry, muzungu, you cannot die from the gorilla because he is habituated to humans, and he cannot do you any harm."

Annoyed that Aristote was lecturing me about a gorilla that he too had only just met, I realized that I was still shaking and now panting. I looked over to see that Chimanuka had his back to us, busily munching away as if nothing had happened. Sensing that the gorillas and I had experienced enough for one day, the rangers said that it was time to go.

We slowly walked away from the group and then turned to look for a nearby road. As I emerged from the forest onto the road, I saw several female gorillas with babies on their backs scampering across the clearing. I photographed them until they disappeared into the adjacent forest, but I did not want to leave. One of the rangers smiled at me knowingly and said that I was very lucky to see the silverback and so many babies during our brief visit. I certainly had to agree, and now that I had experienced Congo's nature so intensely, I knew that I would not be able to resist returning here repeatedly, no matter what the obstacles.

As we slowly walked back to the headquarters at Tshivanga, the rangers asked if I would be willing to give them a little beer money. Under normal tourist circumstances, such a visit would have cost about three hundred dollars, so I had no hesitation to say yes, and I gave them each enough for several bottles. We soon returned to the gift shop, where the smiling warden asked if I had experienced a good visit with the gorillas. I told him yes, and when I gave him some additional beer money in thanks, he shook his hand at me and insisted on giving it all to the rangers, who were ecstatic to now have enough money to throw an entire party. I came away from that meeting thinking that there were still some men in Congo who were not corrupt and believed in conservation enough to risk their lives for it. I still believe that, but two years later the warden was fired for illegally selling elephant ivory that the rangers had confiscated from poachers in the park.

It is easy to hear about the enormous challenges facing gorilla conservation and throw up one's hands in despair and say it is hopeless. However, John Mitani, a primate behavioral ecologist who has worked with great apes for thirty-three years, recently opined, "If we do not take action now . . . our children and our children's children will ask with wonder, and perhaps a certain amount of anger, why we stood by idly while these remarkable creatures were driven to extinction."[58] In the final months of Bill Clinton's presidency in 2000, the Great Apes Conservation Act was signed into law, which authorized Uncle Sam to pay $5 million a year for five years for ape conservation, and the act was reauthorized in 2005 by President George W. Bush. Five million a year may not seem like a lot of money, and in the overall scheme of things it is not, but the act strived to match public and private dollars, and the effort helped to raise $25 million in private grants and governmental support from other countries. In Congo, some of that money was used to introduce alternative fuels to discourage gorilla habitat destruction from the charcoal industry.[59] The act seems to have transitioned into the Great Ape Conservation Fund, which is now administered by the US Fish and Wildlife Service, but gorilla conservation efforts need substantially more funding to ensure a lasting impact.

Chifundera finally showed up with the repaired Toyota at Lwiro on June 3, 2008, and we departed for Kahuzi-Biega National Park the following day, excited to see what new species of amphibians and reptiles we might discover. We stopped at Tshibati long enough to pay our respects to the warden and park rangers we had seen the previous year, and then we moved on to the main road that traversed the mountains on the way to the foot of Kahuzi Volcano, for which the park gets half its name. We had also visited the ranger outpost of Mugaba the previous year, and we were hopeful that friendships we had made then would be strengthened by a second visit.

Because it was the rainy season, the going was very tough. In some places, the road had enormous ruts caused by overloaded lorries getting stuck repeatedly in the same spot. At one point, we had to wait two hours for a large truck to be dug out of an enormous mud pit that resembled a giant bowl of chocolate mousse before we could continue. But despite the difficult journey, the view was spectacular. Pristine montane forest could be seen on both sides of the road, and we occasionally passed through tunnels of bamboo forest so dense and bowed over that nearly all the sunlight was blocked. Once or twice the road curved in such a way that I was able to get a glimpse of the spectacular extinct Kahuzi Volcano (10,853 feet or 3,308 meters tall) rising above the emerald forests. Biega, the other extinct volcano for which the park gets its name, formed with Kahuzi at least 10 million years ago during a rise in volcanic activity between Congo and Rwanda,[60] but recent studies suggest the date might be several million years older.[61]

With about 2,316 square miles (6,000 square km) of territory, Kahuzi-Biega National Park includes a great diversity of habitats from subalpine heather at the highest elevations of the Kahuzi and Biega (9,153 feet or 2,790 m) Volcanoes to lowland tropical rainforest as one descends the western slopes of the Albertine Rift. There are also savanna-like meadows, swamps, peat bogs, and large areas of bamboo forest, which are a favorite haunt of the gorillas. In addition to modest numbers of gorillas and chimpanzees, other more common primates include anubis baboon, dwarf galago (i.e., bush babies), Bosman's potto, five species of guenon monkeys, grey-cheeked mangabey, and three species of black-and-white colobus monkeys. The park also has numerous species of duiker and bongo (antelopes), buffalo, hippo, giant forest hog, mongoose, leopard, genet, jackal, serval, and other cats, and scores of species of bats, insectivores, and rodents.[62] Although the road through Kahuzi-Biega receives a fair bit of traffic daily, I was still able to spot brief glimpses of colorful birds as we turned corners through our winding path in the forest.

We arrived at the ranger outpost of Mugaba in the afternoon. A large

The ranger outpost of Mugaba in Kahuzi-Biega National Park.
Kahuzi Volcano is visible in the background.

pet baboon scurried around the crowd that gathered to greet us. The
majority of the people at the outpost were pygmies, and like many places
I have visited in Congo, they were very friendly and accommodating for
the unexpected guests that suddenly arrived out of the blue. They provided us with jerry cans of water and, after some brief negotiations from
Chifundera, a few rooms in a simple rectangular building made from
concrete, brick, and a corrugated metal roof.

I was curious to see the bamboo forest on the slopes of Kahuzi Volcano, so I left Marcel to prepare dinner and set out with Chif, Aristote,
Wandege, Maurice, and a couple of armed rangers on a trail leading up
to the summit. Although there had not been any trouble in a while, Interahamwe militia were known to roam the lowland forests of the park, and
a rebel dissident from the Congolese army had attacked Mugaba in 2005,
kidnapping nearly all of the rangers and stealing their equipment.[63]

The trail first led through a small area of cultivation before ascending
the volcano, and then passed through beautiful patches of montane forest, small streams, and enormous pockets of bamboo forest. The forest
was still wet from the rain, and we had to don our rain jackets to prevent the water on the leaves from soaking into our clothes as our bodies
brushed past the lush vegetation. As dusk set in, the haunting calls of

at least half a dozen kinds of birds echoed through the mountains. We rested on the trail and listened to the changing of the guard as the diurnal forms of life settled into their beds and the nocturnal ones started to stir from their daytime hiding places.

My mind drifted to Akeley's death brawl with the wounded leopard that he had shot twice in East Africa. "Chif, do you think we have to worry about leopards?" I asked. I suddenly recalled pictures from an old *National Geographic* story that showed an ancient species of hominid (human-like ancestor) from East Africa that had been discovered with leopard canine puncture holes in its skull. When the cats attack humans, it is usually from behind and without warning.

"No!" he replied with conviction. "The leopards have been hunted heavily in eastern Congo, for skins for men with money in the Middle East."

I am sure Chif was right that leopards and other animals with commercially valuable hides had been poached heavily during the insecurity of recent decades, but huge areas of pristine forest afforded ample places to hide, and adequate populations of antelope, bush pig, and other mammalian prey still remained in the park. Was Kahuzi-Biega's leopard population really wiped out? In Africa, reliable population estimates are difficult to obtain, because resources to count secretive leopards are scarce, especially in the least-developed countries of the continent, including Congo. Because the cats have learned to live on the outskirts of major cities in Africa and India, it is likely that they are still present in many areas where one would not expect them to be present in the twenty-first century.[64] Either way, leopards would probably be spooked away by our headlamps — probably.

When the onset of darkness was complete, we fanned out to look for animals. I lifted up rocks and fallen branches to see if anything was sheltering underneath, and I used my snake tongs — a metal pole 3 feet (1 m) long with a pistol grip and a chopstick-like end — to probe piles of dead leaves on the forest floor for hiding lizards and frogs. Like countless other times in Congo, it was not our night — we found only a single puddle frog after hours of searching.

The next morning, as the first rays of the sun cast a warm glow on my sleeping bag, I opened my eyes and caught a glimpse of a mouse running across my body. For reasons I have not quite figured out, the Congolese I have interacted with always guffaw hysterically whenever they see or hear about rodents in human habitations. This time was no exception. When I informed them of my early morning sprinter, Chifundera joked that maybe I would have a new, small, furry girlfriend to keep me company at night.

The following morning after a breakfast of cold rice leftover from dinner, Aristote and I got to work photographing the small number of specimens we had collected the previous night. The procedure was always the same. I would use a small squeeze bottle to shoot a fine stream of water onto animals that were dirty, cleaning them off so the photos would capture them at their best. Aristote had a talent for making the frogs disoriented temporarily and flipping them onto their back so that I could snap a quick shot of their venter (belly), which often has species-specific coloration. Small crowds would invariably gather around us during this process, and people speculated about how the muzungu must be getting rich from the process. When we would handle nonvenomous snakes with our hands, people would shriek in shock, and the crowds' chatter would revolve around the topic of me being a wizard, for how else could I handle a snake without dying?

With the photo shoot complete, it was now time to write down detailed information about the photographs and GPS coordinates in my field notes and take DNA samples from the specimens. The rangers provided me with a small table and a chair, and I got to work. As an evolutionary biologist and herpetologist, I am interested to know how, why, where, and when species of amphibians and reptiles evolved and to understand their relationships to each other. I am also interested in looking at species boundaries, or roughly where one species ends, in both geographical space and genetic connections, and another begins. For example, there might be two populations—a group of interbreeding individuals of the same species—of green frogs that live on two separate mountains. The frogs look the same as far as their color pattern, shape, size, foot webbing, and other morphological features. But if one analyzes the mating call of these frogs, or the "song" the males use to attract mates (typically at night), there might be differences in the pitch, frequency, and other quantifiable characteristics between the two populations. If you suspect the two populations might actually be different species, you can analyze the DNA, and you might find that not only are the two populations genetically distinct, but they are more closely related to other previously recognized species than they are to each other. This is an example of "cryptic species," where we think we have only one species based on morphology, but other types of data (especially from DNA) suggest there are actually two, or sometimes even three or more species. Throughout most of the twentieth century and earlier, morphology was typically the only tool available to scientists to distinguish species. If no previous researcher recognized and named the genetically distinct populations identified from modern DNA analyses, it is necessary to modify the taxonomy and name new species to acknowledge this diversity. Importantly, this type of work has conservation implications, because one must know how many and what kind of species occur in an area to understand exactly what one is conserving. If newly recognized species are restricted to tiny geographic areas, they are invariably classified as threatened to some degree.

A lot of this meticulous work takes place in the laboratory after the expeditions are over, because one needs to examine preserved specimens under a dissecting microscope to scrutinize and measure minute morphological details such as scale counts and patterns, even on tiny structures like toes that might be only a millimeter long. Analyses of DNA take hours of work and require expensive, perishable enzymes, and even more expensive machines (DNA sequencers cost hundreds of thousands of dollars) that need constant power sources and dedicated technicians, requirements that unfortunately are still prohibitive in most developing areas of Africa. When you factor in the enormous amount of time needed to synthesize previously published research, often in foreign languages and difficult to obtain, the researcher can quickly become immersed in projects dealing with only one species for months at a time. Sometimes, however, if one is familiar with a particular group of animals, it is possible to recognize the discovery of a new species as soon as you find the first specimen in the wild, because it might have a morphology that is so distinctive that one can be sure it is new. That type of discovery is the most exciting of all and has kept my colleagues and me motivated to work in dangerous, uncomfortable, and unhealthy tropical environments for the last decade. So far, my colleagues and I have described eleven species of amphibians and nine species of reptiles that are new to science, but I expect this number to increase dramatically in the coming years.

After several hours of work, I wiped the sweat off my head and stepped outside to look at the extinct volcano. Several ominous, dark clouds swirled around the summit, casting a long shadow over the jungle beneath it. With the promise of more rain in the evening, perhaps we would have better luck finding frogs.

Suddenly, something jerked my pants behind my knee. Before I could turn around, the resident baboon spun around me and tried to jump up into my arms. I shrieked and staggered backward, causing an eruption of laughter from everyone nearby. The baboon was obviously tame, but it was large enough to cause a serious bite, and the list of hideous diseases carried by primates in Congo is very long. Monkeypox in particular would be a slow, horrible way to die—imagine chicken pox on steroids. One of the rangers, still laughing, took pity on me and shooed the baboon away. I smiled awkwardly at the people who continued to laugh at me and saw a little boy re-creating the event, to everyone's delight. At least I was being a good guest by providing some entertainment.

That night, as we set out to search for more frogs in a steady rain with our armed escorts, we were unaware that our modest luck would turn around in a spectacular way, and we would solve a mystery that had started almost eighty years before. In 1929, a notoriously careless German herpetologist named Ernst Ahl described several species of treefrogs in the genus *Leptopelis* from the neighboring countries of Rwanda and Belgian Congo. It is unclear whether his thinking mirrored that of the gorilla taxonomist Matschie, but only about 16 percent of the frog species Ahl named are considered valid today. It is somewhat ironic that Ahl, who joined the Nazi Party in 1933 and died fighting for it in 1945, named one of these treefrog species for the Jewish explorer Grauer, who had collected some of the specimens.[65] The controversy was about two of Ahl's putative species: *Leptopelis karissimbensis* (described from Mt. Karisimbi in Rwanda) and *Leptopelis kivuensis* (described from Gisenyi on the north-eastern shore of Lake Kivu, also in Rwanda). In the original description, Ahl noted that the former species had a blue throat, whereas the latter's was white. For decades, several prominent herpetologists went back and forth questioning the validity of the two species. Imagine my shock when I heard two distinctly different *Leptopelis* calls (one sounded like Daffy Duck chuckling) from some bushes on the side of the road only a couple hundred feet from Mugaba, and then noticed that one species had a blue throat, whereas the other was white! Although detailed scientific analyses of the DNA and calls of the treefrogs would eventually confirm my suspicion that Ahl got it right in this case,[66] it was exciting to know that I had solved the mystery in the same instant that I found the two species calling together. It was an extraordinary stroke of luck, because I would never find the two species in the same place again.

The next morning, as Aristote and I photographed the frogs from the night before, I observed a defense behavior that Ahl could not have known about from preserved specimens. When Aristote positioned the nearly 2-inch (4.5 cm) animal on a tree stump, it suddenly curved its body upward, raised its legs in the same direction, and opened its mouth. Some Eurasian salamanders and frogs have a similar pose called the unken reflex, in which the brightly colored underside of the body and tail are curved upward to advertise the fact that they are highly poisonous to would-be predators. The treefrogs that posed for us included the white-bellied species *Leptopelis kivuensis*, which suggests that they are not trying to show off bright colors and that instead this performance is likely a death-feigning act. Because the nocturnal treefrogs hide very effectively during the day, the pygmies were astonished to see their bizarre behavior, and I felt gratified that the villagers seemed to be as interested in the frogs as I was.

As we prepared to leave Kahuzi Volcano's shadow, I felt energized that we had discovered so much in such a small amount of time. My mind began to wander to Mwenga, the town on the western edge of the poorly explored Itombwe Plateau where we planned to head next. I would not be disappointed by the animals I would find there in the coming days, but my team and I would pay for those discoveries dearly.

THE WRONG PLACE AT THE WRONG TIME

3 As world opinion was turning against King Leopold II in 1908, the Belgian Parliament was embroiled in a nasty debate about what to do with Congo. In August of that year, the final vote in favor of annexing Leopold's Congo was eighty-eight in favor, fifty-four opposed, and nine abstentions; some of the opposition hissed once they realized they had lost. The Congo Free State officially became the Belgian Congo on November 15, 1908, but for four years, the change in name did not translate to meaningful improvements of policy. One reason was that Belgium had no experience as a colonial power, and it must have been a daunting task to take over administration of a devastated territory eighty times the size of the tiny European country. The only clear goal that Belgium foresaw for Congo was that it should pay for itself, and soon multiple Belgian corporations were granted concessions to exploit the vast mineral wealth, grow cash crops like cotton, and improve infrastructure to bring these products to the international market. A portion of the profits went to the state, and after several years the colony was generating substantial sums of money. Attracted by lucrative salaries, especially for the mining industry in Katanga, thousands of Europeans (and some Americans) moved to Congo to make their fortune. A "head tax" in 1914 forced thousands of Congolese men to work for the state for paltry wages in unsanitary cities (the African death rate in Elisabethville was 24 percent), and although women worked too, they were paid in salt instead of money.[1]

The vast majority of Congolese were treated as second-class citizens by hundreds of *chef de poste* (state

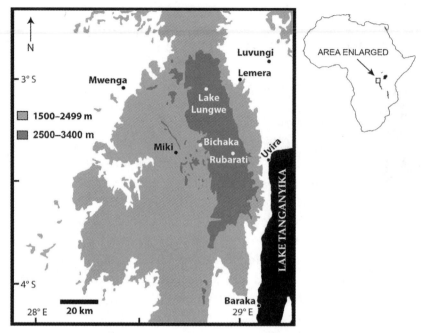

Map of the Itombwe Plateau. Modified from Greenbaum et al. 2011.

officials), who were asked to serve as tax collectors, judges, census takers, construction managers, farmers, and consultants, all with little or no training and often in isolation. A significant number of these European officials had worked in Leopold's Congo Free State, and they had no compunction about flogging Congolese with the chicotte for disciplinary reasons, a practice that was not outlawed until 1955. When the administrators were not trying to accomplish their impossible mandates, they suffered from tropical diseases or fought with each other—Dutch-speaking Fleming and French-speaking Walloon cultural rivalries from Belgium spilled over into the colony. With the outbreak of World War I in 1914, Belgium was rapidly overrun by German soldiers, but in Congo, Belgian officers led African Force Publique soldiers to fight the Germans in their colonial territories in Cameroon, Ruanda-Burundi (one country at that time), and Tanganyika (modern-day Tanzania). These soldiers also fought the Italians in Ethiopia. After the war, a public works program was initiated, which improved Congo's infrastructure, schools, hospitals, electricity access, and housing. Following a temporary economic hiccup that affected most of the world during the Great Depression, Congo's economy bloomed in 1935, and well-paying jobs cropped up around the diamond, gold, and other precious-metals mining industry, which led to the highest standard of living for Africans on the continent. Thanks to Congo's numerous natural resources, including uranium, World War II continued the economic boom, and an urbanization trend saw many Congolese people move to major cities. Large amounts of the money from the economic boom were spent on improving health care, and numerous hospitals, clinics, and pharmacies were built across the country. Deadly diseases like malaria and sleeping sickness that had ravaged Congo since time immemorial were kept under control. Education also improved—97 percent of Congo's children were attending grade school by the late 1950s, and an educated elite class called the *évolué* (the evolved) emerged among the successful, urban Congolese.[2]

In spite of these impressive gains, the Belgians were still firmly in control of their colony beyond the first half of the twentieth century. Most Congolese were purposefully educated in vocational and agricultural curricula, less than 2 percent were allowed to continue to secondary school, and even fewer went on to the university level. The schools, hotels, restaurants, bars (the sale of alcohol to the Congolese was illegal until 1955!), and all places of entertainment were sharply segregated, and many have argued that racial segregation was the official policy of the Belgian administration. Of course Congolese were not allowed to attain positions of power in this administration, and control of the radio and newspapers was in Belgian hands only. Some of the worst Belgians referred to the Congolese as *sale macaque* (filthy monkeys) that "had only recently come down from the trees."[3] During filming of the award-winning movie *The African Queen* in 1951, Katherine Hepburn observed the "psychological imprisonment of being looked upon as inferior" that her Congolese servant Tahili had experienced.[4]

By the late 1950s, the "winds of change" were blowing across Africa, and multiple colonies under European control were granted independence. Belgium was slow to see the writing on the wall, and the administration seems to have been caught off guard when a charismatic and popular *évolué* named Patrice Lumumba demanded immediate independence in December 1958. Days later, when a political rally was planned in the capital Leopoldville (modern-day Kinshasa), the Belgian administration canceled it, triggering violent and destructive riots. A year later Lumumba joined a roundtable meeting in Belgium to discuss Congo's future, where he and his Congolese colleagues were granted almost all of their demands, including nearly immediate independence. But because there were few educated Congolese, none of whom had any experience in state administration, there was almost no preparation for the handover of power. Moreover, there were at least 120 political parties in Congo, many of which had competing interests and tribal rivalries.[5] The stage was set for a disaster.

Lumumba was elected as the first prime minister of Congo, which was officially granted independence on June 30, 1960. King Baudouin of Belgium gave a patronizing speech at the independence ceremony in which he praised King Leopold II. Lumumba responded furiously by saying that Baudouin had presided over "a regime of injustice, suppression, and exploitation."[6] The king was stunned, but the Congolese audience cheered. Within days, many emboldened Congolese soldiers and police rebelled against every white person (including priests, nuns, and children) in sight, and beatings, rape, torture, and killings were rampant. Shortly thereafter, leaders in Katanga declared they were seceding from Congo, and they armed themselves in anticipation of a military response. Europeans fled by the thousands, often with only the clothes on their backs. Lumumba was powerless to stop the chaos unfolding around him, and in an act of desperation, he dismissed all Belgian military officers and put a newly promoted Congolese colonel and chief-of-staff named Mobutu in charge, but the pandemonium continued. A bloodbath ensued, and thousands of Congolese lost their lives as the Belgians retaliated with paratroopers and other military.[7]

Under intense pressure from the downward spiral of his new country, Lumumba's actions became increasingly erratic. He declared war against Belgium, and when international troops from the UN arrived in Leopoldville to restore calm, he demanded that they be put under Congolese control, an unrealistic request that was promptly refused. Desperate, Lumumba flew to the United States to try to rally support at the UN and Washington for an invasion of Katanga, but this request was also refused. The United States and Belgium agreed that Lumumba had to be removed from power, and the novice leader effectively signed his own death warrant when he made a statement on his way out of Washington that "the Soviet Union has been the only great power which supported the Congolese people in their struggle from the beginning."[8] At the height of the Cold War, it is doubtful that Lumumba could have repulsed the Americans more effectively, and when Soviet transport planes started arriving in Congo, the United States hatched a plan to assassinate him.[9, 10]

After Mobutu violently crushed a second secession movement in the diamond-rich Kasai Province, the UN decided to invade Katanga to halt the original secession movement, which ended after its leader, Moise Tshombe, surrendered to their demands. With local European support and white mercenaries, Tshombe would attempt to kick the UN out by force in 1962, but that effort would result in thousands of European and Congolese deaths before failing. Bolstered by American support, Mobutu seized control of Leopoldville in September 1960, easily pushing aside a weak and demoralized Lumumba. In early 1961 the deposed prime minister fell into the hands of his Congolese enemies, but it was a Belgian officer who gave the order to fire when Lumumba was put in front of a firing squad. When Lumumba's death became known worldwide, Belgian embassies in several African nations were attacked, and some race riots even erupted in the United States.[11]

With the death of Lumumba and legitimate Congolese government with him, a power vacuum was created, and widespread fighting broke out in various parts of the country, especially in the east, from 1961 to 1967. Meanwhile, Mobutu's influence steadily increased in the 1960s. As a young man, he had read works by Winston Churchill, Charles de Gaulle, and Machiavelli, and he used that knowledge with his legendary memory to increase his power. In 1963 the rising dictator made a visit to the United States to call on President Kennedy, who gave the new Congolese leader a DC-3 airplane with an American crew (who answered to the CIA) for his private use. One year later, when a rebel group calling itself the Simbas ("lions" in Swahili) took control of an area in eastern Congo about the size of France, Mobutu hired a small army of white mercenaries to take it back. The mercenaries were assisted by bombing runs from American planes, which were also used to fly Belgian paratroopers into areas where Europeans and Americans were being held as hostages. The Simbas tortured and killed dozens of the hostages as the paratroopers invaded, but they were quickly defeated. By the end of 1965, Mobutu was firmly in control of the country, and he continued to violently crush any rebellion or plot that threatened him, including two major coup attempts in 1978 and 1983.[12] He also decided to rename the country Zaire in 1971, and several cities with colonial names (e.g., Leopoldville and Stanleyville) were given new Congolese monikers.

As Mobutu consolidated his power, he learned that it was much easier to buy his enemies off than to fight them, especially because money was pouring into the country from foreign aid and corporate bribes. It is estimated that he stole somewhere between $4 and $15 billion during his three decades in power. He purchased mansions all over the world, including one with a fifteen-thousand-bottle wine cellar near his birthplace at Gbadolite in a remote corner of northwestern Zaire. Taking the hint from their leader, Mobutu's people readily adopted the national Zairean philosophy that would become known as "kleptocracy," and corruption became endemic throughout the country. In one infamous televised speech to his own people, Mobutu declared, "Go ahead and steal, as long as you don't take too much."[13] On another occasion when the dictator decided he would no longer pay his troops, he told them, "Débrouillez-vous" (Fend for yourselves).[14] Bribes were expected for almost all business transactions, to travel through roadblocks, and to enter into universities, regardless of academic competence. Between corrupt state officials who openly stole from public coffers and Mobutu's xenophobic decrees to expel foreign business owners and religious leaders, the economy of Zaire took a downturn in 1974 and continued to decline every year thereafter. Meanwhile, the institutions (e.g., education, sanitation, transportation, and health care) and infrastructure that the Belgians had spent decades building (with veritable slave labor from the

Congolese) started to collapse, and government officials were either too inexperienced or too busy stealing to do anything about it.[15]

In 1989, Mobutu and his entourage took a lavish trip to the United States to visit President George H. W. Bush, who had known Mobutu during his time as director of the CIA. Bush welcomed Mobutu by saying, "Zaire is among America's oldest friends."[16] Most of Mobutu's cash flow originated from the United States, but when the Cold War ended in 1990 and the American money with it, Zaire went bankrupt, many of the country's people did not have enough food to eat, and child starvation rates in rural areas spiked to 16 percent. Miraculously, Mobutu clung to power for several more years — partly through his own political cunning, but also through violence. When a million peaceful protesters took to the streets in February 1992 for the March of Hope against Mobutu, his thugs responded by killing thirty-five men, women, and children and setting others alight with napalm. As inflation skyrocketed, mass riots called *pillages* led to serious economic damage and loss of life in 1991 and 1993.[17] Eventually, the poor economy and prostate cancer weakened Mobutu and his government so much that a rebel commander named Laurent Kabila was able to march hundreds of miles from eastern Zaire to the capital at Kinshasa and seize power as the new dictator. When Mobutu passed away in Morocco from his illness in 1997, Kabila was taking control of a country that had been virtually ruined by his predecessor.[18] As Mobutu had tried to erase the legacy of colonialism by renaming the country Zaire in 1971, Kabila attempted to erase Mobutu by renaming the country Democratic Republic of the Congo in 1997.

On June 8, after returning from Kahuzi-Biega, I was working on my field notes at Chifundera's house in Bukavu when the ground started to vibrate violently. For several seconds I could not figure out what was happening, but then I realized it was an earthquake. It was a vivid reminder that the forces splitting Africa in two via the Great Rift Valley are still active, just like they have been for millions of years. The shaking stopped as quickly as it had begun, and I went to bed early so that I would be rested for the following day's journey.

As we headed west to the town of Mwenga, we passed through shimmering grassy hills that marked the western edge of the great Itombwe Plateau, a poorly explored montane region with scores of rare species. We had grand plans to penetrate deep into Itombwe via Uvira in the east, but for now I wanted to spend a few days in Mwenga because it was near midelevation forests (ca. 4,600 feet, 1,400 m) that promised to have an intersection of species that would be adapted to the lowland Congo Basin, midelevation specialists, and perhaps even some of the highland species that had wandered down to their lowest elevational limit. Although Mwenga served as a territorial headquarters and trading center in the colonial era,[19] it was far removed from the national parks established at that time, and the Belgian herpetologists did not focus much of their attention there. As a result, I was likely to uncover new species that they had missed, and I couldn't wait to see what exciting discoveries awaited in Mwenga's nearby forests.

Our dour driver Mululema stoically pressed the aging Land Cruiser through the winding roads and light rain, and I did not notice when we passed by the small hillside town of Kasika, where at least one thousand people were slaughtered by Rwandan soldiers during the war in 1998.[20] As we neared the city, Chifundera pointed east, toward the immense mountains of Itombwe, which were still covered with montane forest. "The gorilla was living here only ten years ago!" he declared. "But the people hunted them, and now they are gone."

The forest was on a steep hillside, but it looked like one could reach it within a few hours of climbing. I cursed my luck for arriving only a few years after the gorillas and the virgin forest in which they lived had been damaged forever. However, I knew that the smaller animals were the last to go, and my chances of finding unique amphibians and reptiles was high. I looked down on the opposite side of the road and saw a large river snaking through huge swaths of forest that extended into the horizon.

Chif continued to tell me about a semiaquatic antelope called a Water Chevrotain (Hyemoschus aquaticus) that was common in the forest; clearly he was very proud of the beautiful area we were about to explore. I later learned that the chevrotain is a stocky, primitive ruminant that looks like a strange cross between a pig and a deer. It has a beautiful reddish brown coat with white spots and stripes, a bizarre muzzle with slit-like nostrils, and sharp canine tusks used for male-male combat. The animals may have a relatively short lifespan—in captivity they rarely live beyond a year.[21] They frequent forested river valleys like the ones around Mwenga from eastern Congo all the way to West Africa, where they have suffered heavily from poaching and deforestation. Despite being wiped out in western Uganda and its ongoing declines, this antelope species has a relatively large population estimate, and it is not currently considered threatened.[22]

As we passed a small village, a storm rolled in, and people stared at us from the shelter of their huts. A middle-aged woman was standing in the rain shouting at a man who tried to take her by the arm. I could not understand the insults she was shouting, but it was obvious from her slurred speech that she was drunk. Mululema took his foot off the gas so that we could watch the spectacle a little longer as we passed by. I was shocked as I saw her start to slap the man in the face. He continued to try and drag her away, and then she overcompensated with one of her swings and fell face first into a muddy puddle. We were still laughing as we pulled up to an Italian missionary at the edge of Mwenga a few minutes later, just as the waning sun cast an orangish glow over the retreating storm clouds. It would be expensive (about one hundred dollars for all of us) to spend the night at the missionary, which doubled as a hotel, but with darkness approaching we did not have much choice. I was shown to a comfortable room with a large desk and a bed with mosquito netting, all of which are rare luxuries in Congo, so I decided it was worth the premium price for a night. But on my shoestring budget, we would have to find another place to stay the following day.

In the morning after a European-style breakfast of a croissant and some jam, Chifundera left with Mululema to contact colleagues of his from the Congolese wildlife authority, the Institut Congolais pour la Conservation de la Nature (ICCN). Somehow the local boys had already heard that we were looking for frogs, so they started bringing in toads tied with grass to small sticks, and small plastic containers with reed frogs they had found near streams in the city. Most of the species I had seen many times before, but one of the boys showed me a small brown reed frog with a thin yellow line that started at its nose and continued halfway down the body. I asked Aristote and Wandege to go with him to find more while I started to work on the specimens I had in hand. They returned after an hour with several more of the reed frogs, which proved to be a new *Hyperolius* species after I returned to the United States and analyzed the DNA. But that was not all. They introduced me to two pygmies named Butikima and Lukaba who knew the area well and could serve as guides to help us work in the forest.

Because the Italian mission was so expensive, Chif convinced his colleagues at ICCN to let us rent a small and dusty building that they used for office space toward the center of town. We quickly gathered up our things and transferred the operation down there. The place was a bit of a dump, but the price was right, so I cleared away the spiderwebs and rat dung in my allocated room and set up my tent. Aristote, Mululema, and Maurice decided they would prefer to spring for a cheap hotel on the edge of town rather than sleep in the place, so they disappeared to reserve some rooms.

In the late afternoon, Butikima and Lukaba said they could introduce us to the chief of a small village at the edge of Mwenga where the forest starts and that we could probably work there. We left Mululema with the truck after a short drive to the place. It was now dark, so we all turned on our headlamps to guide our path as we followed our pygmy guides to the modest house of the chief. After exchanging a few pleasant greetings, the chief told us that we were welcome in his village and that we could feel free to look for as many frogs as we liked. We followed our guides through the center of the village and down a hill past a fish pond to a stream at the edge of the forest. We shimmied over a tree that had been purposely cut down to fall across the stream and plunged into a forest that was full of ferns as tall as trees. I saw that we were at the bottom of a steep hill, and we started climbing deeper into the forest in search of frogs. Suddenly I felt a little sting on my neck, and I reached up and crushed a tiny black ant. The ant's bite continued to burn for a minute, but I shrugged it off as one of the many annoyances of fieldwork.

It was then that I noticed the men ahead of me were slapping their necks and arms too. "Siafu!" (Ants!), someone yelled. The ants were literally raining down on us from the ferns — we had disturbed a huge nest, and now they were on the warpath. I urged everyone to move up the hill, but the more we climbed, the more they divebombed us. "These insects are dangerous!" warned Aristote.

"Aristote, come on, it's just ants, keep moving so we can get away from them," I said.

But they just kept coming and seemed to be everywhere. I could feel the sting of more and more of them on my neck as they crawled into our clothes. Chifundera ripped off his shirt so he could brush them away. Admitting defeat, I called it quits, and we retreated down the hill and waded through the river to escape. We spent a few minutes slapping each other's backs to kill the ants, and thankfully the painful bites faded away quickly. Demoralized, we decided to call it a night and returned up the hill toward the truck.

After ascending the final hill after the fish pond, we entered the village and I was surprised to see everyone outside of their huts in an agitated state. They started yelling at Chif and Aristote, and I could sense a lot of fear and anger emanating from the crowd. The rants in Swahili came so rapidly that I could not understand what had upset them, but I made out one word: Interahamwe. We tried to explain that we had permission from the chief to be there, but because we met him at night when many people were in bed, he had not been able to spread the word about our presence. Even though at least two dozen people had seen us walk through the village a couple hours earlier, a rumor that we were militia coming from the forest somehow spread like wildfire. The obvious logic that a white man could not be part of a Rwandan militia was lost on them. I glanced at Butikima and Lukaba, but they looked too scared to intervene. We would find out later that Interahamwe militia had emerged from the same forest at night with flashlights only a week before and killed someone from this village. No wonder they were confused and frightened.

We walked away from the angry crowd but were followed by a small number of men who berated us with curses until we reached the truck and drove away. An animated conversation commenced once we were safely away, and we all agreed that we were lucky to have walked away unscathed. A few minutes after I retired into my tent to contemplate the worst day I had ever had in Congo, the police showed up. Our "militia" had been reported to them, and they tracked us down easily. The villagers told the police that I was carrying a gun (my snake tongs), which might have discouraged them from attacking us. Aristote and Chifundera explained everything and even showed them the harmless tongs. The police decided we were telling the truth and left. As the animated conversations over the day's events continued, I went to bed thinking that the worst was over, but I was wrong.

Slightly smaller than the state of Maryland, Rwanda is known as "the land of a thousand hills" because of the undulating terraces of farmland that cover most of the country. Very little land has been spared from conversion to agricultural use, because Rwanda has an extremely dense population and high fertility rates, but it was not always this way. Although the precolonial history of Rwanda is poorly documented, the first settlers in the country were probably the pygmy Batwa and, like their brethren in Congo, were hunter-gatherers in the forests that once covered most of Rwanda. Sometime afterward, the Bantu-speaking Hutu people arrived, and because they were focused on agriculture, they likely initiated the massive deforestation to make room for their crops. A bit later, the putatively Nilotic Tutsi people arrived from the north with their cows to establish a pastoral culture alongside the Hutu, and to a lesser extent, the marginalized Batwa who lost an increasing amount of their hunting grounds. For centuries, the three groups lived relatively peacefully, and eventually they spoke the same language (Kinyarwanda), coexisted in the same social and political chiefdoms, and intermarried freely. Many ethnographers and historians agree that because of this mixing, the Rwandan Hutu and Tutsi cannot be considered separate ethnic groups.[23]

Around 1860, a Tutsi *mwami* (king) named Rwabugiri took control of the Rwandan throne and consolidated his power around a territory roughly equal in size to the current country, and he reserved lucrative positions of power for his fellow Tutsis. When the first Europeans arrived a few years later, they assumed that the "noble" Tutsi race had always ruled over the seemingly subordinate Hutu. They also noticed stereotypical physical differences between the two groups: the Tutsi were tall and light skinned, with narrow noses, chins, and lips, whereas the Hutu were the exact opposite. John Hanning Speke, a British explorer who described the two "races" in detail, concocted the idea that the Tutsi were a Hamitic master race of long-lost Christians from Ethiopia. This so-called Hamitic myth endured for many decades and was embraced by the Germans, who first colonized Rwanda after taking advantage of political turmoil in the wake of Rwabugiri's death. The Germans supported the Tutsi minority, whom they viewed as the superior ruling class, which polarized the distinction between Hutu and Tutsi in the eyes of both the colonizers and Rwandans.[24]

The Belgians continued this policy of Tutsi favoritism when the League of Nations bestowed Ruanda-Urundi to them as a spoil of World War I in 1919, and they went a step further by issuing ethnic identity cards (Batwa, Hutu, or Tutsi) to everyone in the colony. The Belgians bestowed unlimited powers on the Tutsi for advancement in education, politics, employment, and to exploit the labor and financial resources of the Hutu, which predictably led to enormous feelings of resentment by the latter group. These actions had another damaging effect—Rwandans lost their strong sense of national identity in favor of ethnic identity.[25]

In the late 1950s Belgium was pressured by the UN to prepare Ruanda-Urundi for independence. Seeing an opportunity to reverse their fortune, Hutu intellectuals began arguing for majority rule. A cycle of violent attacks and endless reprisals between the Tutsi and Hutu groups led to thousands of deaths and displaced people in the newly independent countries of Rwanda and Burundi for years. In the 1980s, exiled Rwandan Tutsi living in Uganda formed a rebel army called the Rwandan Patriotic Front (RPF), and they collaborated with Ugandan rebels to bring Yoweri Museveni, the current president of Uganda, to power. With this military experience, the RPF crossed the border into Rwanda in 1990 and started a civil war with the Hutu regime, which led to twenty thousand deaths and 1.5 million displaced people. Hutu extremists in Rwanda started stockpiling weapons and organizing "civil defense" youth militias. An economic downturn in the late 1980s had left tens of thousands of young men unemployed and easy targets for recruitment.

One infamous militia called itself the Interahamwe, or "those who attack together." In a system analogous to the Hitler youth movement in Nazi Germany, they gathered at huge, alcohol-soaked rallies where Hutu extremist propaganda commingled with popular music. The men were trained to destroy property and kill people, and neighborhood-sized groups drew up lists of all the Tutsis in their area.[26]

In 1993, under intense international pressure, Juvénal Habyarimana, Rwanda's third president, signed the Arusha Peace Accords, which would allow the Tutsi refugees living in other countries to return to Rwanda, reintegrate into society, and enter the political process. Hutu extremists called the president a traitor. When UN soldiers arrived in Rwanda toward the end of 1993 to bolster the peace efforts, Hutu instigators claimed they were there to help the Tutsi take power by force. Shortly thereafter in 1994, in another eerie comparison to the Nazis, Hutu extremists commenced their scheme for the "final solution" of the Tutsis. In April 1994, Habyarimana's plane was shot down, killing him and the new Hutu president of Burundi. This was the signal for the Hutu-dominated FAR (Forces Armées Rwandaises), Interahamwe, and other extremists to start their killing spree. Only one hundred days later, at least eight hundred thousand people had been killed, mostly by machete. The massacre had occurred three times faster than the Holocaust in World War II. As the evidence of genocide became grotesquely obvious, the world looked to the United States to do something. After all, they had been instrumental in 1946 when the UN labeled genocide a crime under international law. But with the embarrassment of American deaths in Somalia the previous year (i.e., the Blackhawk Down debacle) still fresh in the minds of the president and his foreign policy advisers, they did nothing, and, even worse, they discouraged other nations from intervening.[27]

I woke up suddenly at 3 a.m. with a sharp pain in my abdomen with an intensity I had never experienced before. The violent, painful waves that wracked my body from that moment forward lasted until dawn, and I was very dehydrated, with a wicked headache, by the time I heard loud voices in the next room. Exhausted and weak, I pulled myself together to find out what was going on.

Squinting from the sharp ray of sunlight that flooded in from the building's open door, I found Chifundera and Aristote engaged in a louder-than-normal conversation, and it seemed like Aristote was upset.

"Aristote, what happened?" I asked.

"There was an attack in the night," answered Chifundera. His face had an anger and fear in it that I had never seen before. His resigned tone belied the fact that he had seen such attacks before.

Aristote explained that after the police had left the previous night, he, Maurice, and Mululema had decided to return to the hotel room that they had rented for the night, but some of the angry villagers were waiting with wooden sticks, and they were attacked. Thinking quickly, Aristote said he doubled over to protect our only GPS unit, but the thieves stole three hundred dollars in cash, his headlamp, and a cell phone. Poor Maurice got beaten by a woman, an unfortunate experience that was often ridiculed by the other men for years afterward. Mululema took some licks until he surrendered his driver's license and ID card, and somebody smashed out the back windshield of the truck. Things could have gone very badly from there, but a local military commander named Rama stepped in and put a stop to it. When I saw everyone and the truck the next day, they looked a bit worse for wear, so I bought everyone some good food and beer to restore morale. As we started to calm down, my companions realized that I looked unusually pale.

"Eli, are you feeling okay?" asked Aristote.

"No, I am sick."

Chifundera stepped forward and put his hand on my head to feel my temperature. "You have no fever," he said, trying to sound encouraging.

"Yes, this time it's weird, I have no fever but the headache is bad and my stomach is a mess, so what can we do?"

Aristote and Mululema took me in the truck to the hospital on the edge of town, which looked like it had been built recently. Within a few minutes, I was sitting in front of a doctor and answering his questions in English. We talked about malaria for a while, and how the muzungu is especially prone to catching it in Africa. He ordered some blood to be drawn from me to check. Aristote and I walked down the hallway to the lab, and after seeing the doctor's note on my patient card, the technician motioned for me to have a seat. I looked around the room, and it seemed similar to an old high school chemistry lab. The walls were painted a morbid dark green and covered with public health posters, and there were scores of ancient chemical bottles on the shelves and cabinets. The smell resembled a mixture of postparty frat house and nail polish remover. Some of the glass doors on the cabinets were cracked or missing, and the central work table was stained with countless spills of chemicals, blood, and other unidentifiable fluids. I looked at the floor and saw several large cardboard boxes of medical supplies marked "USAID" (United States Agency for International Development). My nausea was temporarily arrested as I contemplated the irony of being treated with American medical supplies in Congo. Perhaps some of the tax dollars I had paid in the past were now helping me.

As the lab worker approached me with a smile, I eyed the kaleidoscope of stains on his lab jacket. Without bothering to put on any latex gloves, he seized my left index finger and squeezed it until it was purple. He wiped off the tip with a small alcohol pad and then stabbed it with a sterile lancet after opening it from one of the USAID packages. He squeezed my finger again and collected the blood droplets in various small containers, and then he smeared several chipped microscope slides against my bleeding finger and placed them by an open window to dry. He told us to wait outside, so Aristote and I took a seat on the floor around the corner.

By this time I was feeling really nauseous and dizzy, and the thought of food or water made me feel even worse. All I wanted to know was what was wrong with me so that I could get whatever medication I needed and rest. As we waited, I noticed a man and three women chatting on nearby benches and glancing in my direction. I was in no mood to be social, so I tried to ignore them. Aristote told me that they were buzzing with talk about the "great event" from the previous evening. I guess word spreads fast in Mwenga. The man kept talking for several minutes, and then I noticed the women staring at me intently.

"Now what?" I asked Aristote, growing increasingly annoyed.

"This man is saying that you are a muzungu."

"No kidding."

"Yes, and he says that the muzungu does not love the way the black man loves," Aristote continued. "He says that when a muzungu is in love, he can do anything." The man smiled at me when he saw my surprise, and I regarded his kind face as I thought about his unexpected viewpoint. The women were riveted and continued to stare at me.

After waiting for what seemed like an hour, the lab tech emerged with my patient card, and handed it to me without a word. He gestured down the hall, so we returned to see the doctor. After studying the card for a moment, he declared, "No malaria."

Relieved, I said, "Okay, so what is the problem?"

"Maybe it is a virus or you ate something bad."

"Maybe it is the ants," said Aristote. "All of us are sick too."

"What!?" I exclaimed.

"Yes! All of us are sick from the bites of the ants too! I told you they are dangerous."

The doctor looked at me like I was an idiot and said, "Yes, it is *definitely* the ants. You are in the tropics, and we have many animals that you are not used to. Congo is very different from the USA." His condescending tone enraged me.

Angrily I looked at Aristote and asked, "Why in the world didn't you tell me about this *before* we spent several hours at the hospital?" Aristote stopped talking and avoided eye contact with me. I immediately felt bad about scolding him, but I was feeling worse by the minute. The doctor told me that some of the local ants were known to be deadly and that I would simply have to wait for the venom to wear off. I thanked the doctor and apologized to Aristote, and we returned to the office building so that I could rest.

Chifundera insisted that I move back to the more comfortable and expensive Italian mission to recover, and I was too weak to argue. He also told me that everybody had diarrhea from the ants, but that they were not as sick as me, because they had all been bitten before and had some immunity. When we got to the mission, I crawled into bed, and there I stayed, eating nothing and drinking very little. Waves of pain, chills, fever, and intense, dizzying nausea tormented me so much that I could not sleep for more than an hour at a time. Poor Marcel stopped by with

Aristote (left) poses for a photo with Commander Rama, who stepped in during the attack at Mwenga to save his life.

food repeatedly, but I refused to eat. When the effects finally wore off two days later, I felt like I had been beaten.

Somehow I managed to photograph a few frogs that Aristote collected while I was recovering, and he told me that he had become friends with the military commander named Rama who had stepped in during the beating and saved his life and that of Maurice and Mululema. He also told me that the commander had seen who had robbed him and knew the man well. When I suggested that maybe the commander could arrest the man with the police, Aristote laughed and said that my notion of justice was ridiculous. He was sure the money had already been spent on massive quantities of *pombe*—beer—but perhaps his phone or the headlamp could be recovered. In the end, nothing happened.

The commander showed up at the mission during our conversation, and he was wearing an immaculate white training suit. He had a potbelly, but he was solidly built, and I could see how his physical presence had persuaded the thieves to stop their attack two nights before. After I took some photos of him with Aristote, the team accepted an invitation to eat dinner with him, and I bought everybody plenty of beer.

We had made at least one friend in Mwenga, but the collective negative experiences made us eager to leave. A combination of poor communication and hasty planning had almost ended the expedition (and our lives) early, and we all learned from that mistake. I later learned that there happened to be rumors of a white man "man-eater" circulating around Mwenga at the time of this incident. I cannot imagine how our luck could have been any worse. The next day we returned to Bukavu without incident and prepared for the marathon hike that would take us deep into the Itombwe Plateau's forests. That journey would prove to make our misadventures in Mwenga look like a trip to Disneyland.

THE RATS OF MIKI

4 Following our return from Mwenga on June 14, I was enjoying the comforts of Chif's house in Bukavu when I was introduced to a man in his late twenties named Asukulu, who regarded me with a silent stare as we greeted each other. He was a protégé of Chifundera and would be our guide through the rugged mountains of Itombwe, which he knew like the back of his hand. We planned to walk to Miki (pronounced *mee-kee*), the Babembe village where Aristote had grown up.

The following morning, I descended the small hill from Chifundera's house to find Mululema and Asukulu helping the crew from Lwiro, including Maurice, Wandege, Marcel, John, Felix, and Aristote, load the truck with our gear. As Mululema climbed into the driver's seat next to me, he removed his cap and bowed his head in a deferential way that was uncomfortable to me, but I acknowledged his gesture so that we could move on. He fired up the rumbling engine and we were off. People scattered out of the way as he mercilessly honked his horn every five seconds to clear a path for our exit from the city.

Within minutes we had left the crowded streets of Bukavu behind us, and we passed through deforested and rolling hills covered with crops, spindly introduced eucalyptus trees, cattle, and flimsy patches of natural vegetation that wilted over the edges of streams. Our truck bucked and swayed on the rocky road, and the unavoidable potholes jarred us violently. Here and there I observed dilapidated wrecks of old Belgian houses, some of which must have been impressive mansions in their day. I could tell we were ascending the mountains that edged the northern part of the Itombwe Plateau, and the natural vegetation slowly transitioned from bushes and trees to grassland. Parts of the narrow road had accommodated traffic in only one direction in the colonial era,[1] and as it snaked through the undulating hills with sharp turns, Mululema repeatedly jerked the truck to the side to avoid an oncoming vehicle that was impossible to see before it was nearly upon us. After another hour, I could see on the eastern side of the road a precipitous cliff, which plummeted to the spectacular Ruzizi River. The ribbon of water frothed below us as it ricocheted through the valley, and Chif told me that until recently, there had been gallery forest (forest that is limited to the edges of rivers) along the entire Ruzizi, but the people had cut it all down for firewood.

As our elevation dropped I could feel the temperature spike noticeably. Almost immediately after reaching the valley, the rocky mountain pass intersected a well-paved road originating from Rwanda. We were able to increase our speed beyond the slow crawl we had taken through the mountains, and I began to see another change in the vegetation as we continued south. The area was much more arid, and I noticed candelabra-shaped euphorbia trees dotting the landscape of long grass and rocky outcrops. Before the modern world brought firearms to Central Africa, toxins from the leaves of these trees were used by many African tribes to poison arrows for hunting and warfare.[2] When the British explorer Wollaston passed through this valley a century before, he remarked it was full of elephants and lion.[3] I asked Chif if there was a chance we might see some interesting mammals as we headed south.

"The last lion in this area was shot by the Belgians over fifty years ago," he said curtly.

Profoundly disappointed, I glanced at the prehistoric landscape and tried to imagine what it must have been like when roving herds of mammals grazed as far as the eye could see. Despite this, however, the valley was stunningly beautiful and sharply different from everything else I had seen in eastern Congo.

Eventually, we reached an iron bridge that took us over a small river and into the outskirts of Uvira, a hot, dusty town on the northwestern edge of Lake Tanganyika at about 2,450 feet (ca. 746 m) elevation. People were walking everywhere along the edge of the road, many carrying large yellow plastic jugs of water on their heads. Motorcycles were almost as numerous as the pedestrians, and they weaved in and out of traffic, honking their horns at anyone foolish enough to attempt a mad dash across the road. I noticed a haze that loomed above the city, which seemed to be a combination of smoke and dust. Ancient Belgian storefronts had been repainted in bright colors to advertise pharmacies, repair shops, cell phone stores, and even travel agencies. Uvira is only a few miles west of Bujumbura, the capital city of Burundi on the eastern side of the lake, where an international airport serves as a regional hub for air cargo and business travelers. Both cities are also major ports for the northern end of the lake, which is the second-largest freshwater lake in the world, extending 404 miles (650 km) to the south as it passes along the western edge of Tanzania to the northern tip of Zambia.[4]

As I looked to the west, I could see enormous grassy mountains rising sharply beyond the edge of the city. The British explorer Burton gazed upon these same mountains as early as 1858 shortly after he and fellow explorer Speke confirmed rumors from Arab slave traders of an inland "sea" that turned out to be Tanganyika. At that time, Uvira was one of the major stops on the Arab slave trade route out of Central Africa. When the Belgians took control of the city after quelling rebellions at the end of the nineteenth century,[5] they made it into a commercial and industrial center, establishing the port to shuttle goods with steamships from the resource-rich Katanga Province in the south to Bukavu via the road I had just descended. The city also served as a territorial headquarters, a center for anti–sleeping sickness efforts around the Ruzizi, an IRSAC research station for aquatic sciences (including herpetology), and Catholic and Protestant missions.[6] More recently, Uvira became a haven for refugees fleeing from conflict zones from Burundi and areas to the south of Uvira during the war.[7]

Although Aristote grew up in Miki, deep in the Itombwe Plateau, he spent most of his time in Uvira with his mother and extended family, and he was excited to show me the best place to collect frogs on the lake. After obtaining a modest hotel room that was mercifully equipped with an electric fan to mitigate the worst of the heat, we grabbed dinner at a restaurant called the Blue Cat. As we drank large bottles of Congolese Primus beer, Chifundera listened to my plans to visit the lake after dark with Aristote, and he warned me about crocodiles. Although they were now rare around the city, a German woman had been eaten by one a decade before when she had gone for a swim with her husband. Promising to be careful, Aristote and I grabbed some headlamps and Mululema drove us to a place called Mulongwe on the lake's shore.

We were greeted by three drunks imbibing pombe on the crumbling foundation of an old Belgian building near the shore. Aristote answered their slurred questions about our business diplomatically, and despite their shocked exclamations, we proceeded to the flooded reeds adjacent to the lake. As we approached, I heard a deafening chorus of frogs calling for mates from the reeds and in shallow puddles. Still leery from the near-death experience in Mwenga, I decided we should not linger in this place for too long, because our strange lights might garner the wrong kind of attention from the locals. The large number of flying insects that swarmed around our lights also prompted us to hasten our task. In fifteen minutes, our plastic containers were full of twenty-five frogs, ranging from large toads to colorful reed frogs.

The next morning, after Aristote and I began the task of photographing the frogs we had collected the previous night, Chifundera showed up to say that we needed to visit the local military commander to obtain permission for our visit to Itombwe. Our entourage walked to the historic part of the city, where we saw several old Belgian buildings, including an impressive hotel with waterfront balconies.

We turned a corner, and I saw a modest house surrounded by a large wall with barbed wire. There was a jeep parked in the main entrance with several soldiers carrying AK-47s and RPGs. They eyed us suspiciously as we approached the entrance to the compound. Ever the diplomat, Chifundera produced a small pile of paperwork from the government and CRSN to prove who we were and the purpose of our research mission to Itombwe. He had also been busy obtaining signatures and notarized stamps from the local government officials and police chief in Uvira to bolster this paperwork. We were escorted to the back of a house where we were introduced to a Colonel Ngobanya, who had an impeccable uniform, shiny black boots, and a carefully shaved head. He looked to be in his late forties, but he was in excellent shape, and his men stood at attention as his commanding voice directed his subordinates. We learned that he had been a key player in the rebellion that brought Laurent Kabila to power a decade before, and that he had even served as a mentor to the rebel leader's son Joseph Kabila, the current president of Congo.

As Chifundera pointed to the tall mountains to the west and explained the ambitious plan for our fieldwork, the colonel regarded me with thinly veiled amusement. Things seemed to be going well, but as Chif continued talking, a shadow seemed to envelope the colonel's face. He looked sternly at Chifundera and told him that there were many dangerous militia where we were going, and if something happened, we would be too remote to hope for any help from him. After he signed and stamped our paperwork, he shook our hands and wished us luck. Although I knew about the dangers of Itombwe before coming to Uvira, the meeting left me spooked.

Aristote tried to allay my fears by saying, "Do not worry, I know Itombwe very well and with God, we cannot have a problem." I knew he was trying to help, but I did not feel any better. But then Chif told me that Asukulu knew a popular soldier in the rebel militia who was in Uvira and that he was negotiating with him to accompany us into the mountains.

On June 17 after a modest breakfast from Marcel, our truck was stashed safely in one corner of the hotel, the porters arrived, and everything was set, but Chifundera, Asukulu, and our new rebel companion were missing. After an hour of waiting and seeing the sun rise higher in the sky, I asked Aristote to call Chif to inquire about the delay. Chif told him that he was in renewed negotiations with the rebel and that he would come to the hotel soon. Two hours later Chif showed up to say that the rebel had agreed to a price of ten dollars a day, but he wanted a three-day advance now. Not wanting to delay us any further, I gave Chif the money and waited. Hours slipped by with nothing happening, so I went with Aristote to get lunch at the Blue Cat. Just as we finished, Chif showed up to say that now the rebel wanted more money. It was clear to everyone that he had no intention of following through with his commitment, so I ordered everyone to gather up our cumbersome gear (scientific equipment, tents, and food) and depart immediately. It was now noon and the temperature was climbing rapidly.

For two hours we climbed the steep hillside of the city, walking in between small shacks that served as people's houses, and avoiding open sewers that trickled down the hill. The sun had been baking the rocky terrain all day, effectively making the ground an oven, and I sucked down water in copious amounts as the sweat dripped off my body with every step. After a brief rest to enjoy the aerial view of the city and the lake from the towering hillside, we continued climbing, sometimes straight up through a series of loose-rock steps that had been created by centuries of human passage, including slaves. My hands were burned by the hot rocks as I grasped them to climb upward, and when the loose rocks under my feet gave way and caused me to stumble, Marcel exclaimed, "Sorry!" With little time for rest from the punishing climb and heat, we toiled on through the inferno for hours. I was drenched in sweat as we emerged from the rocky stairway onto a steep grassy hill. Chifundera told me that baboon were known to haunt the area, and I looked around to see several worn paths crisscrossing the hills in every direction from years of travelers' traffic. I could also see that to the west beyond the steep hills, the mountains just kept rising higher and higher, but the upper limit was obscured by clouds.

As the sun and temperature started to wane, I could see a waterfall trickling down the side of the mountain, and several huts with banana trees at its base. The tiny village was named Kibenge (ca. 4,900 feet, 1,500 m elevation), and by the time I walked into its center, Chifundera seemed to be best friends with the chief. The children were apprehensive, but the adults smiled at me and I shook hands with everyone as they welcomed this unexpected group of strangers into their midst.

My unconditioned body had no trouble sleeping that night, and the next morning after a breakfast of cold leftover rice, we resumed our seemingly endless climb. This time we had little trouble from the heat because the temperature dipped as we climbed ever higher, but as the air thinned, I noticed I had to breathe harder. At some point the temperature dropped so much that we had to put on our jackets. We passed through a beautiful stand of bamboo forest as we passed the 6,500 foot (2,000 m) mark, and Wandege spotted two chameleons after we surpassed 8,500 feet (2,600 m). In the afternoon we reached a military checkpoint where Congolese soldiers asked me for cigarettes and *biscuit*, a generic cookie imported from India. I gave them a little money for beer so that we could continue, and after climbing to about 9,800 feet (3,000 m), we finally seemed to reach the plateau, but it was hilly, and we started a pattern of descent and climbing that would continue for days.

I noticed a marked change in the vegetation that accompanied the cooler temperature. Instead of the long savanna-like grass we had seen on the eastern side of the mountains, it was now more verdant and much shorter, and there were numerous yellow flowers sprinkled among the green blades. Bonsai-like *Hagenia* trees could be seen in various-sized patches here and there, and a gray moss called Old Man's Beard dangled from their branches in a way that truly resembled a wizard's graying facial hair.

After several more hours of walking, we reached the picturesque village of Rubarati. Small huts with whitewashed walls and brown thatched roofs dotted the rolling green plains. Modest herds of goat and cattle meandered along the edge of the village, which explained why much of the plateau's grasslands were trampled and full of dinner-plate-sized patties of dung. As we approached, a small group of children ran up to stare at me, shouting "Muzungu!" The patties were everywhere, but the barefoot children must have learned to ignore it long ago, and they ran with reckless abandon as all children do, laughing and pointing at the oddly dressed muzungu who had suddenly appeared.

We had reached the realm of the Banyamulenge tribe, some of whom are descended from Rwanda's ancient monarchy. Originally Tutsi pastoralists from Rwanda, the Banyamulenge settled the Itombwe highlands sometime in the nineteenth century, although this time frame has been contested by some Congolese intellectuals.[8] Then as now, their culture and livelihood revolves around cattle farming. They were involved in several of Zaire's conflicts in the mid- to late twentieth century and made up a significant portion of Kabila's forces in 1996. When Bukavu fell out of Mobutu's hands, many Banyamulenge were rewarded with government positions of power, but two years later, a backlash by Kabila's Congolese supporters from other ethnic groups resulted in many deaths. In 2004, many more Banyamulenge were killed in Bukavu during a failed coup attempt. Culturally and linguistically distinct from other Congolese and Rwandan Tutsis, the Banyamulenge are currently concentrated in Itombwe. Because their identity as Congolese citizens has been called into question multiple times in the recent past, some Banyamulenge have formed their own militia to protect their land and interests.[9]

Aristote approached me with a middle-aged man wearing a light gray checkered suit jacket, a red argyle shirt underneath, dark gray suit pants, black rubber boots, and a large, black cowboy hat. He was the village's chief. He welcomed me to his village and proudly showed off a large brick church that was under construction. He invited me inside a large hut, where a fire was blazing away in a pit in its center. I shook hands with everyone inside, and the chief ordered food to be cooked for us. After several minutes I realized that there was no ventilation in the hut, and although a small amount of the smoke escaped through the top of the thatched roof, the air inside was as thick and dark as storm clouds. My eyes and throat started to burn, and I had to repeatedly escape outside to get some fresh air. It was obvious that I would not be able to spend the night in the hut, because the fire would continue to burn to keep everyone warm. Everybody was surprised when I insisted on setting up my tent outside, but they seemed to understand that I had not grown up inside smoky huts as they had.

The next morning at dawn as I shivered in my tent, Chifundera invited me back inside to warm up by the fire, talk to the chief of the village, and with luck, not suffocate from the smoke. I did not realize I was walking into an ambush. Chif's eyes were bloodshot and glassy from the smoke, and he looked very serious as he began translating a series of questions from the chief. At first it was just small talk to ask how I had passed the night and if I was enjoying my stay in Rubarati. I did not reveal that the bitter cold had made my sleep restless despite the physical exhaustion of the climb.

"The chief says the village is working hard to finish construction of the church that you saw outside. Can you make a very small contribution, maybe two thousand dollars, for the construction?"

I explained that I was very grateful for the chief's hospitality, but two grand was a lot more money than I had for the entire jaunt into Itombwe. I told him I would be happy to make a more modest contribution to the church.

"The chief wants to know how old are you," Chif said.

"Thirty-three."

"The chief wants to know how many children you have."

"None that I know of."

"Are you married?"

I frowned and glared at him. Chif knew that I was single, and I was beginning to get annoyed with the personal interrogation. Without an answer from me, Chif told the chief no.

"Would you like to marry one of the girls in this village?"

I suddenly noticed that several teenage girls were hovering around the entrance to the hut, taking turns peeking at me through tiny holes in the wall. When I caught one of them staring, she giggled and shyly retreated from her vantage point, only to have a bolder girl take her place and stare at me with doe eyes. It seemed like I was the only one in the village who had not been forewarned of the matrimonial proposition. I looked at Aristote, and somehow he had a straight face, but his bloodshot eyes betrayed the slightest hint of amusement. I wanted to laugh, but everyone in the hut was solemn, and I knew the marriage proposal was genuine.

Seeing my hesitation, Chif translated the chief's pitch that was aimed at closing the deal. "The women here are very good workers and will make a good wife for you. They will bear you many children and maybe someday you can be chief. You should get married now because if you don't have children soon, you will die before you can see your grandchildren." It was definitely time to leave Rubarati.

I responded by telling the chief that the women of his village were very beautiful, and I was sure they would make excellent wives, but it would not be possible to take them with me back to the United States. Thankfully, logic ruled the day, and the chief had to concede that I was right. After a modest breakfast and a little time to pack up our gear, I kept my promise to make a donation to the church, and the chief wished us farewell.

For hours my body struggled with the altitude, endless ravines, and steep ascents that dipped up and down for hundreds of feet at a time. Because we were on the move, there was not enough time to make a fire and cook some food, and with the exception of a little fruit, we ate nothing. Later that morning, we ascended a grassy hill to find a small shelter constructed out of bamboo. A couple of the local chiefs were inside, and after we greeted them, Chif started explaining why we had come. We told them that Itombwe is a unique place in eastern Congo, and we supported growing efforts to turn the plateau into a protected area. One of the chiefs shook his head and said that it was not a good idea to protect the forest, because it should all be cut down to ensure there are enough crops for all the people. He pointed out that the people around Kahuzi-Biega National Park were supposed to be benefiting from ecotourism of the park, yet after decades they were still poor. What, he asked, would be the benefit of making Itombwe into such a protected area? At that moment before I had really contemplated the issue, I didn't have an answer that would resonate with him. I wish I could go back in time to that meeting now.

———

It is true that making Itombwe into a protected area would not transform the lives of the people in and around the area, at least for several years. But if peace can ever come to eastern Congo, the Congolese people will have an opportunity to embrace the win-win strategy of conservation, scientific research, and millions of dollars in ecotourism revenue that are firmly ingrained in the policies and psyche of the neighboring countries of Rwanda, Burundi, Tanzania, and Uganda. Like the national parks in these countries, Itombwe could become a bird-watcher's paradise, because no other area in Central Africa can boast the bird diversity of the plateau and its western transitional forests. Perhaps the remaining gorillas could be habituated for tourism as well, and who knows, someday even elephants might make a comeback. And then there is the unparalleled beauty of Itombwe's forests, grasslands, and mountains — many foreign hikers would pay for the privilege to walk through it. All of this is the natural heritage of the Congolese people, and perhaps the next generation will come to understand that in Itombwe, they have a unique and fragile national treasure that must be protected for future generations.

But what about the hard skeptics who see no direct human benefit from the forests and do not care about its natural beauty or the animals that live in it? Numerous studies have documented that tropical forest deforestation leads to increased greenhouse gases, alteration of local weather patterns, and increased risks of disease, flooding, erosion, and fires. At the local scale, tropical deforestation is correlated with warmer temperatures and decreased rainfall, which can negatively affect agricultural activities of subsistence farmers that live near these forests. Indeed, rain gauge and satellite data from 1979 to 2004 suggest precipitation has decreased by 20 percent or more in the region from the Congo Basin to the East African coast, especially since 1992.[10] On the plus side, tropical forests perform many highly valuable services for nearby human communities, including natural filtration of water and providing a diverse array of mammal, bird, and insect pollinators for crops.

Because most recent human population growth on our planet has been happening in the developing world where educational and employment opportunities are often limited, terrible damage has already occurred to many of the world's tropical forests, where the majority of terrestrial plant and animal species are found. Several biodiverse countries have lost staggering percentages of their tropical rainforests, including Haiti, 97 percent; Madagascar, 95 percent; and the Philippines, 95 percent.[11] The rate of deforestation for countries that still have sizable areas of rainforest has been increasing in recent years—a 2016 report from the World Bank estimated that the world has lost approximately one thousand soccer fields of forest per hour over the last twenty-five years.[12] Much of this loss has been occurring in sub-Saharan Africa. Nigeria, for example, destroyed 80 percent of its forests between 1990 and 2005,[13] and as a whole, 80 percent of the original forest of West Africa is now an agricultural-forest mosaic inhabited by over 200 million people.[14] Because tropical forests store huge amounts of carbon and other greenhouse gases such as nitrous oxide (nearly three hundred times more powerful than carbon dioxide) that are released when they are razed, about 10 percent of global anthropogenic greenhouse gas emissions are attributed to tropical deforestation, and thus the destruction is making global climate change worse.[15]

Most of the devastation is being driven locally by a need for more land to grow crops to feed the planet's skyrocketing tropical human population. But we must also look in the mirror to explain much of the rest. In the Neotropics, cultivation of coca and poppies for the illegal drug trade, partly fueled by American consumers, is responsible for as much as half of the deforestation.[16] A recent study found that, in general, about 30 percent of global species threats are attributed to international trade in commodities, mostly to developed countries, including the United States, Japan, and European Union. These commodities include coffee, tea, sugar, textiles, fish, and various manufactured items such as wood-based furniture.[17] According to an interactive map developed by the latter authors,[18] the United States is responsible for eight threats to species in the Congo via energy production, mining, hunting, fishing, and forestry. Plantations for palm oil, the world's cheapest and most widely traded vegetable oil, are replacing tropical forests on four continents, including Africa, and although little deforestation to make way for palm oil plantations has occurred recently in Congo, most likely because the war, corruption, and poor infrastructure scared away investors, models suggest large swaths of the country's eastern forests could be destroyed in the coming years as climate change makes them more suitable for plantations. Because palm oil is used in a wide variety of products including junk food, sodas, cosmetics, soaps, and personal care products, American pension and retirement funds are investing billions into the industry, exacerbating deforestation across the tropical world. A database run by Friends of the Earth and As You Sow[19] reveals several US retirement fund companies are heavily involved, especially in tropical Asia where most damage from palm oil has occurred.[20] It is likely that most of the oil palm plantations that occur in Congo today are left over from the colonial era, but even when the forest has been allowed to slowly reclaim abandoned plantations for half a century, my team has found that the biodiversity of these sites is still very low, and the abundant trash species that occur in them are identical to the ones found around villages.

In the case of the tropical forests of the Albertine Rift, the most species-rich region in continental Africa,[21] the environmental devastation from deforestation for agriculture, illegal drugs, cattle ranching, and mining (including gold and other rare minerals for US and European markets) is extensive. With one of the highest human population densities in the world, the region is defined by a juxtaposition of bountiful natural abundance and too many people to share it. Thanks to its ancient geological processes, the Rift has exceptionally fertile soil and minerals, a cool highland climate that has fewer tropical diseases than the lowlands, poor or even nonexistent law enforcement, and large swaths of political instability, all of which has fueled illegal land grabs, including from parks and reserves.[22] Mafia-like collusions with militias have contributed to worrying levels of deforestation in Virunga National Park. Because of the Itombwe Plateau's relatively large size and diversity of habitats, and from the sheer numbers of endemic and threatened species, it is by far the most important site in the Rift for conservation of unique biodiversity, including amphibians and reptiles.[23] In the colonial era, the Belgians did not sanction enough exploration of the plateau to understand its importance, and Itombwe was not recognized as a reserve until 2006. But the borders of the reserve were not finalized until input from local stakeholders was combined with conservation analyses in June 2016.[24]

Yet despite the dire status of tropical forests in the Rift and around the world, the deforestation rates in Central Africa are three to four times smaller than in Amazonia or Southeast Asia, and on a global scale, Africa contributes to only 11 percent of gross deforestation.[25] A 2016 *Science* study that examined biodiversity loss across the planet pointed out that the Congo Basin, the second-largest tropical rainforest in the world, half of which occurs in Congo, is one of only three relatively intact and large "wilderness areas" (the other two are rainforests of Amazonia and New Guinea) in the world that continue to harbor "safe" levels of biodiversity.[26] Because Africa's World War displaced and killed millions of people who would have otherwise cleared a plot for their families to grow crops, much of Congo's forests were spared, a premise known in some circles as "gunpoint conservation."[27] During the twenty-year period from 1990 to 2010, militias exploited resources (e.g., charcoal, mining) from areas under their control, leading to some deforestation, but protected reserves and national parks maintained much of their integrity.[28] The terrible postcolonial state of road and bridge infrastructure, corruption, as well as political and economic instability, are likely responsible for the relatively slow pace of logging in Congo, which has inflicted heavy damage on forests elsewhere in Africa.[29] Recent studies of deforestation based on satellite data from the first decade or so of the twenty-first century suggested that Congo has lost only about 2.6 percent of its total forest, a modest percentage compared to other tropical countries, including Malaysia (14.4 percent), Paraguay (9.6 percent), Guatemala (8.2 percent), Cambodia (7.1 percent), Belize (5.6 percent), and Ivory Coast (4.7 percent).[30] And so in the overall scheme of things, the lion's share of forests in Congo remain intact, and we should use this welcome news to redouble our efforts to conserve what is left, because only about 12 percent of the country's forests are currently protected, and even these areas require improved law enforcement.[31]

But why should the average person care about this? One reason for Americans to be concerned about deforestation in Central Africa is that, amazingly, the consequences can affect us directly. We know the region has global importance to weather patterns because it is the second most important convective "engine" of global atmospheric circulation after the Maritime Continent (in Southeast Asia), and it has a higher frequency of lightning strikes than any other place on the planet.[32] A study in 2006 used complex 3D mathematical models that link the atmosphere, oceans, and land surface, commonly known as general-circulation models (GCMs), to examine the phenomenon of so-called teleconnections, climate anomalies (temperature, rainfall, etc.) that are linked across large distances of Earth. A renowned example of a teleconnection is the El Niño effect, where warming of the Pacific Ocean can lead to unusual weather patterns around the world. The study examined global teleconnection patterns and found that deforestation in the tropics is linked to rainfall declines in the United States. More specifically, deforestation in the Amazon decreases rainfall in Texas, deforestation in Southeast Asia decreases winter precipitation in northwestern US states, and deforestation in Central Africa decreases rainfall in the Gulf of Mexico (centered on Louisiana).[33] Because so many variables and a diversity of methods are involved in modeling climate at the global scale, not all subsequent studies have agreed with some of the details of that 2006 study. But in 2015, a review paper in the journal *Nature Climate Change* examined many of these studies and found that several of them agree on the link between tropical deforestation and decreased rainfall in multiple areas of North America. Moreover, abnormal fluctuations in temperature and rainfall that are linked to deforestation might affect agricultural productivity in the United States, India, China, and other areas with large human populations,[34] which could in turn lead to famine and conflict. Nobody knows for sure when we will approach a tipping point, or what will happen to our climate as tropical deforestation continues. That should concern everyone on the planet.

What else do we stand to lose if we let the tropical forests of Congo disappear? If we focus on the biodiversity that can only live within these forests, the answer is that we have no idea, because most of this biodiversity is virtually unknown. However, if an unknown threshold of extinction is crossed, it might lead to an irreversible shift in the local or even global ecosystem. Elephants, for example, bulldoze paths in the impenetrable forest that are used by many antelope species, create gaps to allow herbaceous plants to grow for other herbivores, and disperse seeds (sometimes exclusively) for a great diversity of ecologically important trees and other plants.[35] The rainforest will likely lose many species that rely on elephants as the pachyderms are wiped out across Central Africa. Compared to other areas of the world, we have almost no understanding of Central African ecological species interactions and food webs, especially for amphibians and reptiles in Congo,[36] and because my team's research suggests we have underestimated the number of herpetological species by at least a factor of three (especially for frogs), we cannot begin to understand what is happening in the ecosystem if we do not even know how many species might be key players in it. British scientist Richard Fortey put this another way: "Just as you need a vocabulary before you can speak a language, so it is necessary to have a dictionary of species before you can read the complex book of nature."[37] That said, the "insurance hypothesis" of theoretical ecology posits that high levels of biodiversity protect against ecosystem damage, because if some species are pushed to extinction, other ones with overlapping ecological niches will maintain the integrity of the ecosystem. Unfortunately, this hypothesis has not been tested rigorously in tropical rainforests, and nobody knows for sure what catastrophe might befall these ecosystems as their biodiversity disappears.[38]

Human health can be improved from the biodiversity that resides in tropical forests. There are a potential cornucopia of pharmaceutical products awaiting discovery in tropical forests if scientists can explore them before they disappear. About 25 percent of medicines that have been patented by the Western world were identified from tropical forest plants in use by indigenous people.[39] In the case of venomous snakes, the complex toxins they use to subdue prey and deter predators include an enormous amount of molecular diversity that can be used to develop lifesaving drugs. For example, peptides (chains of amino acids that form the building blocks of proteins) from the venom of African *Dendroaspis* mambas, including Black, Green, and Jameson's Mambas, are showing promise to treat heart disease and pain. Venom from vipers, such as the colorful Rhinoceros Viper my team encountered in Virunga National Park, are already being used to develop new drugs for heart disease, hypertension, and to control bleeding during surgery. One Asian viper species' venom has even been used for an antiwrinkle "Syn-Ake" cosmetic cream. The planet contains about one hundred thousand species of venomous animals, most of which are actually insects, and because venom is a complex cocktail of many peptides, these species synthesize a combined arsenal of about 20 million biochemically active compounds. But biochemists have identified only ten thousand of these toxins, of which only one thousand have been studied in depth to see if they have medicinal value.[40]

Toads and other frogs are another source of potentially useful peptides. Bufotoxins, a type of toxin secreted through the paratoid glands on the back of toads to make them poisonous to predators, have powerful heart, antitumor, antivirus, anti-infection, and analgesic effects.[41] Bufotoxins from the Colorado River Toad (*Incilius alvarius*) in the United States and Mexico even have powerful hallucinogenic effects.[42] My preliminary phylogenetic analysis of toads in the Central African rainforests suggests that at least a dozen new cryptic species need to be described, many more new species discoveries are likely from unexplored areas, and one can only imagine what benefits their bufotoxins might have for humanity. Other groups of frogs, including African Clawed Frogs (*Xenopus*), are known to secrete an "antiobiotic library" of skin peptides that will be important to fight the worrying and increasing number of antiobiotic-resistant bacteria that threaten human health in the twenty-first century.[43]

So what can we do to help endangered species survive poaching, competition from invasive species, and environmental devastation? First and foremost, we need to establish more protected areas, including national parks, with effective law enforcement and management. If the establishment of national parks is America's best idea as suggested by documentary filmmaker Ken Burns, shouldn't we be promoting it in places that will be gone in a generation? In general, protected areas, including national parks, do a relatively good job of preventing deforestation and saving threatened species from extinction. However, a discouraging study that focused on biodiversity loss in protected areas worldwide found that four-fifths of reserves are losing biodiversity, and 50 percent of these reserves are suffering "relatively serious" declines. The most important factor for reserve health was effective management and on-the-ground protection from rangers, which minimized the damaging effects of illegal deforestation, logging, fires, and hunting. But the study also found a worrying connection between negative ecological changes just outside reserves (human population growth and associated activities) and negative changes within these reserves,[44] which raises concerns about parks like Virunga that are surrounded by altered landscapes and large human populations. Another study found that poachers are able to move in and out of most of the world's protected areas with impunity, and although many conservation efforts are focused on creating new national parks and reserves, it is clear that law enforcement and management are the most important factors for effective conservation.[45] This is especially true in the case of the Congo's crown jewel of biodiversity, the Itombwe Natural Reserve, which has a sizable area under its protection, but not enough rangers and resources to enforce the law effectively.[46]

One of the obvious ways we can help these conservation efforts is to provide more money, but there can be problems if the relevant institutions lack oversight. The Green Climate Fund, just one of many ideas to fund conservation efforts, aims to raise $100 billion a year by 2020 to effectively compensate developing tropical countries from chopping down their forests. The major concern with this well-intentioned program is that large transfers of cash to corrupt governments may not result in the goal of reducing deforestation. In a Corruption Perceptions Index of seventy-four biodiverse countries from 2010, Congo was almost at the bottom of the list—only Myanmar, Burundi, Equatorial Guinea, Somalia, and Sudan ranked lower. Even when income poverty is taken into account, there is a strong link between high levels of corruption and failing measures of conservation effectiveness for developing countries in the tropics.[47] With a decades-long legacy of corruption epitomized by Mobutu, some have asked how funds intended for conservation efforts will not evaporate into the morass of corruption in Congo and elsewhere in Africa. Although many conservation organizations (see "How Can I Help?" for a list) are accomplishing a great deal in Congo, corruption, poor governance, and lack of infrastructure remain formidable challenges. But with enough determination, these challenges can and must be overcome.

After doing everything I could to convince the chiefs that Itombwe should be protected, I handed over some small presents of beer money and we continued our trek through the rolling and grassy hills. In the early afternoon we reached the village of Magunda, where an English-speaking Congolese doctor emerged from a small clinic to greet me. When he heard I was a biologist, he explained that the Interahamwe had destroyed the forest during the war, and only ten years before, many wild animals could be seen in this area on a regular basis. Now there was only the hacked and burned wreckage of tree stumps, and most of the land was now used for grazing cattle and goats, with a few patches for crops. A small group of Congolese army soldiers with AK-47s watched us pass through the outskirts of the village, and a small puppy played in the arms of one soldier. We rested in the shade of a small number of huts for a few minutes, and then we continued our ascent through successive patches of forest, agricultural areas, and rocky hills.

We had been walking, climbing, and scrambling for about ten hours when we took a brief break in the edge of a marsh, and as Asukulu eyed me, he said that there was a village called Bichaka ahead, but there would be at least one more descent and steep climb to reach it. I was exhausted, but I could hear thunder in the distance, and I knew we would have to hurry if we wanted to reach the village soon. We continued to march on well after dark, and during one of the sharp descents, we were hit with a downpour of rain. The rocky trail turned to muddy sludge, and when I was only a few feet from the bottom of a hill I slipped and fell forward, scratching my hands as I broke my fall. Cursing everything from the rain to my crazy drive to come there in the first place, I started to ascend the final steep hill and realized that it was so slick with mud and draining rainwater that I had to crawl on my hands and knees to climb it, occasionally losing my footing and sliding back several feet during the effort.

I carried on through a path in the forest, passing through cleared areas with crops, and I climbed over a couple of bamboo fences meant to exclude domestic and wild animals. When I finally stumbled into the village of Bichaka a few minutes later, I realized I had gone ahead of everyone and I was alone. The rain was so heavy that I could not see anyone in the village, but I sat down next to one of the huts under the edge of its thatched roof to deflect most of the rain from continuing to soak my body. During brief streaks of illumination from the lightning, I could see an enormous wall of forest at the far end of the village. Grateful to be off my feet and somewhat sheltered from the cold rain, I let my head droop to my knees and watched the rainwater bounce off my boots.

A middle-aged man approached me from the shadows and said something to me in Swahili, but I could not understand him over the roar of the storm. He reached out his hand to me, and after I took it, he helped me to my feet. He guided me to a nearby hut, where I found a crude bed constructed out of a bamboo frame. I thanked him as I sat down on it, and the water dripped off me onto the floor, creating a small muddy pool. He disappeared for a minute and then returned with a small metal bucket of sorts that contained hot coals, and I warmed my hands as the rest of the team started to enter the village. One by one everyone ducked in to see that I was okay, and then they disappeared to other huts where they would have more room. I was amazed that the people of this tiny village welcomed our exhausted band of strangers into their homes in the middle of the night during a violent storm. If that was not enough, they started bringing us food too. I have never forgotten the kindness that they showed us on that difficult journey, and I would learn that such behavior was the norm and not the exception in Itombwe.

We hung around the next morning for a few hours to search the nearby forest, which looked nearly pristine. The village chief told Chifundera that the elephants had been gone for years, but he still saw several kinds of antelope and chimpanzees from time to time. After a bit of searching, we found two species of chameleons, including a *Rhampholeon* dwarf chameleon, which has the shape and yellowish-brown coloration of a dead leaf to camouflage itself from predators. The bizarre creature buzzed and vibrated its entire body as a last-ditch defense when it was handled. When Aristote and I overturned a large log, we found several semi-fossorial skinks in the genus *Leptosiaphos*, which resemble small snakes with minuscule legs. In this part of their range, they are a mixture of brown, yellow, and red, and the underside of the belly and tail are often bright yellow or orange.

We trekked through the increasingly forested landscape for about six hours, and reached the small village of Lusasa, where the children had never seen a white man before. As it started to rain, they yelled and danced around me as I approached, and led me to a courtyard in the center of the village. The ancient chief welcomed us, and after hearing that it would take at least five hours of climbing over a mountain in the rain to reach Aristote's village of Miki, we decided to pass the night there. In exchange for a modest amount of money, a young man rented his bamboo and mud hut for my use, and within minutes I had a small laboratory constructed inside of it to work on the specimens we had collected at Bichaka. As a drizzling rain started, I glanced outside and saw a man with a machine gun over his shoulder as he passed through the village. There was a weathered look to his dour face, and he wore green army fatigues with black rubber boots. He was striking to me because his complexion was noticeably darker than anyone I had seen in Congo, and he seemed to be much taller than the villagers. Curious, I stood in the doorway of the hut and saw a column of several more heavily armed soldiers with a similar appearance as they passed through the village. One of them looked at me with surprise, but they continued on their way without stopping to talk to us.

"Interahamwe," Aristote said as he saw my expression. I knew the nasty militia was in the area, but Aristote told me that in this region of Itombwe they were on their best behavior. We had reached the area controlled by Aristote's Babembe tribe, and he explained that a few years before, following their escape from Rwanda, the Interahamwe had been read the riot act. The Babembe warriors had informed them that every single one of them would be killed if they did not stop their stealing, raping, and killing of people in the Babembe's area. Because the Babembe had home turf advantage and they are excellent fighters, the Interahamwe heeded the warning and a fragile peace was established. I was betting everything that the truce would hold.

The next morning as we continued to Miki, I felt myself slowing down as my unconditioned body continued to suffer the consequences of poor nourishment and fatigue. After climbing to the top of an especially steep hill in the forest, a man emerged from the side of a trail with a rifle and four scrawny hunting dogs. He was a poacher in search of antelope. As we caught our breath from the climb, Chifundera chatted with the man to learn about the health of the mammal population in the area and learned that there were good numbers of several species of ungulates (relatively large herbivorous mammals). A survey of Itombwe from 1999 recorded two species of hogs, water chevrotain, buffalo, bushbuck, sitatunga (a swamp-dwelling antelope), five species of deer-like duiker, and Bate's Pygmy Antelope—nearly all of them have declined in overall numbers in recent years.[48] As the hunter disappeared down the trail we had climbed, I wondered how many more men like him were in the mountains and how long the animals could survive.

For several hours, our weary party descended the western edge of the plateau. Aristote pointed to a village that we could see in the distance below, and proudly announced that we were approaching Miki. The evening rain had made the trail muddy and slippery, and as my stiff legs struggled to support my weight as I carefully used rocks and tree roots to negotiate the sharp decline, I felt my footing slip again and again. With the exception of Aristote, who faithfully waited for me as I slowly continued, everyone else advanced with haste so that they could reach the village and rest. I was trying not to slip on an especially steep and slippery stretch of the trail when I heard the sound of jingling metal and several rapid thuds of feet on the earth. I looked behind me and was surprised to see a small column of Interahamwe literally running down the muddy trail with their rubber boots. They passed me in silence, and I marveled at their catlike agility as they rapidly and effortlessly descended the treacherous hillside in footwear that surely had less traction than mine.

Aristote and I finally reached Miki, where he received a hero's welcome. Several of the children shouted "Muzungu!" and danced around me as we made our way through the town. There were several small brick buildings mixed in with the huts, and the town was large enough that several vendors were selling cheap plastic toys, cookies, sodas, and even bottles of the popular Primus beer at little bamboo-framed tables. Goats and chickens walked freely among the dirty thoroughfare, and almost everyone, including the goats, stopped to stare at me as I passed by. One of these onlookers was a scowling Interahamwe with an AK-47 strapped over his shoulder. He looked at me with a combination of suspicion and menace, but I greeted him in Swahili, and his expression immediately transitioned into modest surprise. He raised his hands in tacit greeting, and his hollow eyes lingered on me as I walked on.

We emerged from a sharp turn in the main path through town and ascended a gentle grade in the hillside to see several larger brick houses, complete with chimneys. Aristote told me that the Belgians built these houses in the late 1950s to exploit the mineral wealth near Miki, which still includes gold and coltan (a commonly used nickname for columbite-tantalite ore mined in Congo), a metal with unique properties that is essential for everything from smart phones, game consoles, and other electronic devices to hip replacements and ammunition. The Congo supplies around 8 percent of the world's tantalum, and during a price surge in

2000, militias made millions of dollars by extorting money from artisa-
nal miners. Child laborers and teachers abandoned schools en masse to
mine coltan, and because the process requires a lot of water to separate
the ore from soil, the list of environmental effects is catastrophic. Water-
ways are diverted and polluted, forests are cut down, topsoil is washed
away (making the land unsuitable for agriculture afterward), erosion is
increased, and many endangered species are hunted to provide food for
miners in remote areas. During the war, militias controlled large por-
tions of Kahuzi-Biega National Park to mine coltan, and within a few
years, the elephant population was reduced from 350 family groups to
only two by 2001. After the chimpanzee, gorilla, antelope, and buffalo
populations nose-dived, the miners moved on to poaching smaller species of antelope, monkeys, birds, and even tortoises.[49]

As I looked more carefully at the old houses, I noticed that several of
the brick walls had caved in, but some of them were still relatively whole,
and we walked up a tiny path to one of the more intact ones. Marcel
had started a fire in the large fireplace and was fluttering around with
his pans and utensils in an effort to start cooking. After shaking hands
with some of the locals, including the current landlord of the house, I
was shown to a large room with a couple of twin-sized beds. The house
had several other bedrooms, each with its own fireplace, the remnants
of a kitchen, and a bathroom that had once held a tub, sink, toilet, and
mirror, but was now completely destroyed. When I inquired about the
location of the toilet, my guide pointed to a path that led up a hill to an
open pit. I returned to the cobweb-infested room I was to share with
Aristote, laid a sleeping bag out on one of the beds, and collapsed onto
it. Miki was at 7,200 feet (2,200 m) elevation, and since leaving Uvira,
we had walked about 31 miles (50 km) in a straight-line distance, but
perhaps nearly twice that distance was traveled when one considers the
numerous hills and valleys we crossed during the trek. I closed my eyes,
and when I opened them again, the sun was rising the next day.

I relished a hearty breakfast of rice and beans, and Aristote, Chifundera, and I went to meet the local leaders. I was introduced to a well-
dressed man in his thirties who said he was effectively the mayor of the
village, and several other local officials. They were very polite and cor-

dial, and after handing out some small gifts of money and food to foster goodwill, I thought my political duties were finished. But then Aristote said we would have to meet the other leader in the village, the local commander of the Mai-Mai rebel militia. The Mai-Mai had formed as a response to the First Congo War that broke out in 1996, and at first their main focus was to protect themselves from the foreign armies that had invaded their land. At that time, Aristote had been a commander in the militia, and he defended his people bravely. But over time after the war ended, the militia endured, and now its purpose was not as clear. Some factions allied themselves with the Interahamwe, who were infamous for committing atrocities of all kinds to enrich themselves.

Aristote led us down a small hill to a modest brick building that was blaring rumba music from a radio with a jerry-rigged antenna that snaked up the wall to the roof. I was introduced to the local Mai-Mai commander, who was sitting in a white plastic lounge chair in sweatpants and a T-shirt. He looked to be in his late twenties and had a stocky, athletic build that reminded me of a football running back. He smiled widely as I shook hands with him, and his eyes scrutinized every inch of my appearance as his subordinates scrambled to get chairs for his new guests. Aristote and Chifundera diplomatically explained that we had come to Miki to look for amphibians and reptiles and that, if things went well, I would return in the future, perhaps with other biologists.

"Ndiyo!" (Yes!), he exclaimed. The commander then told us that we were welcome in Miki, that we would have no problems with security while he was there, and that he hoped our mission would be successful. I guess these words of acceptance and support were the cue for me to return the goodwill, because Aristote asked for money to buy everyone some bottles of the local Primus beer. Because we were so isolated, the beer fetched a steeper price in Miki, and I ended up spending about twenty dollars to make everyone happy. The commander then asked if I could bring a radio transmitter on my next trip to Miki, because his biggest problem was communication with the rebel leadership in Uvira and Bukavu. Then he jumped into an animated and forcefully opinionated conversation about Mobutu, Kabila, and politics. Chifundera asked some questions, which elicited a wagging finger and loud proclamations from the commander. This went on for some time, until Aristote decided that we had heard enough, and then we politely wished everyone well and took our leave.

As we walked back to the house, I asked Aristote what he thought of Mobutu. Aristote said he was a peacemaker, an apparently popular idea in Congo. Perhaps the dictator's modus operandi of buying off his enemies was a way to keep the peace, but his ascent to power had been anything but peaceful, and the United States had been a willing accomplice for three decades. At the close of the twentieth century, as Africa's World War was devastating Congo, Mobutu's biographer Michela Wrong wrote, "It is worrying to imagine that, one day, Congo's predicament may become so bleak its citizens will actually wax nostalgic for Mobutu, just as under Mobutu they talked with fondness and selective amnesia of the ghastly colonial years."[50] It seemed that her words had been prophetic.

We ascended the small hill to the house as the sun began to wane, and I looked at the beautiful forested hills that extended into the distance as far as the eye could see. Few biologists had ever gazed upon this awesome sight, and my imagination started to contemplate how many unknown species the forests still harbored. I would not have to wait long for the answer.

A group of women and one man were waiting to greet us at the house. They were part of an agricultural cooperative, and they brought us an enormous basket full of flour, vegetables, and a chicken. I gave them some money in thanks, but it was obvious that they had not expected payment—they were only trying to welcome us to their village. Marcel cooked a restorative meal from their generous gift, and my weary body relished every bite.

As the team ate the meal, we discussed the plan for surveying the area. A few hours' walk to the west there was a village called Kiandjo that was the type locality (the exact place where a new species was discovered) for a very rare genus of dwarf toad called *Laurentophryne*, named in honor of the Belgian herpetologist Raymond Laurent, who had been based at IR-SAC in Uvira in the colonial era.[51] He had discovered the bizarre-looking frog with his Congolese team in 1949, when it was still possible to drive

Belgian
herpetologist
Raymond Laurent
in 1977. Photo
courtesy of
William E.
Duellman.

through Itombwe with a road maintained by colonial mining companies. The tiny toad was only about an inch (2.5 cm) long, and it had an
unusually pointy snout and very rugose (warty-looking) skin. It had been
placed in its own unique genus because of several unusual skeletal features, but after its initial discovery, it was never seen again. Nobody knew
how it was related to other lineages of dwarf toads (only fresh DNA samples could unlock that secret), and because the animal had not been seen
in nearly sixty years, it was within the realm of possibility that it could
be extinct. I really wanted to find out. We agreed that on the following
day Chifundera would take Asukulu, John, Felix, Wandege, Mululema,
and Maurice to Kiandjo to collect for two or three days. In the interim, I
would work with Aristote to see what we could find in Miki.

While I watched the sun descending into a flame-orange sky, I felt my bones seemingly melt into the soft cushion of my sleeping bag, and I listened to the conversation of the people who had retired into the small huts just outside the house. Babies cried, spouses argued, a radio crackled with static, cooking fires sputtered, and in the distance I could hear haunting echoes of birds, bats, and unknown creatures in the forest as they either retired or began their nightshift. The smell of smoke fluttered into the cracked window of the room, and it soothed me into a relaxed state. Just as I thought I was going to fall asleep, somebody decided to pick up a megaphone and make announcements to the village, and the ringing squawk of the man's voice jarred me to attention. At one point during the squeaky shouting, the announcer paused as he tried to read out my name to welcome me to the village. "Ellleeeeee Guh-rain-bayum!" he yelled.

Several minutes after the news anchor of Miki retired for the night, I heard something stirring in the corner of the room, but I was too tired to look for my headlamp. At first it was a single scratching sound on the far wall, which I tried to ignore. But then I heard more scratching from other parts of the room, then squealing, then the sound of little feet scurrying across the concrete floor. Then I heard the creatures climbing around loudly on plastic bags, on my baggage, and especially around the fireplace. Too alarmed to ignore the noise any longer, I turned on my headlamp and saw several rats fleeing from the light.[52] One of them was at least a foot (30 cm) long. My bed was on a wooden frame raised several inches off the floor, and, having no alternative, I shut off the light and drifted to sleep as my furry roommates continued to explore the interesting new items that had entered their territory.

When I awoke shortly after dawn, I discovered why the rats had congregated around the fireplace. Marcel had decided to store all of our food there, including large sacks of potatoes and rice that the ravenous rodents had chewed through with ease. I called him into the room to show him the damage.

"Oh!" he exclaimed, and then he started laughing. Once again the presence of rodents had elicited hilarity. When he saw I was not amused, he said, "No problem, chief!" He reached into one of the bags and pulled out a half-chewed potato. He laid it on the floor at the front of the fireplace and said, "*Ouilla!* Zey will eat zis and not our food tonight!" He smiled at me proudly for coming up with an ostensibly clever solution to our dilemma, but I just grinned at him as I contemplated whether he was really serious. I realized that there was not another place that would be safer from the rats and possible human thieves, so I allowed myself to pretend that Marcel's pointless offering would be effective.

I waved goodbye to the Kiandjo team and was eating a modest breakfast from the previous night's leftovers when Aristote showed up to say that he found a bush viper at the edge of the forest. As word got out that I was looking for amphibians and reptiles, a slow trickle of people started coming by the house with tiny plastic containers with animals they had found in or near the village. One boy captured eight African clawed frogs, which are a completely aquatic and ancient group of frogs that are as slippery as fish and very difficult to catch without a net. An old woman showed up holding a stick with a three-horned chameleon at the end of it. Some enterprising individual had even beaten a harmless wolf snake to death in Lusasa and brought the corpse all the way to Miki in the hope of a reward. Needless to say, I spent most of the day photographing and processing specimens.

My legs were still weary from the long journey from Uvira, but curiosity was killing the cat about the animals in the forest, and I decided to do a preliminary search with Aristote and a teenage boy that wanted to tag along. Just after dusk, we walked for only five minutes before reaching a slippery trail at the edge of the forest. The mud was so thick that I sank in to my knees, and Aristote had to show me how to take advantage of logs that had been laid on the trail to help people avoid the deepest pools of mud. I invariably slid off them into the mud anyway, and I eventually gave up trying to use them and accepted the splotches of black ooze on my pants as I waded through.

We reached a stream that meandered across the trail, and we decided to investigate it after hearing several species of frogs. Almost immediately I spotted a medium-sized frog on the side of the stream, and I easily pounced on it before it could hop away. It was an *Amietia* river frog, but it had a pattern of black spots and stripes that I had never seen before. As

I followed the stream deeper into the forest, I found a dead bush viper near the edge of the water. It did not have any visible wounds, but more likely than not, it had been killed by someone earlier that day. Aristote called out that he had found some treefrogs, and I joined him to collect a few *Leptopelis karissimbensis*, the same species we had found at Kahuzi-Biega National Park, as they called for mates from trees and bushes near the stream. The forest certainly seemed to harbor a healthy population of amphibians, and we found several more frogs during our search.

After struggling uphill through the muddy trail to return to the house, we ate Marcel's dinner of rice and chicken. Following one last look at the specimens to marvel at the incredible diversity we were uncovering, I entered the bedroom, startling several rats as I did so. They dove into small holes in the edge of the wall to escape, but I was so tired I did not care.

The next morning I worked away on the specimens that we had collected the previous night and the ones that continued to trickle in from the surrounding villagers. Aristote said that a short walk from the village there was a good patch of pristine forest where we could spend some time looking for frogs. We planned to be gone for only a few hours when we left in the early afternoon. We walked for three hours past some fields of crops and open pits where the locals had tried to find gold, and reached a beautiful area of natural forest, but even here, there was evidence of mining, snare traps for hunting, and worn paths through the trees and unusually large ferns. We searched along a stream but found nothing. Suddenly, Aristote spotted a toad hopping along the forest floor, and when he showed it to me, I did not recognize the species, which had bold dark-brown spots on its back. As we passed through a beautiful swath of forest, my hands unknowingly brushed against the leaves of a plant with some kind of toxin. I felt a mild burning sensation on my hands a few minutes later and was surprised to see little red boils forming on the skin. We traversed several forested hills, occasionally stumbling into a recently deforested patch where someone had a mind to plant crops, but after hours of additional searching, we had only a few common species of frogs and it was getting dark.

By the time we returned to Miki several hours later, my legs ached with cumulative fatigue, and I had a difficult time deciding whether I was too tired to eat, even though I had eaten nothing since breakfast. Marcel was very excited because someone had brought him some pig meat, a relatively expensive food in Congo. After cleaning the mud off my pants as best as I could, I sat down next to the fireplace in the living room, and Marcel brought me a bowl of rice with several pieces of meat in a red sauce. I eyed the hairy skin that still clung to the flesh of the pig meat and hesitated to eat it, but I was too hungry not to. I stole a quick second peek at the frogs we had found that evening and fell asleep thinking about the amazing things I had not yet discovered.

A few hours later I awoke to a flash of lightning that streaked through the cracked windows onto the water-stained walls of my room. The rats were scurrying around the room as usual, and I could hear heavy drops of rain ricochet off the corrugated-metal roof. I felt nauseous, and sharp sensations of pain tormented me as I felt my stomach twisting itself into knots—the pork was bad, and now I was suffering the consequences. I made multiple trips out to the pit in the pouring rain as I slipped repeatedly on the steep and muddy path that led to it. Just before dawn, exhausted and drenched, I finally fell asleep again.

A short time later I awoke to the sound of Aristote opening the door to the bedroom. He slowly walked over to his bed before deliberately sitting down in an odd way.

"Everything okay, Aristote?"

"No, we have a small problem, but I think it can be okay."

"What's the matter?"

"One of the commander's men came to the house. He is waiting just outside. He said the commander is asking for fifty dollars from you."

"Why?"

"He just says you have to pay him fifty dollars," said Aristote as he looked down, almost embarrassed about the demand.

After thinking about the expensive beers I had provided on the day I arrived, I was disappointed that my kindness was seen as a weakness. There was something about the arrogance of the commander's demand that reminded me of every childhood bully I had ever dealt with. Somehow I was certain that if I gave in now, he would sense my apprehension and come back for more.

I studied Aristote's solemn face for a few moments as I contemplated my answer, and then I said no.

"No?" he asked.

"No. If I give him some money today, then he will ask for more to-morrow, and more the next day, and more the day after that. Then I will have no more money to pay anyone's salary, including yours, or for food, or for pombe [beer], or for anything!"

"Oh!" said Aristote as the reality of my position struck him. Obviously, the prospect of no beer was most shocking.

"If he comes here and holds an AK to my head, okay, I will pay him. But I don't think he is serious if he is not coming here to demand the money himself. You can tell Commander Fifty Dollars that I don't have any more money for him, and that's it." Between this, the rats, the bad pork, and my exhaustion, I had reached the point where I was almost in denial about the seriousness of my situation.

"No, Eli," he said forcefully. "You *must* pay the commander this money, or we can have a *matatizo* [big problem]!"

"What does the mayor think of this request?"

He paused for a second. "I don't know."

"And what about the other village officials I met? Do they think it is good for the commander to ask me for fifty dollars?"

Aristote seemed to consider my questions for the first time. "I don't know."

"Why don't you go ask the mayor what he thinks?" I suggested. "You can tell him I am asking if he thinks it is good for foreign guests of his village to be told they must pay money to militia. Ask him if he thinks more guests will come if I go home and tell everyone about the matatizo I had in Miki."

"Okay," he said, and then he left as quickly as his legs could whip his body out the door. I waited on edge for a few minutes, half thinking that the soldier would burst in to demand the money at gunpoint. But after nothing happened for an hour, my fear subsided and I went back to sleep.

A few hours later, Aristote returned to tell me that my first war of Af-rican politics had ended in victory. The mayor and all the village officials had gone to visit the commander to tell him that they did not agree with his demands. Apparently one of the officials knew a senior leader of the Mai-Mai who would not like to hear about a complaint like this, so the commander was forced to relent. The best part was that Commander Fifty Dollars would be coming to the house in person, *to apologize*. Aristote's eyes got big as he told me this last part, as though he could not believe what he was telling me. It was as if I had used a pair of 2's to bluff my way to the jackpot of a poker game when my opponent had four aces.

I continued to recover the following day, the commander visited me to apologize, and Chifundera showed up with Maurice and Mululema. They had many specimens of frogs from Kiandjo, some of which I had never seen before. Asukulu and Wandege had stayed behind with the Akuku brothers to collect in a nearby village called Kitopo. As I examined the catch, I noticed several species of brown, green, and red reed frogs, and a few treefrogs that looked like *Leptopelis kivuensis*. They had also found some treefrogs in the genus *Phlyctimantis*, commonly called the Wot-wot for their distinctive whooping call, distinguished by their bumpy jet-black skin with flaming orange bands on their thighs. They had not found any *Laurentophryne*, but they certainly documented several rare and possibly new species. That evening as I rested, one of the *Leptopelis* started to call in its container. Instead of hearing a call resembling Daffy Duck (typical for *Leptopelis kivuensis*), I heard a variation of quacks in a different pattern, so from my bed I recorded the call of the animal, which eventually proved to be a new species, *Leptopelis mtoewaate*.

A day later, after a massive photo shoot with Aristote, Chifundera arrived to announce that we had been invited to "take pombe" with some of the villagers. Aristote emphasized that we must not decline the invitation, even if I was still somewhat ill. Grateful for an excuse to take a break from the work, Chif and I followed him to a dusty brick building near the center of town. When he directed me inside it, I found a couple of benches facing each other, and one of them was empty. The room was only lit by the indirect sunlight coming in from the outside, and I could see numerous particles of dust and debris floating around in the air inside. When we sat down and our eyes adjusted to the dim lighting, I saw several people crowded onto the bench opposite from us, including the mayor and several village elders. There was an old woman named Alenge Namakulu whom I recognized from the agricultural cooperative group. Her hair was dressed in a white head wrap, and I noticed a perfectly straight scar that started from the middle of her forehead and continued down between her eyes to the middle of her nose. Similar scars were evident on her cheeks. When my eyes peered at the plastic drinking glass that dangled from her fingers, a cracked smile formed on her face. It was now obvious that I had been invited to a party that I was expected to bankroll.

"Muzungu!" she yelled with a slightly slurred and gravelly voice. She listed on the bench from side to side as she yelled out a proclamation in the local Kabembe language. Aristote translated that she was so pleased that I was feeling better and could now participate in this great party to celebrate my recovery. Apparently my illness was common knowledge. The mayor and other village elders smiled at me sheepishly. I passed some money to Aristote, and he returned with several bottles of beer from the vendor waiting just outside the door. I told Aristote to make sure the old woman got lots of beer, because she reminded me of one of my relatives. When Aristote translated my comment, her eyes got wide, and she stumbled to her feet and slapped me on the shoulder, agreeing loudly. Everyone started to laugh a little as she began a ranting story about a Belgian miner she had known in Miki during the early 1960s.

Realizing I had an opportunity to learn about the history of Miki, I asked her more questions. She said when she was a girl there were wild elephants everywhere, but the last time she had seen one was in 1996. She mentioned warfare with neighboring tribes, the arrival and hasty departure of the Belgian miners, and the most recent warfare that ended only a few years before. Curious, I asked her where she had traveled outside Itombwe. She said she had been to Mwenga and Uvira once or twice, but that was it. I tried to imagine this woman's perspective of the world based on her sixty years of experience in Itombwe. Her lifetime must have bridged the gap between a way of life that was thousands of years old, to a devastating cycle of violence in the wake of colonialism. Aristote later told me that the scars on her face were traditional markings for women of the Babembe tribe to make them beautiful, but the scarification practice had been outlawed by the Belgians, so that way of life would pass away with her generation. I told Aristote I thought that was sad.

As we departed the party with tipsy stumbles, Aristote asked for a salary advance so that he could buy himself one more bottle of beer and some fish. I relented, and he happily escorted me back to the house with his beer and a plastic bag of putrid, dried fish. Seeing that I was genuinely interested in the culture of his tribe, Aristote told me that the Babembe people were known throughout Congo as fierce warriors but that they were also a kind and intelligent people. From what I had seen in Miki, I had to agree. He also told me stories about wooden masks and idols that could speak—similar claims were noted for multiple tribes in Gabon by du Chaillu.[53] I asked Aristote about a statement in George Schaller's book *Year of the Gorilla*: "The Wabembe in this region [Itombwe] believe that the gorilla, the *kinguti*, is not an ape but a man who long ago retreated into the forest to avoid work."[54] Aristote confirmed Schaller's statement and added that this is why his tribe is a champion of ape conservation.

When we entered the room, Aristote hung his bag of fish on a nail on the wall that we were using as an anchor point for a clothesline. When I asked him where the fish was from, he said, "Lake Tanganyika."

"Can't the fish be rotten by now, Aristote?"

"No, the fish was dried in the sun at the lake, and it will be very good for many days."

"Well, I don't think I will ask you for any—that fish smells very bad. My favorite fish is sushi."

"Okay, no problem, muzungu, more fish for me then. What is sushi?"

I explained that sushi is raw fish prepared in a Japanese style. Now it was his turn to be repulsed. "Maybe someday you can visit me in America, and then you will understand. And if you do, you can also drink *rivers* of American pombe!" To this suggestion he grinned widely and agreed, and then took another swig of his Primus.

I had trouble falling asleep after dusk because the rats seemed to be in a frenzy over the enticing smell emanating from the unreachable fish. But then to my disbelief, I heard something gnawing at the plastic bag. When I turned on my headlamp, I was amazed to see that one of the intrepid rodents had managed to drag himself across the clothesline to the point on the wall where Aristote's fish was suspended. The light scared the tightrope-walking rat, and it dropped to the floor and ran, but only twenty minutes later I heard gnawing on the plastic bag again. As I debated what to do about Aristote's fish, he suddenly opened the door and, seeing the rat eating his prized dinner, immediately grabbed it by the tail and killed it instantly with a swift jerk of his wrist. When Aristote cursed the corpse for stealing part of his dinner, I could not help laughing.

The next day Wandege, Asukulu, and the Akuku brothers returned from Kitopo with an impressive number of frogs, chameleons, and two snakes. One of the snakes was a beautiful *Hapsidophrys lineatus*, a harmless emerald-green snake with large black eyes that resemble bug-eyed sunglasses. They had found more specimens of the new species of *Leptopelis* and forest toad, a puddle frog I had never seen before, and several species of *Hyperolius* reed frogs. Absolutely delighted, I spent the better part of the day photographing everything. As I worked, I noticed a small crowd of men talking to Aristote and Chifundera. They looked very serious as they walked over to me.

"Eli, we must talk about how to get from Miki back to Bukavu," said Chifundera. "The easy route is to follow the old Belgian road west to Mwenga, which is only one day's walk away."

"Oh, good!" I said. Instead of walking at least two days over the plateau to get to Uvira, walking downhill for only one day certainly sounded better.

"But the way to Mwenga has many Interahamwe," he added.

At this point Aristote chimed in with his opinion. "These men are dangerous! The route is outside the area of the Babembe, so they can do whatever they want. They can steal everything, or maybe even kill us." Aristote continued to tell me that many people from Miki took the shorter route to Mwenga but that they were often harassed, and sometimes robbed or beaten. I made the obvious choice to return to Uvira via the difficult route we had taken to get to Miki. Nobody argued with me.

Because I was still weakened from the pig-meat infection, our return was a bit slower, but after two days of hiking, climbing, and opportunistic collecting, we reached Magunda. This time, instead of seeing a few government soldiers, the village included a few Mai-Mai soldiers. We talked with them for a few minutes, and Aristote and Chifundera

Pale and thin from illness and a difficult journey, the author pauses for lunch with armed Mai-Mai militia and fellow travelers on the Itombwe Plateau. Chifundera is seated behind the author's right shoulder, John Akuku is behind his left shoulder, and Aristote is to his left. A man in the right background balances a heavy load of mined coltan on his head; he planned to sell it in Uvira. Photo by Wandege M. Muninga.

informed me that there was a problem on the route back to Uvira. Apparently the government soldiers had not been paid in several months, and to make ends meet, they had started robbing travelers as they passed over the plateau. Several small groups of men and women were stranded in Magunda as they waited for the situation to resolve.

I scratched some flea bites that I had picked up in a hut the night before, contemplating our next move. We had the greatest collection of amphibians and reptiles to come out of the Itombwe Plateau in sixty years, and I'd be damned if I would lose it after all we had endured to get it. When Aristote suggested we hire a small team of armed Mai-Mai to escort us to the safe part of the plateau, I agreed immediately. Word spread quickly among the other travelers, and within a few minutes, our entourage swelled to about two dozen people. We now had the dual advantage of Mai-Mai protection and safety in numbers, and after several hours of hiking, we passed through the danger. We paused for a quick lunch and parted ways with the Mai-Mai and most of our fellow travelers.

We then continued the difficult return journey to Uvira, but as we were climbing a grassy hillside with rocky outcrops, I spotted a lizard darting through the foliage. Wandege and Maurice had seen it, and after dropping their packs, they used a machete to dig it out of a burrow. I studied the animal for a few moments and immediately saw that it was in the genus *Adolfus*. We had collected a handful of the widespread and common species *Adolfus vauereselli* at slightly lower elevations of Itombwe, but we had always found them near the edges of montane forest, and the color pattern of this one also seemed odd. Suspecting we had just discovered a new species, we spent a few minutes looking for more, and eventually we collected a second specimen. I needed more for an adequate sample size for statistical analyses, but, running out of daylight, we had to move on.

As dusk fell, we descended a "path" of loose rocks that shifted under our weight like marbles. My stiff and weary feet slipped repeatedly as we began the descent down the eastern slopes of the plateau, but we reached a small village named Munanira before darkness overtook us. The chief kindly provided us with an enormous hut that was large enough for all of us to pass the night, and luckily for me there was no fire pit.

Shortly after dawn on July 1, we thanked the chief for his hospitality and made the final leg of the journey to Uvira. Along the way we passed through an increasingly hot series of rocky outcrops that baked in the sun, and several patches of maize and cassava crops. It seemed surreal as we descended into Uvira in the afternoon, and everyone stared at the dusty and rugged muzungu as I walked through the maze of shacks and small buildings on the edge of the city. Exhausted and hungry, I treated everyone to a feast of grilled chicken, fish, and beer at the Blue Cat, and we celebrated our success. We had hiked, climbed, and crawled through endless miles of mountains, and I was at least 15 pounds (7 kg) lighter to prove it. The next day we returned to Bukavu, where we planned the final stage of the 2008 expedition to Virunga National Park.

A VAMPIRE IN VIRUNGA

When Parc National Albert (modern-day Virunga National Park) was created in 1925, it was the first of its kind in Africa. One of the main forces driving the establishment of the park was to create a sanctuary for the mountain gorillas concentrated in the volcanic highlands. In the years that followed, a series of royal decrees from the king of Belgium expanded the park's territory to include pre-established hunting reserves and additional land. The decision to increase the park's territory was based mainly on the distribution of large mammals, and the territory was added in a way to minimize the impact on local peoples' need for hunting, fishing, and agriculture on traditional lands. This process was not perfect, and negotiations with indigenous tribes resulted in a series of concessions and changes to the park's boundaries into the 1950s.[1]

Designing the park's purpose after the American model, the Belgians realized that scientific studies would be needed to understand exactly what they were protecting and that tourism could help fund this endeavor. The first intensive study of the park's biodiversity was initiated in 1933 by a Belgian herpetologist named Gaston F. de Witte, who documented twenty-three species of amphibians and sixty-three species of reptiles from the park—one of the amphibians and one of the reptiles were described as new to science.[2] Eight additional major studies were completed by independence in 1960 in areas ranging from anthropology to botany. Now that the park's flora and fauna have been studied more thoroughly, we know that Virunga harbors more species of animals (including endangered species) than any other national

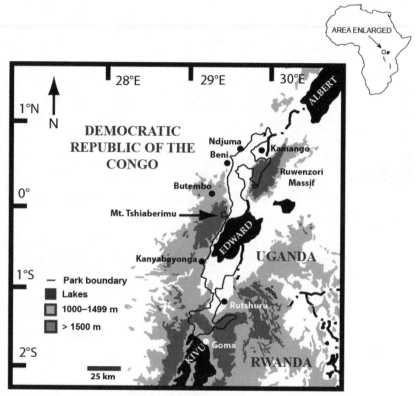

Map of Virunga National Park.

park in continental Africa. Included in the park's two hundred species of mammals are the African icons of elephant, lion, leopard, hippo, buffalo, and several species of antelope. But the park also includes over seven hundred species of birds, several endangered species of reptiles and amphibians (including Nile Crocodiles), approximately one hundred species of fish, a diverse but poorly studied invertebrate fauna, and a staggering diversity of plant life, making Virunga among the richest troves of biodiversity in Africa and the world. This fact is astonishing when one considers that Virunga is 186 miles (300 km) from north to south, and averages only 14 miles (23 km) from east to west, for a total area of only 3,011 square miles (7,800 square kilometers), which is only a little larger than the second tiniest US state, Delaware.[3]

How is it possible that all this biodiversity could be crammed into such a small space? The answer lies in Virunga's location at the western edge of Africa's Great Rift Valley. The valley started forming about 30 million years ago when two large plates, the African and Arabian, split apart from each other, forming the Red Sea. As this plate tectonic activity continued, the African plate split into two "protoplates," the Nubian and Somalian, which started drifting west and east, respectively. Over millions of years, as the distance between the protoplates increased, the Rift Valley formed; it now extends for thousands of miles from the Red Sea to Mozambique. Volcanic activity at the periphery of this enormous rifting activity led to the formation of numerous mountains, including the nearly continuous chain of Albertine Rift Mountains along most of the eastern edge of Congo's border. These forces also resulted in the formation of numerous craters within the Albertine Rift, which eventually filled with water to form some of Africa's Great Lakes: Albert, Edward, Kivu, and Tanganyika from north to south. In fact, Virunga means volcanoes in Kinyarwanda (the national language of Rwanda), and the park includes two of the most active volcanoes in the world in its southern sector—Nyiragongo (11,358 feet or 3,462 m high) and Nyamulagira (10,045 feet or 3,062 m high). Nyiragongo in particular has erupted multiple times in the recent past, often spewing forth large lava flows that destroyed parts of the nearby city of Goma on Lake Kivu's northern shore. Relatively frequent earthquakes are another consequence of the active rift. Hutu mythology attributes these frequent eruptions and tremors to violent outbursts of evil spirits living in the volcanoes, where tormented souls of departed ancestors linger in the African version of Hell.[4]

Because Virunga occurs along the eastern edge of the Albertine Rift, it includes territory from the mountains at about 9,842 feet (3,000 m) elevation through the precipitous drop down to Lake Edward at about 2,624 feet (800 m) elevation. This great range of elevation encompasses numerous habitats from bamboo forest on the mountains through a gradient of montane and submontane forest to the forest/savanna mosaic and flooded grasslands in the valley. This is impressive enough, but in addition to its volcanic highlands, Virunga also contains the spectacular Ruwenzori Massif,[5] a chain of mountains that sprung up from nonvolca-

Scrubby vegetation gains a foothold on a lava flow that emerged from Nyiragongo Volcano during one of its many eruptions. The volcano is just visible through rays of sunlight in the background.

nic geological processes 2–3 million years ago. The massif peaks at an astonishing 16,794 feet (5,119 m) and includes a glacier that once covered over 2.3 square miles (6 square kilometers). Because of its great height, Ruwenzori includes several types of vegetation that are absent from most, if not all other sites in Virunga, including tree heather, groundsels and lobelias, and afro-alpine vegetation characterized by moss and lichen. Given this incredible diversity of landscapes and vegetation, it is easy to understand why Virunga is renowned for its biodiversity and beautiful scenery.[6]

Despite Virunga's status as a UNESCO (United Nations Educational, Scientific and Cultural Organization) World Heritage Site, it is not the same place that it once was in the early twentieth century. During the diversion of Belgian attention and resources that occurred in World War

II, many local Congolese entered the park to exploit its resources. One iconic mammal species, the African Wild Dog (*Lycaon pictus*), was extirpated (destruction of a population of a species) in Virunga by the late 1950s, most likely because of conflicts with livestock.[7] In the aftermath of the Rwandan genocide in 1994, a million refugees fled into eastern Zaire, where many of them cut down Virunga's eastern forests for firewood. An influx of automatic weapons and lawlessness that accompanied the First Congo War in 1997 resulted in wholesale slaughter of Virunga's most emblematic animals. Elephant populations nose-dived from 8,000 in 1960 to about 400 today, a decrease of 95 percent. Virunga once had the largest population of hippos in the world with a peak of nearly 30,000 individuals in the lowland rivers and Lake Edward in 1974, but a survey in 2005 recorded less than 900.[8] Militias and corrupt officials continue to damage Virunga's remaining forests for the lucrative charcoal and marijuana black market. A satellite-imagery study noted that Virunga lost 2.6 percent of its forests in the first decade of the twenty-first century.[9] Yet the wildlife officials who defend Virunga's integrity never give up, even when militias like the Interahamwe attack park stations and kill rangers. If peace can come to Congo soon, there is an excellent chance that Virunga's wildlife will recover, and tourism can provide much-needed income to local communities that surround the park.[10] However, if the current trend continues for only a few more years, the fauna and ecology of the park will be irreversibly damaged.

In 2008, I hoped to renew herpetological interest in Virunga by looking for long-lost species that had been described by Belgian herpetologists from the park during the colonial era and, in some cases, had never been seen again. Gaston-François de Witte spent nearly two years in Virunga making an enormous collection of amphibians and reptiles, which resulted in a large monograph about the park's herpetofauna, including the description of a nearly 3-foot-long (87.5 cm) black snake, *Melanocalamus leopoldi*, surely named in honor of King Leopold II.[11] Three decades later, Laurent used some of these specimens to name several new species of amphibians from the park, including the reed frog *Hyperolius xenorhinus*, which was described from only a single specimen with a distinctive flat snout.[12] Were these poorly known species taxonomically valid? Were they extinct? Could the enormous and diverse territory of Virunga harbor additional, undiscovered species? To answer these questions and update the list of species known from the park, we needed to sample as many amphibian and reptile species as possible from different habitats of Virunga, including its lowland jungles and montane forests. I was exhausted from the long trek in Itombwe, but these unanswered questions and a desire to see some of Virunga's iconic mammals motivated me to press on.

It was July 4. After resupplying in Bukavu, we spent a long day on a bumpy, winding road that passed from Bukavu to the border city of Goma on Lake Kivu's northern shore. Our truck rocked through some narrow roads that were cracked and blackened from an old lava flow that had oozed down from nearby Nyiragongo Volcano a few years before. We stopped outside the iron gate of a relatively large house, and Chifundera got out of the truck to knock. After a few loud reverberations with his fist, somebody responded from inside. Chif impatiently demanded that they open the gate. When this was done a moment later, he returned to the truck and told me that this was his house. Soon after, I was surprised to learn that he had a second wife from an older marriage in the house, along with several of his children in their early twenties, whom I had never heard him mention before. Apparently he had called ahead, because his wife already had a delicious meal prepared for us, including cold cokes and beers that she had in a refrigerator. It was obvious that Goma enjoyed a better standard of living than other cities I had seen in Congo, including amenities like running water and more reliable electricity. I took advantage of those luxuries by taking a hot bath, my first since entering the country, after my delicious meal.

The next morning, after grateful thanks to Chif's family, we left the city and headed north. The main road briefly passed through Virunga's southern sector, which in this area included a beautiful combination of green forest, acacia trees, and savanna. Despite the park's seemingly pristine scenery, people crowded the roads with vehicles, homemade wooden bicycles called tshukudu (unique to the area around Goma), and carts transporting all kinds of goods, including firewood and large sacks of charcoal. It was obvious that the wood and charcoal could only have come from Virunga, because as the road continued north outside of the park's official boundary, rolling plains of thatched huts, fishponds, and crops could be seen in every direction, and there was hardly a tree in sight.

We continued north, again crossing into Virunga, and this time the acacia trees became more numerous in the grassy plains that crowded the edge of the road. It looked like the Africa I had seen in numerous nature shows about the Serengeti of Kenya and Tanzania. We crept along slowly as Mululema attempted to avoid large cracks and craters in the road, but I did not mind because Chifundera mentioned that there were still a few lion and elephants in this area. Before the war and the influx of automatic weapons and starving people that came with it, I probably would have seen scores of grazing mammals along the side of the road. But now our search for wildlife was in vain. We soon reached an outpost called Rwindi Station with several dilapidated buildings that had once served as the park's headquarters and provided lodging for tourists.

As I scanned the scene, I saw a group of two dozen bedraggled women and children surrounding our truck with bread, boiled eggs, fried dough, sodas, dried fish, and other snacks as they shouted out prices. Several other trucks laden with heavy loads of goods and people idled on the side of the road. Just as in Kahuzi-Biega National Park, a major road passes through the middle of Virunga, and I realized my chances of spotting wildlife on such a noisy and well-traveled route would be slim to none. But then Aristote pointed out a small troop of baboons foraging near the road. They had obviously become accustomed to the presence of people, and I saw a couple of them picking through some plastic bags that had been discarded by passing travelers.

We continued on past a UN outpost in the middle of nowhere that was surrounded with razor wire. I asked Mululema to stop the truck as I spotted a small herd of Uganda Kob (*Kobus kob*), a common deer-like antelope species with tan-colored hair and spiraling horns in males. After a skittish retreat from the edge of the road, they paused to look back and stare at us with nervously twitching heads. Next to them was a small pond of water filled with several large species of scavenging birds, including Marabou Stork (*Leptoptilos crumeniferus*) and White-backed Vultures (*Pseudogyps africanus*). Because both species are scavengers, I wondered if an animal had been killed or died in the pond. I took several photos of the scene, but the searing heat from the plains drove me back into the truck and we continued our journey north. Although we continued through the park for several more hours and I spotted a few colorful birds that sprung up from the grass as our truck passed by, I did not see any more wildlife.

Eventually the road started to climb the steep ascent known as the Kabasha Escarpment. At first it was very subtle, but then the road started making hairpin turns as it snaked up a steep mountain. When we neared the top, we paused to look at the stunning beauty of the valley below us. The grassy basin of the Great Rift Valley continued as far as the eye could see into Uganda, and I smiled as I observed that there seemed to be a complete absence of man in that valley—no roads, houses, cars, or fires. But then as I turned my gaze in the opposite direction, I looked at the spine of mountains that continued parallel to the road. Because these mountains contain deep and fertile soils and a cool climate that is free from the most dangerous tropical diseases, the Belgians settled here in great numbers during the colonial era. They cut down the montane forest to make way for their crops and herds of cattle and sheep, and many of the colonists prospered and raised families. By the late twentieth century, almost no forest remained in this area, and now I was contemplating a search for the tiny patches that had somehow escaped the axe. As I returned to the truck, I could already feel the heat and humidity dissipating from our position at a higher elevation.

We soon passed through a road barrier that marked the edge of the park, and suddenly hordes of people, small huts, and crops were everywhere. We had entered the town of Kanyabayonga, and I could see a veritable ocean of shacks and small houses on every hill within sight. Remnants of the Belgians could be seen in faded French writing on old brick buildings that had served as churches, police stations, and schools. The sides of the road were bordered by enormous eucalyptus trees that had been planted by the Belgians for shade and aesthetics, but in random places the locals were cutting down the trees to get access to firewood, which was now very scarce because of the ever-increasing human population and deforestation.

We continued north through the mountains west of Lake Edward, and I saw enormous Belgian mansions on the hillsides that overlooked the road. Some of them were in immaculate condition and sat in the middle of lush green meadows that still contained small herds of European cattle and sheep. An ancient, faded sign at the entrance to one of these properties advertised cheese, yogurt, and other dairy products. I could not help marveling at the beauty of the place and wondered what it must have been like to enjoy the local delicacy of strawberries and cream in the colonial era.[13] But it also seemed absurd that the Belgians had re-created rural European farms in the middle of Central Africa.

When we reached Lubero in the late afternoon, I observed what must have been a central marketplace in the past. There were crumbling buildings that had served as shops, a hotel with broken windows and verandas covered in black mold, and several old Belgian houses on hills in the distance. A few women and children were selling vegetables and other food from small wooden stands on the side of the road, and a metal road barrier prevented us from continuing into the town. Chifundera got out of the truck and greeted a man who refused to wave us through, and they disappeared into one of the old buildings to talk to the police chief as I waited. I noticed a man in a full-length woman's fur coat glaring at me from behind the barrier, and with a confident swagger he walked up to my window and demanded to see my passport. Although he had no uniform, badge, or any visible clue of his official status, he said he was with the police. Aristote tried to tell him that Chif had gone to see the chief of police about our visit, but the putative cop continued to insist that I give him my passport. Not wanting any trouble, I relented and watched as he disappeared with my most precious possession into the crowd of people on the other side of the barrier.

Chif returned to the truck and commanded Mululema to continue, but when I told him that the man in the coat had taken my passport, he cursed and returned to the building to look for it. Twenty minutes later he returned with my passport in his hand, complaining that I had to reimburse him for a fine that he had to pay to get it back. By the time we left, a beautiful sunset had come and gone, and our truck hummed into the grayish light that faded with every passing minute. When the darkness finally overtook us, everyone became quiet and I felt a weariness creep into my body.

I perked up a little as our tiring journey continued through a small remnant of forest, and when I heard frogs calling on the side of the road, I decided to make a quick pit stop to see what they were, but it is always dangerous to travel after dark in Congo, and we did not want to linger too long. I could hear the quacky call of *Leptopelis*, but when I saw a strange, mustard-yellow species of *Hyperolius* reed frog, I told everyone to focus on them since we could only stop for a few minutes. As I looked at one of the frogs carefully with my headlamp, I realized that it must be a Side-striped Reed Frog (*Hyperolius lateralis*), a species described from a small lake adjacent to Nyamuragira Volcano near Goma. Laurent described the species in 1940, but within a decade he described several related subspecies based on aberrant color patterns. The one I had just found seemed to fit a subspecies (*Hyperolius lateralis pleurospilus*) that he described from a nearby place in Virunga National Park just after World War II.

Energized from the interesting find, I was wide awake as we entered the small city of Butembo later that evening. Ravenous from lack of food, we immediately drove to a restaurant where we had a rendezvous with a jovial man named Jean Claude Kyungu, who was in charge of the tiny fragment of montane forest at Mount Tshiaberimu in northwestern Virunga. Three years earlier, when Chifundera was warden director of the Mount Tshiaberimu Gorilla Conservation Project, he had spent a lot of time with the gorillas to habituate them for tourists and knew all too well how precarious their existence was in their tiny and isolated forest patch. As we ate a meal of grilled chicken and *frites* (french fries), Jean Claude told us that two of the eighteen remaining gorillas had recently died of an unknown illness at the site, and as a precaution, we would not be able to see the remaining group.

When George Schaller spent two weeks at Tshiaberimu in the late 1950s, he counted eighty-five gorilla nests, most of which were constructed at the tops of bamboo stands several feet above the ground. At times, Schaller would use winding paths made by elephants in the forest to look for gorillas and find his way back to the camp. Although he noted the presence of terraced agriculture and concentrated areas of human settlements near Tshiaberimu, the site was certainly more pristine at that time. Well before the turn of the twenty-first century, the elephants disappeared, the gorilla numbers plummeted, and the pristine world that Schaller had glimpsed was changed forever.[14]

In the morning I talked with Jean Claude about the gorillas and how their tiny space often led to conflict. Lone males would leave the group in search of females to make their own group, but the overall population was now so small and cramped that the males often bumped into the main group, causing conflicts with the dominant silverback that sometimes led to injuries.

When we left Butembo, the road to Virunga curved ahead in such a way that I could see Mt. Tshiaberimu in the distance. The forest clinging to the edges of it was indeed beautiful, but I also noticed that the surrounding area was densely covered in human settlements and crops. A narrow, teardrop-shaped corridor of land connects the isolated mountain to the main mass of the park in the east, and it is obvious that Tshiaberimu is effectively isolated in this way. With no gorillas coming in or out through the corridor, I could not help thinking that the Tshiaberimu population is only one minor disaster away from annihilation.

When we reached the edge of the forest in the late morning, I saw colonial-era metal signs reading "Parc National Albert" that were riddled with bullet holes. We walked along the edge of the forest to a small group of houses, where we were introduced to several park rangers. Jean Claude invited me into one of the houses because he wanted to show me something. I followed him to the doorway of the house, where he pointed at some bullet holes in the wall. A park ranger had been killed there recently by militia who wanted to get access to the natural resources at Tshiaberimu, including animals for food, firewood, and bamboo for building materials. I felt a chill run down my spine as I focused on the place where the ranger had died, but I also felt angry that one small group of bullies with guns felt they were entitled to destroy everything that the park represented for temporary personal gain. Fear crept into me as I wondered about the security in the area, but there was one more grisly sight to see before we began our climb onto the mountain. We passed a graveyard for gorillas that had died from the mysterious illness at Tshiaberimu recently. Jean Claude looked somber as he told me that when a gorilla died at Tshiaberimu, everyone was very sad because it felt like a member of their family had died.

Wanting to put the negative energy behind me, I started climbing and hiking the mountain trail as soon as Jean Claude pointed it out to me. It was a steep ascent for at least half an hour, and I searched for lizards and frogs in the leaf litter on the side of the trail as I paused every few minutes to catch my breath. Within an hour, we had crossed a couple of streams and were deep in the forest, and the afternoon light was much dimmer as it filtered through the closed canopy above us. It became especially dim when we passed through patches of thick bamboo at least 50 feet (15 m) tall, and in a few places I saw telltale signs of gorillas that had passed along the trail very recently.

After scurrying over some logs that had been strategically placed to help the rangers pass over a flooded area of grass that resembled a bog, we emerged from the forest into a small clearing with a cabin called Kalibina Station. I was sweating from the two-hour hike, but the air was noticeably thin and chilly now that we had reached the elevation of 9,022 feet (2,750 m). After some more introductions to the rangers living there, my team was provided with a few rooms in the cabin, and I worked with Aristote to photograph the *Hyperolius* reed frogs we had collected the night before near Lubero.

When dusk fell on the camp, clouds rolled into the clearing, and I could smell the water in the thick air. We walked into the flooded grasslands near the station, and within minutes we found and recorded some calling *Hyperolius* reed frogs and a chameleon that Chifundera found sleeping in some tall grass. An increasing crescendo of thunder and lightning forced us back to the cabin for the night, and despite a double layer of a warm sleeping bag and an extra blanket, frigid temperatures made me shiver all night until I could get some hot coffee the next morning at dawn. Over the next few days, we found several more interesting species that I had not seen in other areas of the Rift, including a chameleon with a mohawk of spiny scales on its back and an emerald *Leptopelis* of uncertain identity. As we searched during the day, we also saw many species of birds and even some nighttime nests that black-and-white colobus monkeys had used. It was heartening to see that the animal fauna at Tshiaberimu seemed to be healthy and that we had likely found some species endemic to this part of the Rift. Our discoveries also underscored the importance of continued conservation for the mountain, even if the animals in its sanctuary were now cut off from neighboring populations in the park.

After saying our goodbyes to the kind people at Kalibina, we descended the mountain and retraced our drive to Butembo. We drove north as the road slowly descended from the mountains, and the air became increasingly hot and thick with humidity. We passed through several unremarkable towns, each surrounded by bleak, deforested landscapes of crops, and we pulled into the city of Beni in the late afternoon. Beni had been a small outpost in the middle of the rainforest a century ago, but now it was unquestionably the most developed place I had seen since Goma. There were several shops, hotels, restaurants, and even some banks, and I could see power lines providing electricity to most of them. People were walking around everywhere, and I noticed the presence of Congolese military and UN cars. Chif directed Mululema to a small set of well-tended buildings near the center of the city—the local headquarters for ICCN. I was surprised to see a stocky white man walking in the courtyard, and as our truck coasted to a stop, he turned around to look at me.

I greeted the man in French through my open window, then stepped out of the truck to shake his hand. He introduced himself as Stuart, a biologist from the Zoological Society of London. Each of us was delighted to meet a fellow scientist who could speak English, so we were soon engaged in an animated conversation about each other's work in Congo. Stuart had come to the northern sector of Virunga to set up camera traps in the lowland rainforest to see if the park still had a healthy population of the elusive and rare okapi, a relative of the giraffe. I made plans to meet up with him later that night.

After a quick search, we found a cheap but comfortable hotel in the middle of the city. I could not resist capturing a *Hemidactylus mabouia* house gecko, the same species I had encountered at Lwiro, which scurried across the wall of my room as I entered. After getting settled, I decided to rinse off in the bathroom. Although there was a shower stall, the reliability of running water was so unpredictable and intermittent that the hotel staff had simply left a large bucket of water to be used for washing. Of course this standing water is a perfect nursery for mosquitoes. I turned on the faucet and, as expected, a small amount of air hissed through the empty pipes before going silent. There was no electricity either, so in the dim gloom I splashed myself with water from the bucket until the dust and mud from several days of work had been washed away. Feeling refreshed and relaxed, I was only too happy to join Aristote when he knocked on my door to tell me that Stuart and another white man had showed up at the hotel bar.

Now that darkness had fallen, most of the city's electricity was on, and I rounded a corner from my hotel room to find a well-lit restaurant with several white plastic tables and matching chairs. A large TV screen was blasting Swahili music videos from an artist named BB DJ,[15] and several people were eating dinners of chicken, fish, and cassava with beer. Stuart waved at me from the bar, and I noticed a tall white man with glasses next to him. After I shook Stuart's hand, he introduced me to his friend and colleague Simon, a fellow Brit who had come to assist him with the camera trap survey of Virunga's northern lowland forests. All three of us were genuinely thrilled to be on the verge of starting to work in one of the most biodiverse places on the African continent, and our imaginations ran rampant with possibilities of what we might discover in the coming days.

The animal that Stuart and Simon hoped to capture with their camera traps, the okapi, is by any definition a mysterious and unusual creature. The animal has the chocolate-brown body of a horse, zebra stripes on its legs and buttocks, and a head that is shaped somewhat like that of its closest living ancestor, the giraffe. Male okapi have two cone-like horns on the top of their head, and the hair of both sexes includes brown pigmented oil, which seems to be an adaptation for waterproofing in the rainforest's wet environment. Okapi are diurnal (active during the day), but they are very shy and prefer to live in the most remote parts of the forest, where their coloration helps them blend into the dark shadows under the closed canopy. Special glands at the top and front of each hoof secrete a waxy substance that might be involved in olfactory communication. Like their cousin the giraffe, okapi have long tongues (up to 18 inches [46 cm]) that they use to browse on leaves from over one hundred species of understory shrubs, lianas, and tree saplings on the forest floor. Okapi make a wide range of human-like sounds when communicating with each other, and, like elephants and rhinos, they are also capable of making infrasonic sounds (not detectable with the human ear) for communication across long distances in the dense vegetation and humid air of the forest. The animals reach sexual maturity at two to three years, and in captivity they can live to be over thirty years old. Females can give birth at any time of the year to a single calf (sometimes twins), and in between nursing sessions, the calves are left to hide in shelters deep in the forest while the mother browses for food.[16]

Because the okapi is so secretive and the Congo Basin lowland forests were virtually unknown to Westerners, rumors about its existence did not surface until the late nineteenth century. In his 1890 book *In Darkest Africa*, Henry Stanley repeated tales from Mbuti pygmies that a "donkey" called *atti* lived in the forest and that the pygmies sometimes captured these animals in great pits camouflaged with vegetation. Stanley later said he caught glimpses of the animal on the western side of the Semliki River in the Ituri Forest. Sir Harry Johnston, British governor of the Uganda Protectorate and friend of Stanley in the early twentieth century, decided to mount an expedition into neighboring Congo to look for the animal in 1900. Guided by pygmies, Johnston managed to obtain two okapi tails from men in the Bambuba tribe near Beni. These striped tails were sent to the Zoological Society of London, where the secretary Dr. Philip Sclater examined them and decided the animal was an unknown species of mammal that might be related to the zebra or giraffe. Some people even speculated that the creature might be the mythical unicorn. The following year the animal was erroneously described as a new species of zebra, *Equus johnstoni*. Later that year Johnston obtained a skin and two skulls from Congo, which he forwarded to scientists at the British Museum of Natural History. They determined that the animal was a relative of the giraffe, but it was so unique that it belonged in its own genus, and it was renamed *Okapia johnstoni*. The find caused a sensation in the press, and many people rightfully asked how such a large animal could have been missed for so long.[17]

If something the size of a horse could evade scientific detection until the turn of the twentieth century, what other amazing animals could still be hiding in Congo's vast forests? Consider that the lowland Congolian rainforests and swamp forests in Central Africa form a nearly continuous stretch of 619,192 square miles (1,603,700 square kilometers), an area over twice the size of Texas.[18] Much of this area is so isolated from roads and navigable rivers that they have never been explored by scientists. Tens of thousands of gorillas were found in the swamp forests of Congo-Brazzaville in 2008, underscoring a truly shocking lack of basic knowledge about the Congo Basin's biodiversity in the twenty-first century.

As we drank our beers, Stuart started telling me an intriguing story related to his previous projects with gorillas. A European man based at the Institute for Scientific Research in Central Africa (IRSAC) in Lwiro during the colonial era developed a talent for capturing entire families of gorillas for zoos. Stuart said one could still see the large nets he used for the captures at present-day Centre de Recherche en Sciences Naturelles (CRSN). While examining the man's field notes, he came across an entry that would be ridiculous in any part of the world except Congo. The man wrote he had found the tracks of a bipedal ape in the forest, and although he tracked it for some time, he failed to find it before the trail was lost.

The man Stuart described was most likely a Swiss animal trapper named Charles Cordier, who lived in an isolated forest clearing near Kabunga, a mining site north of present-day Kahuzi-Biega National Park. George Schaller confirmed that Cordier used large nets manned by one hundred Congolese men to trap gorillas, and at the time it was a lucrative endeavor: in the late 1950s a single gorilla could fetch five thousand dollars, equivalent to about fifty thousand dollars today. Schaller repeated stories from Cordier about the *Kakundakari*, a man-like ape that Schaller likened to the Congolese version of the abominable snowman. Local Congolese told him the ape is covered in hair and walks upright, and males are 5.5 feet (1.7 m) tall, whereas the females reach only 4 feet (1.2 m). At night Kakundakari sleep on beds of leaves in caves, and they eat crabs, snails, and birds. Cordier told Schaller that he had seen the footprint of the apelike creature (thus backing up Stuart's story), and on another occasion an individual wiggled out of a bird snare before it could be captured. Cordier even claimed that a Kakundakari was killed in 1957 in a mining camp.[19]

Is all of this really outside the realm of possibility? Given the shocking gorilla discovery in Congo-Brazzaville in 2008, it is certainly possible that more ape populations await discovery. Mankind's closest living ancestors are found in Central Africa, and during the Miocene (5–23 million years ago), at least forty different kinds of apes lived in Eurasia and Africa.[20] In 2014 a team of scientists reexamined a single intriguing molar tooth that had been collected in the 1950s at Ishango, near the northern shore of Lake Edward in Virunga National Park. The fossil beds where the tooth was found dated to the early Pleistocene, about 2–2.6 million years ago, but it is unknown whether the tooth belonged to either an early human (genus *Homo*) or a separate "australopith" species in the genera *Paranthropus* or *Australopithecus*, both of which would have been bipedal with apelike facial features.[21] Could a living, unknown species of ape really have escaped notice for so long? Probably not, but spectacular, new species undoubtedly await discovery in the vast and unexplored Congo Basin forests.

The next morning we left Beni shortly after dawn and took a road that corkscrewed down a steep hill. I tried but failed to capture an alert, malachite blue-and-green tree lizard sunning itself on the side of the road, and during our brief stop I paused to look down the hill at the beginning of the vast and flat Congo Basin. A mixture of palm trees and natural lowland rainforest vegetation stretched into the horizon as far as the eye could see. This was the eastern edge of an enormous bowl-shaped depression of rainforest and swamps that continued with few interruptions to the Atlantic Ocean on the western coast of Central Africa, over 2,100 miles (3,500 km) to the west. My heart raced as I contemplated what secrets could be hiding in the ocean of green lying before me.

Once we completed the descent, the road became exceptionally wide, level, and flat. There were few potholes, and it seemed obvious that a work crew had recently improved the road, installing culverts and ditches on the sides to channel away the enormous amounts of rain that surely

A view of the road through the lowland rainforest of the
Congo Basin at Ndjuma, Virunga National Park.

fell there. After a few minutes of marveling at the enormous trees on
both sides of the road, we arrived at a place called Ndjuma (Djuma on
the old Belgian maps) near the edge of Virunga National Park's northern sector. There was a pair of modern-looking buildings to house the
rangers stationed there, and in front of them I noticed a sign bearing the
USAID logo, suggesting that American money had funded the construction. I saw a handful of small huts where three curious women were
hanging laundry and cooking food. As a former warden at Virunga,
Chifundera recognized the rangers and greeted them enthusiastically
as the rest of us slowly left the vehicle to shake their hands. After a few
minutes it became clear that Chif wanted us to set up our camp there,
because this was the last human habitation of any kind for many miles,
and he wanted us to be near the rangers to ensure our security.

I looked at the vegetation around me, and although I could see many species of trees that were obviously endemic to the rainforest, including some at least 100 feet (30 m) tall, I could also see a few crops, several places where large trees had been cut down, and some thick concentrations of palm trees, which can occur naturally in the forest but are also grown commercially for the nutritious nuts and valuable palm oil. I realized that we were at the edge of secondary forest, a term used by ecologists for an area that has been recently disturbed by human activities, and would be unlikely to harbor species that are truly endemic to the primary, pristine rainforest. Somewhat disappointed, but not willing to challenge Chifundera's concern for our safety, I agreed to set up our camp next to the huts. Within a couple of hours we had cleared a small area for our tents, Marcel had started a fire, the friendly women had filled our plastic jerry cans with water from a local stream, and we even managed to suspend a large plastic tarpaulin between some trees so that I could have a rain-free place to work. One of the rangers also volunteered a chair and small table for my modest open-air laboratory.

Following a decent lunch of plantains from Marcel and an afternoon thunderstorm, dusk descended on our camp, and the voices of retiring monkeys and birds gradually transitioned to the nightshift chorus of bats, insects, and frogs. Within minutes, we found several species of reed frogs, treefrogs, puddle frogs, spiny reed frogs, rocket frogs, aquatic *Xenopus* clawed frogs, sleeping lizards, and toads. I recorded the call from several frogs calling from perches at the edges of small ponds, grassy reeds near the water, and, in the case of a Wot-wot, even 10 feet (3 m) above the ground in trees. We worked for hours, but I felt very tired when we finally returned to camp, and I fell asleep immediately.

A few hours later, I awoke with a throbbing headache. There was also a sharp pain in my abdomen, and the cramps and other unpleasant symptoms continued until dawn. When Marcel emerged from his tent and saw me on one of my return trips to the latrine pit, he smiled and said, "Bonjour, Chief!"

"Ninagonjwa" (I am sick), I replied with a dour expression.

"Ooh la la!" he replied. As I left the camp again, I heard him greeting

Chif through the side of his tent. When I returned, Chif was drinking his morning coffee, and he eyed me seriously.

"Hello, Eli. Marcel says you are sick."

I looked up at him and must have appeared green, because without a word from me he said, "Yes, you are sick! What's wrong?"

I told him I had painful cramps and a foul odor in my mouth.

"Ah!" he exclaimed. "Does your breath smell like rotten eggs?"

He had hit the disgusting nail on the head. "Yes. How did you know that?"

Very matter-of-factly, Chif informed me that I had giardia. He was quite sure of the diagnosis because giardia is one of the most common gastrointestinal human parasites in the world (only absent from Antarctica), with infection rates reaching 30–50 percent in the tropics. The organism is a single-celled protozoan that has the ability to reproduce via a two-stage life cycle within the small intestine of human hosts. Giardia are distinguished by the presence of four pairs of flagella (each one similar to the whip-like tail of sperm), two functioning nuclei (most eukaryotic, unicellular organisms have only one), and a unique disc-like structure that they use to attach to the lining of the small intestine. The sulfurous exhalations are a result of the parasite's ability to stop the absorption of fats (and sometimes sugars, carbohydrates, and vitamins) in the gastrointestinal tract of the host—the undigested fats essentially rot in the gut and produce the nasty odor. The disease is most common among infants and children, and the malabsorption effects can exacerbate malnutrition, stunting growth and development, but giardia infections are not fatal. Cysts are transmitted through fecal-contaminated water, food, or direct transmission from person to person, and the incubation period is one to two weeks.[22] Given the timing and unsanitary conditions, I had probably picked up the parasite during my jaunt through Itombwe.

Because the disease is so common, Chif happened to have some pills to treat it. I gratefully took his medication and returned to my tent to catch up on some rest, but within a few hours the heat and humidity rendered my tent an oven. Aristote was waiting for me when I emerged to escape the heat, but Chif and Wandege were off looking for animals in the forest. Not sure what to do next, I looked over at my jungle laboratory and was reminded of the large number of specimens we had collected the previous evening. Sick or not, it was time to get to work photographing specimens. As I sat working in the chair, the thick humidity prevented my sweat from evaporating, and I could feel a constant drip of perspiration tickle my ribs. The slow and steady work focused my attention away from my illness, and after a few hours, I decided to risk eating some bananas.

As the day wore on, Chif and Wandege returned with a handful of animals. One of them was a spectacular rhinoceros viper, a venomous species endemic to the lowland Congo Basin. Reaching about 3 feet (1 m) in length, these nocturnal snakes spend most of their time lying motionless in wait to ambush their prey, which includes small mammals and amphibians. When disturbed, they emit the loudest hiss of any African snake, which has been likened to a shriek,[23] and Aristote warned me that the strike is so powerful that when threatened the snake can jump off the ground to attack. Chif and Wandege had also scoped out a flooded field at the edge of the forest that looked promising for frogs in the evening. We heard a truck pull up to the ranger outpost, and I spotted Stuart and Simon emerging from it to pay me a visit. They told me that they had been working hard looking for okapi tracks and setting up camera traps, and they had found some evidence of okapi activity in the area. Then the conversation turned to my illness, which was still physically obvious from my pallid color.

"How long have you been in the Congo now?" Stuart asked.

"About six weeks."

"And how many times have you been sick?"

"Well, aside from some gastrointestinal problems from bad food, this is the first major issue I've had."

Stuart looked surprised. "You don't know how lucky you are," he said. At that particular moment in time, with my limited experience in Congo, I did not fully realize how right Stuart was.

Simon chimed in and told me about his unpleasant experience with giardia. As we continued to chat about the difficulties of working in Congo, an otherworldly screech reverberated through the forest. Although I could not see the animal that emitted the bellowing call, I heard its large wings whooshing just over the canopy above us, and it was obviously a large bird. The haunting sounds in the primeval forest made me think of a giant pterodactyl.

"A hornbill!" exclaimed Stuart. He suddenly produced a pair of binoculars to look for the bird, but the canopy was too thick to get a glimpse of it. Simon yanked the binoculars away to see if he could have better luck.

Although about twenty-five species of hornbill occur in Africa, and more than thirty are found in Asia and Melanesia, the species I heard was most likely the Black-casqued Hornbill (Ceratogymna atrata), which is relatively common in Central African forests and is known for the whooshing sound of its wings, which span nearly 3 feet (1 m) in adult males. As the name implies, most of the bird's plumage is black, but there are bright, cobalt-blue patches around the eyes and throat, and a large tube-like structure (the casque) extends from the top of the head along most of the length of the bill.[24] The omnivorous birds live for a relatively long time; are likely monogamous, breeding every one or two years (depending on how much fruit is available); and lay one or two eggs. Like many other hornbill species, the Black-casqued Hornbill nests in cavities of the largest and oldest trees in the forest, which unfortunately are often the first to be felled by commercial loggers. To minimize the risk of predation, females enter the cavity, and both sexes use mud to seal the female inside so that only a small narrow slit connects her and the eggs to the outside world. She puts the life of herself and her chicks in the hands of the male, who tirelessly flies back and forth to the nest to bring food. Because the hornbills' main staple is fruit, they are absolutely essential for seed dispersal for many species of trees and, as a result, maintain the forest's ecological structure.[25]

The three of us exchanged well wishes for productive fieldwork, and then I watched the two Brits depart in the lengthening shadows of the late afternoon. With renewed vigor, I finished my lab work and accompanied my Congolese colleagues to the promising pond they had found earlier that day. Toads and spiny reed frogs were calling everywhere, and I spent several hours recording the mating song from a dozen individuals of several species. By the time we returned to our tents after midnight,

I had forgotten about the giardia and slept through the night without any issues.

The next morning, shortly after dawn, I awoke to the sound of Chifundera, Marcel, Aristote, and one of the rangers in a heated conversation. Concerned that there might be a problem with security, I dressed quickly in my sweaty clothes (they had not yet dried from the previous night's work) and prepared to poke my nose from the tent to see what was happening. As soon as I opened the zipper I could see and smell numerous small piles of red-hot coals sprinkled all over the campsite. Chifundera was motioning toward the ground, and Marcel was following in his wake with a pot full of coals, dumping them wherever Chif pointed with his wild gesticulations. Following the direction of Chif's curses, I could see the cause of the problem: army ants.

The forward column of about 20 million female ants[26] was snaking through our campsite, zigzagging here and there where Marcel had blocked their path with burning coals. When I listened carefully, I could hear the sound of countless tiny ant feet marching over the dead leaves on the forest floor. I had seen such columns once or twice before as they crossed a footpath or road, and then, like now, I could see enormous soldier ants with wicked-looking mandibles guarding the flanks of the roving masses.

Unlike most of the thousands of known species of ants, many army ant species do not typically build nests, but instead congregate in temporary aggregations called bivouacs to shelter the vulnerable queen and larvae. The Dorylinae subfamily of African army ants lacks stingers, instead relying on a swarming mob attack to overwhelm, disable, and dismember prey. The nomadic ants may roam up to three weeks at a time in search of food, but they have sedentary cycles as well and sometimes stay put for weeks at a time to reproduce or when food is abundant. In Africa, all the known species are mostly or exclusively carnivorous, devouring any invertebrate or small vertebrate species that cannot escape an attack. Although the army ants can be thought of as one collective superorganism with impressive predatory abilities,[27] they also serve an important role in the overall ecology of the forest. Many forest animals take advantage of prey weakened by ant attacks or even the ants themselves, including birds, snakes, lizards, mongeese, gorillas, and chimpanzees. Butterflies feed on the bird droppings, parasitic flies infest invertebrates fleeing from the column, and mites sometimes hitch a ride on the roving columns.[28]

I added to Chif's curses as I realized that the ants were too close to the laboratory for me to work, and I could see that the burning coals were only effective for a few minutes before they cooled off and the column ignored them in their relentless search for food. Just as I began to think that we were ultimately powerless to fend off the hordes, a man ran up to the campsite with a plastic bowl full of some kind of liquid. He started shouting at Marcel to stop throwing down hot coals, and I quickly figured out why. The strong odor of gasoline soon filled the camp as he dribbled the fuel everywhere, and this time, the ants took a detour to avoid the foul smell. Still woozy from the giardia, I jumped out of my tent as quickly as possible, because I did not want to burn alive if the fuel strategy backfired. Within a few minutes, we were ant free, but it was very unpleasant to work all day in the midst of the fumes. I was also not pleased that we had used gasoline to fend off a natural part of the forest, but nobody had asked me for my opinion, and I did not react quickly enough to protest.

Hours later, the fumes subsided, and I realized that despite the difficulties with the ants, I was feeling better and my appetite had returned. I ate several bananas, and Marcel cooked me some cassava with chicken meat. As morning transitioned into afternoon, my Congolese colleagues wandered in and out of camp with several interesting frogs. Aristote brought me a brown white-lipped frog with sharp creases on its back. Wandege appeared with an *Amietia* river frog that had an unusual black mask around its snout. As darkness fell, Chifundera directed me to a flooded field at the roadside where *Afrixalus* spiny reed frogs were calling, and I spent a few hours recording the males' love song. Aristote decided to follow some pygmies he had befriended deep into the forest near our camp, and when he returned a few hours later he showed me a container with three *Chiromantis* treefrogs that were lime-green, with skin so bumpy it looked like they had a bad case of chicken pox. The frogs belong to a family (Rhacophoridae) that engage in the amphibian equivalent of an orgy. Several individuals typically mate on a branch of a tree while kicking their legs to form an enormous frothy, foam nest that includes various secretions, sperm, and eggs.[29]

Before retiring for the night, we decided that Ndjuma was yielding a few interesting finds, but the area was too damaged by human activity to find many species truly endemic to the pristine forest. It was time to move on to the Ruwenzori Mountains, just a few hours east of us. I wrapped up my work the next morning as quickly as I could, but it still took us several hours to pack everything into our truck. After saying our goodbyes to the rangers and the women at the campsite, we started our journey through the forest, and I focused on the road to see if I could catch a glimpse of any wildlife. But with the exception of a roadkilled forest cobra — the largest cobra species in Africa (8.9 feet, 2.7 m), and highly aggressive,[30] which I am just as glad not to encounter on its own turf — I saw nothing. The jungle soon gave way to a mixture of forest and savanna, until we left the protection of the park and drove through areas where humans had devastated the natural vegetation.

It was late afternoon when we reached the village of Kamango in a marshy floodplain that occurred in an unprotected donut hole between Virunga's lowland rainforests to the west and its towering Ruwenzori Mountains to the east. Several brick and mud buildings with either corrugated metal or thatched roofs dotted the landscape of marshes, crops, and wandering chickens and goats. Women in colorful kitenge sarongs with babies strapped to their backs and wooden hoes balanced on their shoulders stopped to stare at our truck as we pulled into the center of the village. Someone had spared a tall palm tree in the middle of a field of crops a few feet away, and its leaves were sagging from the weight of dozens of black-and-yellow weaverbirds and their Bocksbeutel-shaped nests. They chirped noisily as they flew back and forth from the tree, undoubtedly collecting food for the growing chicks inside the nests.

Following a pleasant dinner with Kamango's chief, Chifundera wandered off to look for a guide, and I sat down on a log next to Aristote to wait. As dusk arrived and people walked by on their way home from the fields, I noticed a barefoot middle-aged man loitering near us. He seemed to be mumbling to himself, and Aristote chuckled quietly. They exchanged a few words, and as Aristote started laughing harder, the man sat down on the ground next to us and used his finger to scratch into the mud. Wandege joined us, and he giggled slightly as he stood next to me. Aristote said that the man was mad and that he was going on and on about women. When I asked him to clarify, Aristote said the man disliked women because they are "too expensive," apparently because they are always asking for new shoes.

As I contemplated whether it would be interesting to start a conversation about the price of couture shoes in New York City with him, something moved in my peripheral vision. I glanced over, and slithering across the path in front of me was a dark snake about 2 feet (0.6 m) long. "Nyoka!" (Snake!), I yelled. The village idiot shrieked and scurried away rapidly, and before I could get to my feet, Wandege clicked on his headlamp and ran after the serpent. By the time Aristote and I had our own headlamps on and caught up with Wandege, he had the snake in his hands, a sure sign that it was a nonvenomous species. As my light illuminated the animal, I could see from its purplish-black color and the odd, pear-shaped head that it was a *Gonionotophis*, commonly known as a file snake for the triangular cross-sectional shape of the body. These harmless nocturnal snakes are especially common around human habitations near lowland rainforests, and they are almost exclusively predators of other snakes. We spent the rest of the evening collecting an impressive diversity of frogs from a nearby marsh.

When the first rays of sunlight caressed my tent the next morning, I unzipped my flap to see several children already gathered nearby to witness my emergence. We ate some bread and stale cookies with coffee as I told Chifundera where I wanted to explore for the final stage of the expedition. We were just west of the Ruwenzori Mountains on the border between Congo and Uganda, and I wanted to enter the foothills on the western side to look for the long-lost reed frog species *Hyperolius xenorhinus*, which had been described by Laurent from a unique, wide-snouted specimen collected by his colleague de Witte in 1955 at a place called Mount Teye.[31] I took out a map and showed him where I wanted to go, and Chif commented that we would need to buy supplies at a town at the end of the road, where we could look for a guide and porters into the mountains. When we arrived, we were so close to the Ugandan border that many of the locals spoke English, and we had some trouble with our Congolese francs because they only wanted Ugandan shillings.

I waited for Chifundera and Aristote to sort out the logistics issues, and I leaned against the truck and stared at the green foothills of the mountains, which ascended to unseen heights in a thick crown of white clouds. Because the peaks of the mountains are habitually cloaked in a combination of clouds and smoke from burning grass in the surrounding plains, they were the last of Africa's great massifs to be noted by white explorers, and the clouds obscured the true extent of the mountains during some of the first glimpses by outsiders. The Ruwenzoris were rumored to exist as early as 500 BCE, when the Greek poet Aeschylus wrote of Egypt being nurtured by snow.[32] The first putative Western eyewitness account was written in 120 CE by the Syrian geographer Marinus of Tyre, who recounted the travels of a Greek merchant named Diogenes. The merchant claimed to have made an inland journey from East Africa, where he observed two great lakes and a snowy mountain range that he thought were the sources of the Nile. Thirty years later, Claudius Ptolemy used the Diogenes account to make a famous early map of Africa, which showed two great lakes just south of the equator being fed by Lunae Montes, the Mountains of the Moon.[33]

When the first European explorers entered Central Africa seventeen hundred years later, the mysterious legend of the snow-capped mountains persisted. The British explorer Sir Richard Burton referred to them as the Lunatic Mountains because of legends of men going crazy in their search to find the mythical highlands.[34] When Burton's fellow British explorer Speke passed by the Virunga Mountains in 1861, he noticed they were partially covered in clouds and thought he had found the legendary mountains, but he was too far south. The first white man to glimpse the mountains was the legendary explorer Henry Stanley, who described a distant and enormous blue mass in 1876; not realizing its significance, he named the obscure highland Mt. Gordon Bennett after the man who financed his second expedition to Africa. Later that year, the clouds again obscured the view for Italian explorer Romolo Gessi, who described "a strange vision in the sky" during a trip to Lake Albert. Finally, in 1890 Stanley published his book In Darkest Africa, in which he recounted his first clear view of the snow-capped summit of Ruwenzori, which at the time he did not realize was the same Mt. Bennett he had named twelve years previously.[35]

Together with Lake Albert and the Semliki River Valley, the Ruwenzori Mountains are now considered to be a major source of the Nile River. The Ruwenzoris are of nonvolcanic origin and arose from the base of the Albertine Rift about 2–3 million years ago,[36] at least 20 million years later than the rest of the rift's highlands.[37] The youth of the Ruwenzoris helps to explain their great height and steep slopes. Centered on the Congo/Uganda border, the Ruwenzori Massif is approximately 68 miles (110 km) long and 31 miles (50 km) wide, with six major mountains named after famous European explorers (Stanley, Speke, Baker, Emin, Gessi, and Luigi di Savoia) that contain twenty-four peaks exceeding 15,000 feet (4,600 m) in elevation. They are also among the wettest mountains in the world: they are exposed to an exceptional amount of precipitation, exceeding 15 inches (40 cm) in some months. This water is soaked up by a thick sponge-like carpet of colorful mosses that keep the ground moist for a staggering diversity of plants, many of which are unique to Ruwenzori. The saturated moss forms extensive moss/bog zones, which transforms runoff from the massif's glaciers into rivers that are a major component of the source of the Nile.[38] Thanks to global climate change, however, Ruwenzori's glaciers have been melting since the 1950s, and they are projected to be completely gone by Virunga National Park's one-hundred-year anniversary in 2025.[39]

The Banande people have lived on the slopes of the Ruwenzoris for centuries and were rumored to be as wild as the mountains. When the British explorer Wollaston passed this way a century before my visit, he remarked, "The Belgians claim in theory to administer the left bank of the Semliki right up to Ruwenzori; but in practice their control stops with the river, beyond which they never venture, except to travel along the road by which we had come from Lake Albert Edward [now just Lake Edward]. The natives inhabiting the east bank of the river and the west slopes of Ruwenzori are, in the Belgian phrase, révoltés—that is to say, they refuse to recognize the authority of, or to work for, the State."[40] Although a fair number of tourists climbed the western slopes of Ruwenzori in the 1980s and early 1990s during a relatively peaceful period of Mobutu's Zaire, few if any had done it since militia moved in during the war,[41] and in the area I wanted to go to, it was likely that no Westerners had visited for half a century. We had to be very cautious.

Within an hour everyone returned to the truck, and we had the supplies and a local guide ready to lead us into the foothills. He said there was a village called Mbili at the end of an old road to the east where we could hire porters. We had barely crossed the eastern edge of the village when we encountered a small group of women and children descending a small footpath from the mountains. One of the teenage girls looked wide-eyed at me, then said something in Swahili that included the ever-present word *muzungu*. Aristote must have thought she was cute, because he stopped in front of her, gently wrapped his fingers around her chin, and lifted her face so he could get a better look at her. Following a stern comment from Aristote, she swatted his hand away and looked extremely perturbed as she slowly walked away, pausing every few steps to look back at him with an angry stare. I told Aristote that he should not be so rude.

"Noooo," he said with his typical drawn-out accentuation of the word when he felt very strongly about something. "She said something bad, so I had to correct her."

I recalled that she must have said something about me and asked him what it was.

"She said, 'Look, there is a muzungu! He must have come to drink our blood!'"

"WHAT?!" I was not expecting that at all.

"Yes!" Aristote continued. "She thinks you have come to kill the black man and drink his blood so that you can be strong."

"Why in the world would she possibly think that?" I asked in shock.

"This is what they are taught in the schools—*everybody* knows that."

"Are you kidding me, Aristote? That is completely crazy!" Dumbfounded and unsettled, I asked him if we should rethink going into the mountains. I stopped walking to wait for his answer. But without stopping, he simply made a dismissive gesture and said that I should not worry about it. For a few moments I was paralyzed with fear and hesitation, and I could not bring myself to continue climbing up the side of the mountain. But as I watched everyone disappearing into the distance above me, I decided to have faith in Aristote and started walking again. My trepidation caused a surge of adrenaline, and I gasped for air as the combination of nervous energy and uphill climbing taxed my weary body.

What I did not know at the time was that there is a long history of Africans believing that white men, particularly colonizers, had come to drink the blood of Africans. Suspicious of white workers in the medical field, some African rumors suggested the colonizers were using the blood of slain African patients to treat Europeans with anemic diseases. In other cases, colonial white firefighters wore black overalls and were rumored to drink the blood of Africans because of a similarity in clothing to blood-sucking "Mumiani men," who were akin to vampires and supposedly gained strength by drinking human blood. The origins of these rumors are not entirely clear, but they seem to have started in the late nineteenth or early twentieth century and might be associated with colonizers' technologies that Africans did not understand. One of these disturbing technologies was associated with medicine: some Africans were astonished by the use of chloroform for operations, because the chemical seemed to mysteriously paralyze black patients.[42] Given the innumerable injustices perpetrated by European colonizers against Africans, it should not be surprising that unexplained phenomena of the former gave rise to negative stories by the latter. But the astonishing thing to me was that these twentieth-century rumors persisted and were apparently perpetuated in Congolese schools!

Not wanting to fall behind my companions, I quickened my pace and caught up to Aristote, who had faithfully paused on the trail when he realized I had fallen behind. We climbed along a narrow and rocky footpath that passed through a mosaic of grassy fields, thatched-roof huts, and small agricultural plots. After half an hour of walking, the trail became more challenging, and the hot afternoon sun peeked out from the rainclouds. I sucked down copious amounts of water as we climbed a nearly vertical path that zigzagged upward through large boulders.

When I reached a hill at the top, I found Chifundera and all the porters breathless and taking a rest as they enjoyed the panoramic view of the village and foothills beneath us. In the distance ahead I could see the verdant mountains towering above us.

Slowly we plodded on, sometimes climbing very steep paths, other times merely walking along curvy trails that slowly and steadily rose ever higher. As the late afternoon approached, our caravan reached a grassy hill where about thirty people, mostly women and children, had gathered for a makeshift market. Under the shade of a few trees that were remnants of the rainforest that probably stood there years ago, they sold dried fish, fruit, various other foods, and cheap plastic goods imported from India. Everyone stopped what they were doing to stare at me, and even the porters who had been with me for most of the day regarded me with cold and suspicious stares. I greeted some of the children in Swahili and waved, but none of them were brave enough to approach me. Aristote started talking to some of them, and after a few minutes he told me they had never seen a white man before. With the white vampire rumors so extensive, I could not blame the kids for their caution. But when they learned that I was looking for frogs, chameleons, and snakes, they grew very excited and seemed ready to help. After purchasing some fresh fruit from the women, we continued on our way, and the children danced and ran circles around me as they pointed to a village that I could see at the edge of pristine forest a few miles away. After walking for another hour and descending into a small valley with a stream that looked promising for frogs, we climbed one last steep hill to reach the remote village of Kisanzi, sitting at about 4,900 feet (1,500 m) elevation, near Mount Teye.

We were greeted with shocked looks from the people, and some of the younger children started crying when they saw me. Someone brought me and Chifundera traditional, wooden chairs that had long sloped backs; a configuration of branches at the small base of each chair was almost a tripod. When we settled into the chairs, I found them comfortable, but I was supported only a few inches above the ground, and my knees were almost at eye level. Aristote, Wandege, and Marcel cautiously sat on the ground near us as everyone in Kisanzi, and several people who had followed us from the market, stared at us with wonder and chattered away

Local people at a market stop to stare at the author as he takes this photograph in the foothills of the western Ruwenzori Mountains, which are visible in the right background. Most of the children had never seen a white man before, and they were terrified by tall tales of whites who drank the blood of black men. Marcel is visible seated in the grass with a cap and black suit jacket, Aristote is standing just behind him, and Wandege is standing on the trail in the right background with a flannel shirt and black cap. Just visible behind Aristote is Chifundera, who is wearing a white cap and bartering for food.

in a language that was obviously very different from Swahili. Chifundera started speaking in a slow but relatively loud voice so that everyone could hear. A hush came over the crowd as he carefully explained who we were and why we had come. I could hear some of the people hem and haw skeptically as the conversation continued. The tension was tangible.

Through Chif's translations, I learned that the chief of the village welcomed us to Kisanzi. He went on to say generally polite things about our mission. And then he cut to the chase: he and several other residents of Kisanzi were wondering if I could buy them a bottle of pombe. When I asked Chif if they had some beer, he clarified that someone in the next village made a special kind of moonshine that was supposed to be of excellent quality but was relatively expensive. Because I wanted to make a good impression and we were approaching the end of the expedition anyway, I handed over enough money to buy several bottles. Everyone smiled at me and gave the thumbs-up sign, and I told them, "Haraka, ne na kiu!" (Hurry, I am thirsty!). Everyone erupted into laughter, and Aristote said that I had done a very good thing because he had heard some of the villagers wonder out loud whether I was a good muzungu or not. Apparently I had assuaged their fears to such an extent that I was now being heralded as a hero. Offers of food and good places to set up our tents soon followed, I caught some of the women batting their eyelashes at me, and several children became brave enough to approach me and shake my hand.

Over the next couple of days, the people of Kisanzi helped us find many interesting animals. The most spectacular find was a colorful and heavily casqued Carpenter's Chameleon (*Kinyongia carpenteri*) that had not been recorded at such a low elevation before. I also found more *Leptopelis* treefrogs, tree lizards, and a rocket frog. Unfortunately, the black snake named for Leopold and *Hyperolius xenorhinus* never turned up, probably because we were near the edge of the park, and the forest had been heavily disturbed by humans and domestic animals. When we left Kisanzi on July 15, I presented a large package of vanilla wafer cookies to the women of the village who had helped us the most by providing food and water. They screamed with delight and, with tears in their eyes, told us that we must return to their village soon. Our successful expedition had come to an end, and when I checked my email before boarding the flight back to Europe, I learned that I had received funding from the National Geographic Society and would be returning to Congo the following spring.

6

As a newly hired evolutionary geneticist, herpetologist, and taxonomist in May 2009, I planned an especially ambitious expedition for that summer so that I could sample multiple field sites in the highest elevations of the Albertine Rift, which would demand a healthy constitution and a fit body. However, the stress of my first year as an assistant professor had not bestowed me with either requirement, and as a result I would experience many hardships. A year of laboratory work on the previous year's specimens suggested many new species had been discovered, but in many cases my sample sizes were too small for publication, and I needed to find more to bring them to the attention of the world. I also wanted to visit sites that had been explored by Belgian herpetologist Raymond Laurent in the early 1950s. Many of the species he discovered were never seen again and, in many cases, had never been photographed. Once again, I would need to sample as many sites and habitats as possible to get a better picture of the amphibian and reptile species that occur in the poorly known region of eastern Congo.

My journey to Africa in May 2009 was a bit more eventful than the previous year. After an eleven-hour flight from Atlanta, Georgia, to Lagos, Nigeria, the customs official did not understand I was in transit and took me to the airport police, because I did not have a visa to enter the country. There I sat for several miserable hours until someone took pity on me and let me escape to my gate for my next flight to Nairobi, Kenya. Two days later after additional headaches, I had a beautiful view of Lake Kivu as I descended from the clouds over western Rwanda and came to the end of my air journey at Kamembe airport near Cyangugu. Thirty minutes later Chifundera and Aristote showed up on motorcycles and smiled widely as they saw me. I greeted them in the traditional way by touching my head to theirs, first on the left, then on the right, and then in the center.

I told Aristote in his native Kabembe, "Oolay esambo yanaay" (You are my best friend). Very pleased, he hugged me and repeatedly told me, "Welcome!" And then after studying me carefully, he added that I had become pudgy again. Several stressful months of adapting to my new job as an assistant professor had taken their toll on my waistline, but I just laughed because I knew I would soon shed those pounds.

Both of my friends and colleagues were very pleased to see me, and during the short cab ride to the border, I excitedly told them about some of the interesting discoveries my students and I had made during our work with the samples we had collected the previous year, including the new species. When we reached the border, a dour Rwandese man stamped my passport, and several teenage boys jockeyed with Chifundera to get the job carrying my baggage across the rickety bridge over the Ruzizi River into Congo. My passport was soon stamped on the Congolese side, and following a twenty-minute ride through the center of Bukavu, we reached Chif's house, where his five smiling children greeted me in turn. They could barely contain their excitement as I requested a large bowl and poured in more than half of a large bag of chocolate-covered peanuts, which they devoured in seconds. To Chif I presented a new GPS unit for the expedition, and a gift of a new DVD player, with several movies that I had obtained from the French Amazon store so that he could watch them with his children in French. I bestowed a point-and-shoot camera on Aristote and told him that he was in charge of documenting the expedition, and he was absolutely thrilled with his new profession.

The vehicle we had used the year before broke down on the last day of fieldwork in 2008, and weeks before my arrival in May 2009, I had wired Chifundera a significant chunk of my grant money to buy a new engine and make other badly needed repairs. I was annoyed to learn that the engine had only just arrived and was still being installed in the truck, a similar repeat of the frustrating situation from the previous year, but there was nothing to do but hang out for two days and watch some of the movies while I waited for the repairs. One by one, other members of the new expedition arrived from Lwiro to greet me and prepare for the ambitious journey ahead of us. Our cook Marcel arrived first so that he could be at hand to prepare our food. He still had the red baseball cap I had given to him the previous year, although it was now a bit worse for wear. Even though his attention was focused on getting the truck repaired, Mululema popped in and out during the day to say hello, give us progress reports about the mechanic's work, and ask for advances on his salary for beer money.

Next to arrive was Wandege, who impressed me with his warm smile and a little English—the previous year he could not speak a word, but I had left him my English/Swahili dictionary, which he had obviously put to good use. He was accompanied by Maurice, who I was not expecting. Although he looked to be in his late fifties, Maurice was really in his late seventies, and he had struggled to keep up with the group during our difficult journey through Itombwe the previous year. Chifundera and I had decided via email that it would be best if Maurice did not rejoin us this year, but here he was, fully expecting a pay raise from last year, as did the other veteran members of the expedition. I did not have the heart to send him back to Lwiro after he had obviously come with the promise of a job, and Chif told me later that Maurice had expended his political capital as a tribal chief to get Chif to promise him a job this year. However, we would only use his services for a few weeks before going to Itombwe, where it was obvious that Maurice could no longer work. John and Felix Akuku also showed up from Uvira, along with the pensive and intelligent Asukulu, who looked the same except for a goatee, which made him seem a little older and wiser. He greeted me seriously, then introduced me to the only new member of the team, a shy and stocky young man named Mkengywa, who was also from Itombwe.

After three days of resting and adjusting to my new time zone, I was beginning to grow impatient that our field vehicle was not yet ready. It was also costing me money to feed everyone, and they too were disappointed that they were not yet earning money for the promised work. That night as I voiced my displeasure about this to Chif, he assured me that the vehicle would be ready the next day and that we could leave for the field right away. Satisfied, I finished my dinner of cassava and goat meat and retired under the mosquito net suspended over my bed to rest. Unfortunately, Chif's last-minute mechanical logistics would delay us much longer.

Five frustratingly long days after my arrival in Congo, we finally left Bukavu. We followed the steep mountain pass parallel to the Ruzizi River, and as we continued south, the rough road ended at a village called Kamanyola. We had returned to the blazing hot valley between Lakes Kivu and Tanganyika, and we stopped to pick up some soft drinks. Some of the local boys got curious and started talking to us, and we explained that we were looking for reptiles and amphibians and planned to stay in Luvungi that night. Sensing an opportunity, one of the boys took Aristote to a small abandoned building, and he returned with a house gecko. I bought the boy a soda in thanks and we continued south, stopping briefly near a bridge over the Kamanyola River so that I could photograph a monument to Congolese soldiers. Kamanyola had its own monument because it was one of the few victories attributable to Mobutu's corrupt and undisciplined Forces Armées Zairoises (FAZ). In 1964, Mobutu and the FAZ captured the Kamanyola Bridge, which had been under the control of Congolese rebels.[1] In addition to the monument, Mobutu had memorialized the victory by naming his luxury yacht, an army division, and Kinshasa's sports stadium Kamanyola.[2] Bullet holes pockmarked the wall of the monument, and I could see that a statue in the center was missing. Aristote told me that Rwandese soldiers had shot up the monument and torn down a statue of Mobutu when they entered Congo during the war.

We continued south for an hour or so and reached the town of Luvungi, which was little more than a small collection of huts and simple brick buildings with chickens, goats, and children running around everywhere, including the busy road that bisected the town. We stopped at the house of a kind doctor in his midtwenties, a friend of Chifundera's son, who was also a doctor. He had erected a half-circle of vegetation around the front of his simple house to form a fence, which offered a limited amount of shade from the blazing sun. After brief introductions, we all walked down the road about a mile to conduct a courtesy call with the local police and military commanders. We approached a group of soldiers sitting in plastic chairs under the shade of a tree. Their commander wore shiny mirrored sunglasses, and he smiled at me as I approached and accepted their offer of a seat. He was an enormous man in an impeccable green military uniform with shiny black shoes. A red sash over his shoulder clearly distinguished him as the guy in charge.

With a subtle gesture from the commander, some of the men deferentially abandoned their chairs and offered them to Chifundera and the doctor and to the chief of police, who suddenly materialized from the opposite side of the road. The skinny soldiers slung weathered AK-47s over their shoulders and eyed us suspiciously as Chifundera cleared his throat and introduced us to the commander. He shook our hands with a smile, and when he said "Bonjour," his voice seemed to be deeper than Barry White's. Chifundera started to produce a collection of paperwork from the government and CRSN with all our necessary authorization to conduct research in Itombwe, and everyone began to scrutinize the collection of signatures and stamps as they passed it around. Everything was going well, but then the commander's cell phone rang.

"Oui!" (Yes!), he said in his baritone voice. The conversation started mildly, but quickly deteriorated. As he listened to the man on the phone, the commander's face transitioned from jovial to serious to a pained scowl in seconds. Cutting the man on the phone off, the commander burst forth with a bombastic tirade in Swahili that put everyone on edge. As the conversation continued, he grew louder and angrier, pointing his finger and gesticulating at an imaginary enemy in front of his body. I felt my body tense up in fear as I witnessed the powerful wrath of the infuriated man, and I was glad I was not one of his soldiers. When he turned his head to call to one of his underlings, I noticed a hideous gash of a scar on the back of his neck. Someone had obviously attacked him with a machete and carved out a large swath of flesh and, judging by the wound's depth, some bits of vertebrae. This guy had certainly proven himself in battle to attain his current position of authority.

After about five minutes of yelling, the conversation finally ended, and everyone was silent as he continued to scowl at the phone for a few moments. He seemed to curse, and then angrily said, "Militia." He shook his head and explained to us in French that the rebels in the area were creating a lot of problems. He slowly eased back into his chair, relaxed a little, and returned his mirrored gaze to me. Chifundera grew brave enough to return to our original conversation, and the commander looked resigned as he listened to our ambition to do some work around Luvungi and then return to the Itombwe Plateau, which was visible as green mountains shimmering above the sunbaked yellowish savannas on the western horizon. Chif quickly finished explaining our mission, and an animated conversation ensued between him, the commander, and the chief of police. The end result was that we would have an armed escort to look for frogs at night around Luvungi, but when it came to Itombwe, we would be on our own. The important people added their signatures to the paperwork, and we all shook hands again. When we parted, the commander told me "Good luck" in English, and he smiled widely as if the angry conversation just minutes before had never happened.

When we returned to the doctor's house, Aristote told me that the boys from Kamanyola had phoned him to say that they had caught some lizards and were en route via bicycle, apparently egged on by the gift of my soda. Two hours later they arrived with several geckos, skinks, chameleons, and toads, some of which I had never seen before. I rewarded them for their trouble, and Aristote and I got to work right away with photographing. As dusk fell, I doused myself with mosquito spray, but my Congolese colleagues had learned long ago to detest the smell of it, and everyone refused when I offered them some protection from the hordes of insects we would surely face in the swamp that evening.

With the arrival of a few policemen and their chief, we walked a short distance in the darkness to the Luvubu River (transliterated from the local Kifuliru language)[3] at the edge of town. A small crowd of boys were too curious to resist following us, and they watched with shrieks of laughter as we descended from a bridge over the road into the muddy swamp adjacent to the river. Our legs sank into the mud to our calves, making walking awkward and difficult. Even with plenty of mosquito spray, scores of insects flew into my eyes, ears, nose, and mouth and tickled every place in between. My colleagues cursed and swatted at the bugs, but after a few minutes, we resigned ourselves to their annoying touches, and our eyes started picking out a great diversity of frogs on the reeds at the edge of the river. Many of the males were calling, and I made several excellent recordings of tiny *Afrixalus* spiny reed frogs with cream and brown stripes, and several *Hyperolius* reed frogs with a dazzling variety of brown, black, yellow, and red colors. Aristote managed to catch some *Ptychadena* rocket frogs, and even Maurice managed to snag some toads hopping along at the water's edge. Satisfied that I would have a full day of work to photograph things the next day, we called it a night after a couple of hours.

In the morning I was making great headway with the specimens when three men suddenly showed up from Kamanyola on bicycles. Apparently the boys in Kamanyola had told everyone about the crazy white man in Luvungi. Chifundera talked to them, and I learned that they had captured three snakes alive. I was surprised to hear this, because usually when someone brought us a snake, they had killed it as a potential threat around their house and then decided to bring it to us in case we wanted it. I did not like the idea of nonprofessionals catching snakes, especially since the average person (in Africa or elsewhere) cannot tell the difference between a species that is harmless and one that is deadly. But now that they had gone through all the trouble and biked two hours to get to Luvungi, we would certainly have a bigger problem if we sent them back empty-handed. I insisted that Chif tell them not to catch any more snakes, but we would accept the ones they brought to us.

As the senior snake handler, Maurice confidently opened a sealed pot that had two harmless house snakes. But then I looked over and saw a large woven basket carefully lashed to the back of someone's bicycle. I felt a jolt of adrenaline surge through my body as I heard Maurice say the word "cobra" with a tone of disbelief. How could these men have captured a cobra alive? Up until that point, the only cobra I had seen in Congo was the large, black forest cobra, a species that I had collected twice before from carcasses in or near forests. But since we were now in the middle of a dry valley, the captive serpent had to be something else. I ordered every experienced man to grab a pair of snake tongs to handle the snake safely if it turned out to be deadly.

Everyone's eyes were fixated on the basket as the man carefully placed it in the middle of the courtyard. With one rapid movement, he lifted the lid off the basket and scurried back several steps. When nothing emerged from the opening, Chifundera inched up to it, peered over the top, and said, "Oh, it's a *Psammophis*." I was immediately relieved and excited. Commonly known as sand snakes, *Psammophis* are common in the nonforested habitats of Africa and even range into Asia via the Arabian Peninsula. Although technically they have fangs in the rear of their mouth for subduing prey, the venom is weak and they are not dangerous to humans. We had seen a few of the snakes crossing the roads now and then, but they are as fast as lightning, and one has zero chance of chasing them down unless they are cornered. Perhaps the men from Kamanyola had managed to work in a team to do just that.

Curious to see what species it might be, I confidently walked up to the basket and looked inside. My heart skipped a beat as I saw that Chifundera's preliminary impression was horribly wrong. Instead of seeing a striped snake with a pointy snout as I expected—in other words, a *Psammophis*—I saw a dull brown snake with a distinct round head raised a few inches off the ground. The men from Kamanyola knew what they had captured.

"It's a cobra, watch out!" I yelled. In French I told them to be careful and mimicked the motion of spitting, because I feared this could be a black-necked spitting cobra, which has the ability to spray venom into the eyes of its enemies, blinding them. Wandege looked at me and said, "Ndiyo!" (Yes!), because he and Maurice had surely encountered this species before.

The serpent in front of us belonged to an ancient lineage of highly venomous snakes called elapids, which include the New World coral snakes, African mambas, African and Asian cobras, Asian kraits, tropical ocean sea snakes, and the highly venomous snakes that occur in Australia. Ranging in size from about 2 feet (60 cm) to the 19-foot-long (5.8 m) king cobra of Asia, these snakes differ from the vipers by having a nonmovable, erect fang on the front of the maxilla bone (i.e., the upper jaw in both snakes and humans) and by their elongate, muscular bodies, which allow them to actively hunt prey. The cobras have prominent eyes

The Black-necked Spitting Cobra (*Naja nigricollis*) that emerged
from the basket at Luvungi.

that easily detect movement, and elongated ribs at the front of their body,
which are extended to stretch the skin of their necks forward and to the
side to display the warning "hood" to would-be predators. Zookeepers
who have worked with cobras describe them as belligerent, nervous, and
intelligent, a nasty and dangerous combination for a large venomous
snake that can move rapidly.[4] Some of the African and Asian cobra species have the ability to "spit" their painful and potentially blinding venom
into the eyes of predators who do not take the hint from the hood warning. These spitting species are more likely to stand their ground against
an opponent, and the fangs have spiral grooves inside them that act like
riflings in a gun barrel to force a spin on ejected venom. The opening
of the fang is modified into a smaller, circular, and beveled aperture for
more accuracy as muscles squeeze the venom gland and eject venom toward the threat. In Africa, the evolution of spitting seems to coincide
with cooler climatic shifts in the Miocene (starting about 15 million years
ago) that created more "open" habitats of grasslands, and a few million
years later, even drier habitats with less vegetation. Because the snakes

A dazed Pygmy Kingfisher (*Ispidina picta*) regains its composure while perched on the author's finger.

A drowsy and grumpy Chimanuka, the enormous silverback leader of a gorilla group near Tshivanga, blinks in the morning light after emerging from his nighttime nest.

Extensive color-pattern variation in the Montane Reed Frog. (a) *Hyperolius castaneus* adult male; (b) *H. castaneus* adult female; (c) *H. castaneus* subadult; (d) *Hyperolius constellatus* adult male; (e) *H. constellatus* adult female; (f) *H. constellatus* adult female.

An adult male *Leptopelis karissimbensis* treefrog feigns death near Mugaba. The bluish color on the bottom of the feet and the inside of the mouth might help the animal appear to be dead and rotten to would-be predators.

A view of the shimmering foothills of the Itombwe Plateau as the expedition's vehicle approached Mwenga from the east.

A Great Lakes
Bush Viper
(*Atheris
nitschei*).

A glimpse of the village of Bichaka, where the team was provided with food
and shelter on a stormy night. The kind village chief is in the white shirt in the
right background. The boy in the foreground has bald patches on his scalp,
which is caused by a common skin disease in Congolese children.

A *Leptosiaphos* skink from Bichaka.

The bright colors of this *Phlyctimantis* "Wot-wot" treefrog are likely a warning to predators that the frog is poisonous.

A stunning view of the montane forest from the front of the dilapidated Belgian house at Miki. The rolling hills of pristine forest continue for tens of miles into the background.

A skittish herd of Uganda Kob (*Kobus kob*) stares at the author in the southern grasslands of Virunga National Park.

A captive okapi (*Okapia johnstoni*) at Epulu. This animal, twelve other okapi, and six people were killed during a raid by Simba/Mai-Mai militia in January 2012. The actions seem to have been revenge for a crackdown on elephant poaching and gold mining by ICCN rangers who were trying to protect the integrity of the Okapi Wildlife Reserve near Epulu.

The deadly but beautiful Rhinoceros Viper (*Bitis nasicornis*). The geometric patterns on the back help the snake camouflage itself in the leaf litter of the forest floor, where it ambushes its prey.

Wandege shortly after a Black-necked Spitting Cobra (*Naja nigricollis*) nailed him in the right eye with a "spit" of venom. He recovered with no permanent loss of vision a few days later.

Asukulu at Lake Lungwe, as seen from the surrounding hills in the Itombwe Plateau at about 9,500 feet (2,900 m) elevation. Photo by Mwenebatu M. Aristote.

The beautiful and mysterious frog found by Aristote at Lake Lungwe. Years later it was identified as *Chrysobatrachus cupreonitens*, a unique species that is endemic to Itombwe.

The team poses for a photo on the Kabobo Plateau. Kneeling in first row from left to right: Marcel, Aristote, and Chifundera. Mululema is on the left in the back row with a tan cap, along with the author and five teenage porters/guides. Photo by Wandege M. Muninga.

A horned chameleon (*Trioceros johnstoni*) hisses at the author as he takes its photo near the village of Kilwemapante on the Kabobo Plateau.

An unknown species of *Kinyongia* chameleon from the Lendu Plateau hisses at the author. In 2012 it was described as a new species, *Kinyongia gyrolepis*.

Road between Epulu and Beni, North Kivu Province, Congo.

The expedition truck is ferried across the muddy waters of the Ituri River on a rickety wooden barge. The rainforest is visible in the background, along with the red bus that honked at the author. Wandege is wearing a colorful shirt and a yellow cap near the right side of the truck, and Mululema can be seen grasping the front of the truck with a brown shirt on the left. Photo by Mwenebatu M. Aristote.

The Green Bush Viper (*Atheris squamigera*) captured by the author flicks its tongue at Epulu.

The teenage savanna elephant (*Loxodonta africana*) at Virunga National Park.

The living holotype of Asukulu's Grass Lizard (*Congolacerta asukului*).

could not hide or escape from predators as easily in these habitats, spitting likely evolved as a much-needed defense. Eminent herpetologist Harry Greene suggested spitting cobras first evolved in Asia, possibly as a defense against anthropoids (monkeys, apes, and human ancestors).[5]

Fearless, Maurice confronted the basket, and everyone gasped as he dumped the animal onto the ground. The doctor backed into the open doorway of his house, and everyone else froze as the experienced snake-man used his favorite stick to pin the cobra to the ground behind the head. It wiggled its body as it tried to pull away, but Maurice knew from decades of experience just the right amount of pressure to apply to keep it where he wanted it without injuring it. With his free hand, he slowly wrapped his fingers around the base of the cobra's head, and releasing his stick, picked up the snake with his hands. Wandege rushed to his mentor to help him stabilize the snake's body as it thrashed around in protest of its capture. Thinking Maurice had firm control of the animal, we all breathed a sigh of relief and started to relax.

And then it happened. As Wandege was holding the tail of the serpent, it must have realized that its snout was facing him, because it opened its mouth and squeezed a jet of venom directly into his eye. He immediately dropped the snake's tail and wheeled around toward me. He didn't say a word, but I knew what had happened from the look of horror in his eye. I quickly grabbed a squeeze bottle I used for cleaning my tools for DNA samples and squirted a steady jet of water into his eye. I told him to move the eye around as much as he could as I worked the water onto as much of his eyeball as possible. I did not even look to see what was happening with the cobra and Maurice, but luckily he managed to get the snake safely into a cloth bag.

Wandege never whimpered, but it was obvious to everyone that he was in a great deal of pain. The venom of spitting cobras is designed to be painful so that would-be predators cannot continue an attack. I ran into my room to look for painkillers and ibuprofen, but when I emerged two minutes later, Wandege, Chif, and Aristote were gone. I later learned that Chifundera had grabbed Wandege and found the nearest woman with a young child. The cobra's venom can be neutralized with milk, and thanks to the quick actions of a young mother who was breastfeeding, Wandege averted a potentially serious medical disaster. The woman allowed him to rest his head on her lap and, putting her modesty aside, she positioned her nipple over his head and squeezed until the precious antidote filled his excruciating eye.[6]

When he returned to the house, Maurice whipped up a potion made from a special plant[7] that is supposed to neutralize the effects of snake poisoning, and Wandege drank it immediately. Feeling terribly guilty about what had happened to my employee, I checked in on him every fifteen minutes for the rest of the day to see how he was doing. Even after the milk and potion had been allowed to take effect for an hour, he kept saying no every time I asked him if he was okay. We were too far away from a competent hospital to do anything more for him that night, but he accepted my offer of painkillers and ibuprofen, which seemed to ease his agony.

Late that evening after finishing up all work on the bounty of material we had received that day, I contemplated the team's next move. If Wandege's condition did not improve by morning, we would divert precious money, time, and manpower to get him to a competent hospital, probably in neighboring Burundi, for proper treatment. As I drifted off to sleep under the buzzing of several hovering mosquitoes, the expedition hung in the balance.

THE MURDERER OF MUGEGEMA

7

The horrible conflict that consumed Congo at the close of the twentieth century was incredibly complex, involving multiple foreign actors and shifting allegiances, but the origins of the war can be traced back to Congo's tiny neighbor and the Hutu-Tutsi conflict that had been simmering there since the end of Belgian colonial rule in the 1960s. After months of genocidal killing in Rwanda in April 1994, the tide began to turn against the Interahamwe and other Hutu conspirators who had engineered the slaughter. The exiled men of the Rwandan Patriotic Front (RPF) fought their way into eastern Rwanda from Uganda, hastening the retreat of thousands of Hutus, including *génocidaires*, the worst of the killers (mainly Forces Armées Rwandaises [FAR] and Interahamwe) and their leaders. About 1 million Hutu fled into Zaire by the end of July, and then cholera hit—tens of thousands died in the outbreak. Television coverage of the misery prompted the international community to spend unprecedented sums of money to set up enormous refugee camps, and because it would be difficult to weed out the bad guys, everyone was welcome. In fact, innocent Hutus who wanted to return to Rwanda were prevented from doing so by the militias, because the refugee camps perpetuated the safe haven they were enjoying.[1]

Playing the victim brilliantly, the Hutu militia used the camps to regroup, and within weeks, they had reestablished the same political and social structure in Zaire that had fueled the genocide in Rwanda. Because the camps were so close to the border, some of the militia were even able to conduct murderous raids into Rwanda.

As the months passed, the militias spread out of Goma into other areas of North Kivu Province in Zaire, where they recruited Zairean Hutus and convinced them to attack Zairean Tutsi cattle farmers. In response, Zairean tribal militias were formed and fought back, and the region soon descended into a war zone. Stolen cattle and food aid from the camps was sold on the black market to buy weapons and ammunition.[2]

As Mobutu's Zaire became increasingly unstable in October 1996, Paul Kagame (RPF leader and the current president of Rwanda) and other Tutsi Rwandans urged Laurent Kabila (who was from the unrelated Luba tribe in Katanga, Congo) and other Congolese rebel leaders to meet in Kigali, and the Alliance of Democratic Forces for the Liberation of Congo (AFDL) was formed. In less than a month, the Rwandan-backed AFDL forces ejected the Interahamwe and other extremist Hutus from the refugee camps on Congo's border, massacres ensued, and hundreds of thousands of Hutu refugees either scattered deeper into Congo or returned to Rwanda.[3] With additional support from Angolan and Ugandan troops, and logistics and supplies from the USA, the AFDL (including child soldiers called *kadogo*) would take several major cities, march all the way to Kinshasa (the capital of Congo), and install Kabila as the replacement for Mobutu within seven months.[4] Meanwhile, Rwandan troops and their AFDL collaborators had repeated the genocide on Congolese soil by massacring thousands of innocent Hutu refugees during their advance;[5] the national coffers evaporated, and Rwandans took over all of Kabila's security forces. Kabila alienated many friends and allies as he consolidated his power, but as his authority was recognized across the world, American mining and banking representatives, including people from Goldman Sachs, rushed in with executive jets to negotiate lucrative mining deals. In Kinshasa, the Rwandans were obsessed with political control and resented the liberal cultural differences of the city's people, who were humiliated and whipped by the Rwandans with the colonial throwback chicotte. Increasingly paranoid from assassination rumors and reacting to growing xenophobic sentiment, Kabila's loyalties started to shift and he fired loyal officials because they were Tutsi, stoking rebellious resentment from them in the process. As the First Congo War came to an end in May 1997, a tense peace ensued, but it would be shattered only fifteen months later when Kabila turned against his benefactors in Rwanda and Uganda.[6]

In the summer of 1998, Kabila made his move to create his own army. He started freeing ex-FAR soldiers and Interahamwe so that they could be trained and included in the ragtag Congolese army, fired a Tutsi Rwandan officer named James Kabarebe who had been commanding it, and asked all other Rwandan soldiers to leave Congo. But Kabarebe must have suspected that this was coming, because he had prepositioned units loyal to him with plenty of supplies and ammunition in eastern Congo. Kabila's allies stoked anti-Tutsi sentiment in the capital; this prompted a rebellion by Congolese Tutsi soldiers in Kinshasa; the units in eastern Congo soon followed—and the Second Congo War was under way. During the attack, Kabila declared, "I will not let our great country be dominated by its tiny neighbor. Can a toad swallow an elephant? No!"[7] The Rwandans, backed by Uganda, Burundi, and Congolese enemies of Kabila, formed a new group called the Rassemblement Congolais pour la Démocratie (RCD) in Kigali. They quickly took over strategic cities in eastern Congo, but with backing from Angola and Zimbabwe, Kabila stalled their advance west. In time, allegiances shifted, the Ugandans and Rwandans split into their own RCD factions and started fighting each other in Kisangani, and thousands of Congolese civilians died in the internecine conflict.[8]

As the region descended into chaos, Kabila sent arms and funds to the Mai-Mai militia in eastern Congo, including Aristote's men, so that they could fight Rwandan soldiers. Nine neighboring African nations eventually invaded or meddled in Congo to advance their own motives. As the war dragged on, many of these motivations shifted from politics to plunder. Because the war was incredibly complicated and there were no clear "good guys vs. bad guys," the Western media largely ignored it.[9] Millions would be drawn into the conflict, which became known as Africa's World War, including thirty local militias. At the end of the official fighting in 2003, when all the foreign armies had retreated, the Mai-Mai and other armed militias started fighting with each other to control the lucrative resources that were now ripe for the picking, and some have argued that despite the large UN presence, the war continues in eastern Congo.[10] The Interahamwe also remained entrenched in the remote forests bordering eastern Congo. They have been wreaking havoc there ever since.

Shortly after dawn on May 22, 2009, I checked on Wandege and was relieved to find that the pain from the cobra venom had started to subside, and the doctor confirmed that he would recover without further treatment in a few days. Wandege insisted he could work, and after he confirmed several times that he wanted to stay with the team, our equipment was loaded onto the roof of our battered truck. I took a photo of the team, who looked dour and stoic in the grayish pall of the morning light. Aristote had bags under his eyes and frowned. The Akuku brothers looked dazed, Mululema, Mkengywa, and Chifundera looked depressed, and Asukulu regarded me with his characteristic cold stare. Poor Wandege was pouting, and his eye was now so swollen from the aftereffects of the cobra venom that it looked like he had been in a fistfight, but he was on his feet and ready for the next leg of our journey. Amazingly, the elderly Maurice was on the roof of the truck tying down the last of our gear, seemingly more energetic than the rest of us combined.

Somehow we all crammed into the truck, and Asukulu spoke to Mululema in a whisper as he guided us to a barely visible track in the grass toward the end of town. It was an old road, and the truck listed violently as we hit countless rocks and potholes hidden in the grass. As we headed west, the morning light struggled to penetrate the thick clouds, but I could see a fine gray mist rolling over the olive-green foothills of Itombwe in the distance. Gradually, the waist-high grass of the savanna transitioned to patches of secondary forest as the truck struggled up a muddy and rocky road that became increasingly steep. An hour later as we passed through one particularly thick patch of forest, I saw an enormous tree that had fallen directly into our path, and Mululema eased our truck to a stop. I stretched my legs a little as everyone else tested the weight of the tree and discussed in Swahili the best way to remove the roadblock. A man with an obvious sense of humor approached us as he donned a baseball hat with an artificially enhanced brim at least 3 feet (1 m) long. Chif laughed a little and pointed at his hat as they shook hands and started a conversation. Two women with colorful dresses and heavy loads of vegetables balanced on their heads stopped to watch and throw in their two cents as the conversation became increasingly animated.

I think it was precisely at that moment that I figured out "arguing" is the Congolese national pastime. The more heated the exchange, the more entertaining. For the Congolese, I realized animated arguments with a few witty jokes thrown in were a way of bonding with each other in a teasing way. When the tree was finally removed from our path and everyone returned to the truck, Chif shared the good news that the road to Lemera was good and that there had not been any problems with militia for quite some time.

Lemera was a small town in the foothills of eastern Itombwe that had once been a Swedish Protestant mission in the colonial era. During the Second Congo War, the town changed hands from Mai-Mai militia to other combatants several times, resulting in numerous executions on both sides each time.[11] Chif said there was still a European doctor working there, and I thought to myself that it might be a good place to return to if I got sick in the mountains. As we passed through the town on its only road, I noticed a few old colonial-era storefronts and houses, and some enormous, strategically placed trees that complemented the thoroughfare nicely. We followed the road to the edge of the town until we could not continue any farther, and then Chif said we needed to find a certain pastor to watch over the truck. Confused, I asked why Mululema was not driving it back to Lwiro to wait for us there. Chif told me that he did not want to be separated from the group, even if it meant a difficult climb into potentially dangerous territory. Touched by his sense of camaraderie, I looked at Mululema and smiled, but he cracked only a slight grimace in response. In retrospect, I suspect Mululema wanted to stay with the group so that he could make more money working for me, but I am glad he came.

I glanced up at the towering mountains above us and contemplated the unique frog species that had been discovered there by Raymond Laurent in the late 1940s but were never seen again. Some of the most interesting species, including the spectacular African Painted Frog (*Callixalus pictus*), were common in bamboo forests, and Asukulu assured us he could lead us to this type of habitat. More likely than not, these long-lost species were alive and well, but almost no herpetologists had confronted the daunting challenges for fieldwork at Itombwe since the end of the colonial era, and nobody knew for sure. With ongoing deforestation and a myriad of other environmental threats from Itombwe's growing human population, however, I had to consider the possibility that they had been wiped out. There was only one way to find out.

Within minutes, several teenage boys had been hired as porters, and we slowly started to climb the steep and grassy hill leading out of Lemera and into the mountains. Although the road was no longer passable by car, I could see how the colonial miners must have used the ancient route to drive their trucks into the heart of Itombwe, where they mined gold and other valuable minerals in the mid-twentieth century. I stopped at a wooden bridge on the decrepit road that still straddled a small creek and had Aristote take my photo. We followed the road ever higher until Asukulu guided us onto a rocky footpath that wound its way through grassy hills on a steep grade. I leaned my body forward to make it level with the angle of our ascent, and as the hours passed, I could feel the temperature drop, but my constant exertion kept me warm.

As we climbed past 6,500 feet (2,000 m) in elevation, our path resembled a rocky staircase. I donned a jacket as the temperature became chilly, and we literally walked through clouds that had drifted into the mountainside. The thinning air forced us to take increasingly frequent breaks, and the happy sense of exciting adventure we had experienced in the grassy hills below now transitioned into exhausting misery. Once again, my unconditioned body struggled to deal with the grueling climb, and my only thought was to take just one more step when I thought my energy was depleted. We reached the plateau in the late afternoon, and our narrow footpath disappeared into the middle of a peat bog, but Asukulu confidently pressed on toward a grassy hill in the distance. I heard *Hyperolius constellatus* reed frogs calling from the bog as our feet struggled through the muddy morass, and chilly water seeped into my boots as we crossed a small stream blocking our way. Finally, we emerged onto the crest of the hill covered with innumerable cow dung patties, and in the valley below, I could see several round huts with a few herds of meandering goats around them. We had reentered the realm of the Banyamulenge, the same cowherding people we had encountered the previous year.

As the grayish light of sunset crept onto the surrounding hills, we greeted several tall and skinny men who invited us into one of the largest huts to warm ourselves by their fire. They told us their village was called Rurambo. As usual, I had to retreat from the choking smoke of the poorly ventilated central atrium after a few minutes, but I was shown to an adjacent room with a wooden door where I could spend the night. I cleared the rubbish off the floor and set up an air mattress without my tent, because we were now at 9,200 feet (2,807 m) elevation, and there was no sign of any disease-carrying mosquitoes. I suddenly heard Dolly Parton's unmistakable twang on a radio someone had set near the fire, perhaps in an effort to make me feel welcome. I tried not to shiver in the shockingly bitter cold as the sun's warmth disappeared.

As the temperature dropped over the course of the night, I slept fitfully, and constantly tossed and turned as the frigid cold kept waking me up. After a welcome cup of hot coffee in the morning, I emerged from the hut, and the icy air caused a misty vapor to escape from my mouth as I tried to warm myself in the rising sun. We set off along seemingly endless hills of grass, small yellow flowers, and occasional patties of cow dung where herds of cattle had recently passed. Small rocky paths lay where the tread of untold decades of humans and cows had worn away the vegetation, and they looked like brownish-gray ribbons as they snaked across the verdant hills in the distance.

We had not been walking for more than an hour when we passed into a small dale with a few granitic outcrops. Aristote suddenly lurched into a tuft of grass and emerged with an *Adolfus* lizard, the same one we had found on the Itombwe Plateau the year before. A few minutes later, Aristote and Asukulu pounced on another individual. Delighted to have two specimens of a potentially new species, I hardly noticed as the hours of walking slowly crept by.

Our guide, Asukulu, always seemed to be ahead of us, confidently leading us through seemingly endless and identical grassy hills. When we lagged too far behind, I would see him appear suddenly around a corner of granitic rock, or just beyond a tree, as he waited impatiently for us to catch up. He seemed to regard my leisurely shuffle and gasps in the thin air with an annoyed aloofness. He never spoke to me, but he chatted with Chifundera with animated enthusiasm about everything we saw and experienced. I became drenched in sweat in the noonday sun as I struggled to keep up with him and several teenage porters who donned heavy loads of our scientific equipment, tents, and food. But then I saw him stop to chat with two men who stood at the crest of a hill, and I noticed our teenage porters stopped to rest near them. As I approached the top of the hill, I grew uneasy as I realized the men wore camouflage pants and had AK-47s strapped across their shoulders. Aristote had waited for me to catch up just below the position of the soldiers and explained that they were Mai-Mai militia and were demanding payment for us to pass through their territory. After talking to the men for about fifteen minutes, they happily allowed us to continue on our way after receiving a few dollars from me and some comic books Asukulu had brought from Uvira for just this purpose. He was smart enough to recognize that life for a soldier on any side of the conflict in Itombwe was often boring and that comic books were a popular way to pass the time.

After walking for about six hours, we climbed to the top of a particularly steep and rocky hill to discover a spectacular view below us. Asukulu excitedly pointed to a shimmering blue lake in a small valley to the north, and we stopped to rest and take in the gorgeous scenery. We had reached Lake Lungwe, and on the northern edge of the water I could see picturesque huts nestled into a hillside. Small remnants of montane forest could still be seen on some of the hills surrounding the village, but most of the trees had been felled long ago.

In the late afternoon we found ourselves on level but marshy ground near the lake. I could see the huts of the village more clearly, and several people who had been tending crops or herding goats stopped to stare at us. The children were absolutely astonished to see me, and I began to suspect that no white man had been in the area for a very long time. We climbed up a steep hill toward the village, which we learned was called Komesha. I asked the men of the village when a white man had last visited the area. They seemed to be in their thirties, so I was surprised when they responded that they could not remember and would have to consult the village elders. After only a few minutes, one of them returned with a man who seemed to be in his fifties. He told me that the last white visitor was a botanist who had come to Muhuzi twenty-three years previously. Muhuzi was a large village several hours walk to the north, thus there had been no white man at Lake Lungwe in living memory.

The men granted me access to an abandoned hut in the middle of the village, and our kind hosts even gave me a small table to work on. We spent a few hours collecting in the cold water of the marsh in the valley adjacent to Komesha, but with the exception of some orange-bellied puddle frogs, I did not find anything that was new to me. I returned to the lab in the hut and was setting up my camera for a photo shoot of the animals when Aristote approached me with a frog he said he did not recognize. I took a look at it and immediately saw that he was right. It seemed to be some kind of reed frog, but unlike the dull brown or olive-green *Hyperolius constellatus* reed frogs that seemed to be everywhere, this animal had a completely different color pattern — even the color of its eyes was distinctive. It had a beautiful leopard-like pattern that complemented the neon-green flecks inside its black spots and around the periphery of its flanks. Without the advantage of DNA sequence data, all I could do was admire its unique appearance, take a photo, record the locality data where Aristote found it, and ponder whether it might be a new species. Despite the team's efforts to look for more, we never found another one like it, and I would have to wait years to figure out exactly how rare it was.

That evening, I wanted to see if we could find anything interesting at the edge of Lake Lungwe. Chifundera decided that now was a good time to tell me about a warning that the military commander at Luvungi had given him about the lake. It was said that an evil spirit lived there and we should not touch the water. It had not escaped my attention that there did not seem to be any dugout canoes at the lake, and I wondered if the rumors were true. When we reached the shore, half the boys of the village were already there, waiting to watch what would happen. All of us slowly walked through the muddy terrain to the edge of the lake, which turned out to be a boggy quagmire at its periphery. The only species of frog we could hear calling was the common species *Hyperolius constella-tus*, and after a couple hours of trying to move around in mud up to our knees, we abandoned the idea of finding anything interesting.

When Chifundera and I returned to our loaned hut, we started talking about bamboo. One of the very rare frogs I was looking for, the African Painted Frog (*Callixalus pictus*), was supposed to be common in bamboo forest in the highlands of Itombwe. No photographs of the animal in life were known, but it reportedly had a beautiful chocolate-brown ground color with flaming neon-orange vermiculations (branch-like striations) and spots. The animal was considered so distinct that it was placed in its own genus when it was described in 1950 by Raymond Laurent. In a later publication about frog ecology in Itombwe, Laurent[12] stated that *Callixalus* were commonly found at great heights (6 feet [2 m] or higher) on bamboo stalks and usually near streams. But since we had entered the Itombwe Plateau on this expedition, we had not seen a single patch of bamboo forest. Inside the hut where we were spending the night I could see why—the framework of the hut was made from bamboo be-cause few other trees grew at this elevation. The people living here had exhausted this resource, decimating the bamboo that had been common here in Laurent's time sixty years ago.

With great assurance and authority, Chifundera proclaimed that the last stand of bamboo in the area could be seen at Muhuzi, a village a few hours walk to the north. Although I could not understand much of the conversation in Swahili, Chif seemed to be getting his information from an ongoing conversation with Asukulu. Our young guide seemed to know Itombwe better than I knew my own neighborhood, and he had a sharp eye for detail. Chifundera looked at him with fatherly admira-tion as he quizzed Asukulu about conservation issues, and repeatedly Asukulu had a confident answer. With the enticing possibility of finding *Callixalus*, and with a limited bounty at Lake Lungwe, we went to bed with a solid plan to travel to Muhuzi the following day.

On the morning of May 25, we had a light breakfast and hit the trail. Over the course of several hours, we passed through several especially steep hillsides, and once again I struggled to keep myself from slipping on muddy trails and places that were little more than a jumble of innumerable small rocks. I was sweating in the late-morning sun when we stopped to rest and eat a snack on the side of a stream shaded by remnants of montane forest, including a handful of beautiful trees. I was enjoying my brief rest and listening to the birdsong when I noticed an animated discussion occurring between the porters we had hired temporarily at Komesha and some of the members of my entourage. During the rapid conversation in Swahili I could make out two worrisome words: "bandit" and "militia." Obviously trouble was brewing.

The conversation eventually died down, and Chifundera approached me with a troubled look on his face. He said we were entering the territory of two armed groups, the Mai-Mai militia (nearly ubiquitous in Itombwe) and the Interahamwe, dreaded throughout the region for their cruelty. There was also talk of a third wild card, a bandit named Amahoro whose description resembled that of the boogeyman. Apparently he was even crazier and more bloodthirsty than the Interahamwe. Aristote was of the opinion that we should change direction and either go back, or work in another part of the plateau, but Chifundera was not sure. I did not relish the idea of going back over steep mountain passes to areas we already knew had been devastated by human activity. I recalled a quote from the famous British explorer David Livingstone that a man can pass through the worst tribes in Africa if he is good natured and speaks politely, and after reaching a gut decision to continue, I repeated the quote to Chif. He smiled at me after studying my face for a minute, and then he said, "Okay." Everyone seemed a bit surprised by my decision, but nobody questioned me, and we continued on our way.

Our procession meandered along a winding path through open grassland until we reached the edge of a small village called Mugegema. Several huts seemed to be wedged into a steep hillside, but I could see several more on the top of the hillside, along with the requisite chickens, goats, and wandering children. As we approached, a group of women hastily walked by us and told us that Amahoro had left the village only a few hours before, and he was heading to Bukavu with two companions. The news spooked everyone, including me, and everyone began to wonder if he would travel through Muhuzi, where we hoped to find the last stand of bamboo and the rare frogs that might inhabit it. Apparently, everyone except a small group of Interahamwe had fled Muhuzi to avoid Amahoro. Perhaps the rumors of the boogeyman were not an exaggeration, but I reasoned that at this point we were just as likely to run into him if we went back in the direction of Lake Lungwe.

As we continued along the trail leading through Mugegema, I noticed several well-armed Mai-Mai militia, whom I greeted with enthusiastic friendliness to diffuse the tension on their faces. We spoke to them for a few minutes, and they said it was not a good idea to proceed to Muhuzi. Even if Amahoro was not there, they said, the Interahamwe were likely to be trigger-happy, because they were laying an ambush for him. We stopped to discuss the best course of action. The conversations in Swahili were so rapid and animated that I could not follow the details, but I picked up a few key pieces of information. The Mai-Mai seemed to be friends with the Interahamwe of Muhuzi, and they offered to escort us there on the following day—for a fee. This seemed reasonable to me, but after a few minutes Aristote approached with a dour look on his sweat-drenched face.

"Eli, Chifundera has created a matatizo [big problem] for us now." I looked around and noticed that Chifundera was nowhere in sight. Aristote continued, "The Mai-Mai militias told Chif that we could pay some money to take us to Muhuzi, but he refused, and he started walking to Muhuzi anyway. And so the militias said, 'Okay, you can go ahead and die.'"

A chill of fear crept down my neck. I could not believe what I was hearing. I took off down the path to run after Chif, but after I failed to catch up after several minutes, I decided it would be wise to turn back. Wandege ran by me with a worried look on his face and kept going. Hoping that Wandege would be able to talk some sense into Chif, I returned to the group to find Aristote talking to the Mai-Mai. They offered to let us stay in Mugegema overnight; then we could continue to Muhuzi the next day after cooler heads prevailed. Not only did this seem reasonable to me, but I did not think we had a choice. After a very steep climb up the mountainside, we reached a level plateau, and I could see a handful of huts and about a dozen very curious young boys. We carried our gear to an abandoned hut that they let us use, and in the soft afternoon light, we waited.

About thirty minutes later, I spied Chifundera and Wandege slowly walking up the steep mountainside path to Mugegema. Chif's face was contorted in anger, and I decided not to ask him what happened until later. I turned my attention to setting up my tent in the hut. Although we were still too high for mosquitoes at 8,776 feet (2,675 m), the hut had a messy carpet of straw-like material, an ideal haven for fleas. One by one, the curious children of the village appeared at the hut's entrance to watch me set up the tent. Some of the more intrepid youngsters, with the support of their fathers, even dared to approach me, shake my hand, and mutter, "Jambo!" (Hello!) before retreating back to the growing crowd of onlookers. I smiled at all of them, and my anxiety began to subside as I realized the villagers were more curious than fearful.

Somebody must have asked what I was doing here about this time, because a boy showed up with two chameleons that he had found at the edge of the village. Shortly thereafter, a man gave Aristote a bag of frogs that he had happened to collect that morning for his dinner. The frogs turned out to be *Phrynobatrachus asper*, a fist-sized puddle frog that had not been seen since the middle of the previous century, when Laurent discovered it in another area of the plateau. It had never been photographed. Between this unexpected bounty and the handful of lizards that Maurice found at the edge of the village, I decided it was time to set up another lab so I could work. I was grateful to have the distraction from the tense security situation around us. A table magically appeared, and I got to work photographing everything.

That night Aristote slept near the door of the hut to keep guard. The door was actually nothing more than a few branches and leaves stitched together with liana vines. It had no hinges—one simply slid the rectangular piece of dead vegetation into place against a bamboo frame at the entrance when one wanted to "close" it for the night. Of course a swift kick or two would have destroyed the flimsy facade of security, and I struggled to avoid thinking about angry militia doing just that. At about 2 a.m., I had a little trouble moving it to answer nature's call, and I had not wandered outside very far when the village night watchman pointed his flashlight at me. He pointed me in the right direction to the latrine pit, but I realized that the villagers must have been concerned enough about the security to post a guard. I had never seen such a look-out before.

I tossed and turned until dawn, when Wandege showed up with the man who had given us the bag of frogs from the previous day. After a short conversation in Swahili, Aristote told me that the man would guide them to the forest where he had found the frogs the previous day. When I asked if that was wise under the current security concerns, Aristote scoffed and said there was absolutely no problem, because he was going deep into the forest. I convinced him to take one of the armed teenage militia with him just in case. I would stay behind to work on the specimens we already had in hand, because without preservation, some of the rarest ones would decay.

By the time I finished my scientific work several hours later, Aristote and the rest of the team returned with more *Phrynobatrachus asper*, a river frog (*Amietia*) that I did not recognize, and some large, mystery tadpoles. I was sorry I had missed out on joining them, because they had found the frogs in a beautiful patch of montane forest with a small stream running through it. While they were gone, Maurice and Asukulu had found more lizards on the periphery of Mugegema, including another individual of the mysterious *Adolfus*. When I had finished the photo shoot of all these animals, the men of the village insisted that we take some pictures of them. After a couple of them ran to show off two prized homemade guitars, I obliged them. I dazzled everyone with the playback feature on the digital camera, and we prepared to leave on our dangerous passing to Muhuzi. It would have been nice to stay and explore the nearby forests further, but it was clearly too dangerous to do so. I was glad that Chifundera now seemed calm and ready to deal with whatever might lie ahead.

A light rain started to turn our path into the usual muddy and slippery headache, but we had not walked far when we passed over the top of a hill and looked down on the nearly abandoned village of Muhuzi. I could see a relatively large cluster of huts on the western edge of a meadow, and just a little to the east, a second, smaller group of huts was perched on a small hill overlooking everything. As we descended into the meadow, I could see some men at the small cluster of huts, and they were staring at us. I could also see the telltale sign of guns strapped to their shoulders.

They were definitely the Interahamwe we had been warned about. Most of them had AK-47s, and some of them clutched RPGs and machine guns. Two of them descended from their hilltop position to talk to us, and I felt a surge of adrenaline enter my legs as I realized we were now in a situation we would not be able to avoid if things went badly.

Two of them approached to greet us, and I must have been amusing for some reason, because I could hear them laughing at me, but sinister expressions remained on their weathered faces. Everyone was ordered to set their loads down on the ground, and Chifundera and I were escorted to a small shelter that overlooked the valley. A mustached man in a green military uniform in his early forties greeted us with a frown.

Chifundera handed over all the official documents, and the dour man scrutinized it with a scowl. I wondered how he would regard a document from an authority that had pledged to either kill him or evict him back to Rwanda. At least it would confirm our story of who we were and what we were doing in Itombwe. Without looking up, he started asking blunt questions. Chifundera politely answered everything, but I could sense a nervous tone to his voice. A small group of heavily armed young men watched over everything as they sat on the ground near the shelter, oblivious to the increasing rain that was soaking them. One of the men eyed me curiously with bloodshot and glassy eyes that looked reptilian, and after a moment I realized he was high on some kind of drug. It was unnerving to realize that we were surrounded by drugged-up teens with deadly weapons.

Just as something caught my eye from the other side of the hut, I heard a booming voice barking out commands to the boys around us. I turned to see an enormous man in army green pants, an immaculate bright red fleece, and a multicolored scarf around his neck. As he approached us, I could see he was at least six foot three (1.9 m), in his late twenties, and in one hand he carried an AK-47 with several extra ammo clips taped around the one loaded in place. He was smiling and laughing with his men as he approached, and with a confident swagger and a smile, he heaved his weapon to a minion and made a grand entrance into the hut. I had obviously mistaken who was in charge.

With an enormous grin he extended his hand, and I shook it as confidently as possible while greeting him in Swahili. Pleased, he shooed

Chifundera to the side and took a place on the bench right next to me, continuing to grin as he studied every aspect of my face. I tried not to think of how many people he had murdered as he regarded me with a childlike expression of amazement. He ignored the dour man in the corner as the latter sternly reported who we were and the purpose of our presence in the area. Without taking his eyes off me, he loudly proclaimed something. I nodded in acknowledgment as Chif translated that his name was Commander Kifo (death), which prompted a Cheshire cat grin.

In my broken French I explained that I was a professor from Texas in the United States and that I was in Itombwe to study amphibians and reptiles. I also told him that we had heard about the bandit and were concerned that we did not know where he was.

"Oui!" (Yes!), he replied. He continued to stare at my face with an amused fascination, even as Chifundera explained our purpose in passing through his territory. The commander looked over our documents and asked a few questions, but always returned his glance to me and smiled. He said it was good we had not come yesterday, because the situation had been very bad. After all the villagers had fled to escape the bandit Amahoro, the commander and his men had lain in wait to ambush and kill him. Apparently Amahoro was one of the few Mai-Mai commanders who refused to integrate into the Congolese army, and he was also against all Rwandese forces, including the Interahamwe. The bandit led the life of a nomad, wandering from village to village, supposedly killing those who would not feed and shelter him willfully. But he was no fool: he had slipped past the commander unseen and by now was well on his way to Bukavu.

As the commander studied every inch of my beard from a foot away, he explained that another American scientist named John Hart had passed through this way in the 1990s. Back then, he told me, there was forest as far as the eye could see. I looked around the village, and with the exception of a few lone trees on the top of some of the ridges surrounding us, every tree had been eliminated. My predecessor had been there to study large mammals, which could have only existed in forest that would have probably surrounded the village then. All of the bamboo that Chif and Asukulu had talked about so confidently in Komesha had vanished.

The commander transitioned into a commentary about how the Inter- ahamwe are unjustly demonized by the Western media. I made a com- ment that vaguely acknowledged this, but I did not agree with him. I relaxed a little and asked him what he thought of our new president, Barack Obama. He wondered if Obama would be different from his pre- decessor, because he had kept Bush's defense secretary Robert Gates. For the next twenty minutes, they asked me questions about the United States and what I thought of my leaders. Surprised, I asked how he stayed informed about American politics from here, and he responded that he listened to BBC on the radio. Apparently even here, in one of the remotest places in eastern Congo, news of the world reached interested ears. I was not scared of him anymore, because I could feel a loneliness in his words and actions that belied the difficult life he was leading. I knew that he had probably done bad things to be the leader of this group of Interahamwe, but I could also recognize that he was suffering. The conflicting emotions tangled in my mind and made me forget my own predicament.

When I asked him about his life here in Itombwe, and what he did for fun, his face lit up and I could feel him soaking up the attention. He looked to be about twenty-five. I did the math and realized he had been about eleven years old during the Rwandan genocide in 1994. Could a child that young have participated in the killing? If he had been in Itombwe in the mid-1990s when Hart passed through, he probably ended up there in the wake of the genocide and subsequent violent breakup of the refugee camps. I wanted to know his story, and I am sure he would have told it to me, but when I glanced over at the stoned teen- ager holding the machine gun, the teenager half grinned at me, with an awkward sneer. He reminded me of the unpredictable, drunk guys I knew in college who loved nothing more than to explode into a fistfight. That jolted me back to reality, and I was reminded it was dangerous to stay here any longer than necessary.

Commander Kifo eventually sensed that I was ready to continue my journey to Bukavu, and to smooth the transition I gave them some money for beer and cigarettes as a gift. Everyone nodded their head in approval and thanked me for my generosity. The commander stood up and said he would walk me to the edge of his territory. As we descended the hill, I was grateful for his company, because his minions would never dare to shoot at us with him right next to us. Chifundera and I rejoined our companions at the bottom of the hill, and they seemed relieved that everything was going okay.

All of us engaged in small talk with the commander for a few more minutes. And then he dropped a bombshell that threatened to derail the cordial rapport we had established over the last half hour. With a stern look, he asked Chif and Aristote why I had not learned French or Swahili well enough to talk to him fluently. I had to come up with a good excuse, and somehow the best possible answer suddenly popped into my mind.

In a way cruder that I will repeat here, I told him I had not learned either language fluently because I was too busy making love to my girl-friend. The commander eyed Chifundera suspiciously as he and Aristote laughed heartily at my answer. When my reply was translated, everyone on the hill had a good laugh, including cackles from one of the shifty teens, who nearly dropped his AK-47. My strategy to go for the fifth-grade humor had paid off.

When he regained his composure, the commander asked me if I was married. I said no, but that I had a girlfriend, and maybe someday I could get married. He looked shocked and said that in Congo, this was not allowed. I threw up my hands, gestured at him, said "Congo," gestured at myself and said "America," and then smiled. He smiled back and seemed to accept that we were from different worlds. We slowly started to walk out of the valley we were in toward the northeast. We shook hands, and he turned back as I continued through a long cornfield at the edge of the village.

I was still on edge as we passed through the agricultural field over another one of the endless mountains peaks, but as we descended I was distracted by a truly awesome sight. Off in the distance to the north, I could see Mount Mohi, Itombwe's highest point, at about 11,400 feet (3,475 m).[13] The mountain was roughly cone-shaped and ascended from the middle of the plateau at a steep angle. Perhaps that is why it was still completely covered in absolutely pristine forest. I could only imagine how this beautiful forest could have survived the axe for so long. Perhaps it was too steep to allow the local people to convert it into agricultural use, but that would not explain how they had spared the trees for firewood. The only other two possibilities I could think of were that it was either protected by some kind of taboo, or the local people simply enjoyed its beauty and wanted to keep it intact. At such a high elevation, the forest's trees become shrunken and contorted, which has prompted some botanists to call these type of forests "elfin woodlands."[14] In the short moment I had to stop and admire the unique mountain, I wondered what animals, if any, could be adapted to that woodland. I did not even have time to take a photo, because Chifundera rightfully prompted all of us to move on with haste. As the spectacular sight passed out of view, I could only hope that the forest would remain long enough for me to return someday when the militias no longer posed a deadly threat.

About an hour later when we entered a remote stretch of montane forest, I felt relieved that we had passed through the Interahamwe's territory without being robbed or worse. But we still had three armed Mai-Mai teenagers with us, and even though they helped us pass through the Interahamwe's territory unscathed, I did not completely trust them. We traveled on a winding path that crossed a couple of small rivers until we reached a village called Kizuka at the base of a steep mountain. One of the villagers recognized us from our trip to Miki the previous year, and he provided a roomy hut for me to use. When I looked inside, I could see that it had not been occupied for some time: it was covered in cobwebs and dust. It had the unusual feature of rafters in the ceiling, where I could see that someone was storing random cooking supplies and an enormous amount of marijuana.

To avoid the stares of the locals and get some rest, I retired to my tent and waited for darkness and the opportunity to record frogs near a river we had seen at the edge of the village. As I tried to take a nap, I became aware of some subtle changes in my body. I felt a bit nauseated, and some strange tingling was evident in my arms. And then, in waves, I could feel parts of my arms and chest heating up, as if I was getting a hot flash. These symptoms were all too familiar to me from my expedition in 2007 — it seemed to be malaria. I suddenly remembered the mosquito bites I had sustained when I arrived in Bukavu. It had been exactly ten days since then, the right amount of time needed for the malaria to manifest. I was in denial about my sickness until two hours later, when I was knee-deep in a marsh recording frog calls. I reached a point where I could not continue because of nausea and dizziness. I had some medication to combat the malaria, and I took the pills before falling asleep.

The next morning it was still raining. I put on my boots, walked just outside the hut, and barfed several times as Wandege and several villagers watched in concerned silence. It was the first time I had been sick in that way since childhood, but I immediately felt better. I contemplated our situation for a moment and realized we had found some very interesting frogs, but almost no evidence of good forest, and lots of bad guys. A malaria attack would leave me weakened for at least a few days, and it would be too dangerous to try to go to a completely different part of the plateau from here. I decided it was time to regroup in Bukavu and work someplace that was not so problematic.

I emerged from the hut to see all the villagers gathered around the team to see us off. There was still a light rain, and when I looked at the path leading north, I saw a very tall and extremely steep path leading straight up the side of the mountain to a ridge at least 500 feet (152 m) above us. I groaned as I watched our Mai-Mai escorts effortlessly hike up the slippery trail in their cheap rubber boots. It took me a difficult half hour of climbing, with a few slipping setbacks, to reach the ridge above Kizuka. As the path continued, we walked into a patch of bamboo forest, and when we heard a strange peeping call, we stopped long enough to search for frogs. Asukulu managed to catch two *Arthroleptis* squeaker frogs, a possible source of the calls. Close relatives of arboreal *Leptopelis* treefrogs, most *Arthroleptis* are terrestrial, with a relatively small size, an elongated third finger in males (as long as 40 percent of the body length) that is suspected to have some function in reproduction, and direct development, in which the eggs are laid on land and hatch into tiny froglets, bypassing the typical aquatic tadpole stage and metamorphosis.[15]

I started to feel better as our path continued north through grassy hills and modest remnants of montane forest. But then Chifundera took me aside and said there was a problem with our Mai-Mai escorts. They had agreed to escort us for two days at five dollars apiece, but they claimed

Chifundera leans on his snake tongs at the edge of a river during the team's descent of the Itombwe Plateau.

this was now day 3, and now they wanted ten dollars a day for the trouble. I looked around us at the small patches of forest, with no people or villages anywhere in sight. The simple truth was that they were armed and we were not, and if they really wanted to, they could rob us for everything we had. Chifundera bravely argued with them until they agreed to seven dollars a day, but I realized he did this so that they would not sense our fear and take advantage of our isolation. They escorted us for only two more hours before we reached the end of the plateau, where they, along with one of the porters who did not want to go any farther, demanded payment.

After reaching the bottom of one mountain path and climbing up another one, the trail started crisscrossing a small river through incredible forests with ferns at least 15 feet (5 m) tall. Unbeknownst to us, we had crossed back into a thin slice of Kahuzi-Biega National Park. The pristine forest soon ended, and we spent several more hours climbing through grassy hills devoid of trees except for a few places next to rivers.

The maddening thing about the paths was that they always seemed to return to the river, yet they insisted on taking the most difficult route over the mountains as they zigzagged endlessly. A man who had been dragging a stubborn goat through the mountain trail with us for a few hours guided us along the winding valley trail to a village called Twangiza, where it was obvious we would have to spend the night. It started to rain again at dusk just as we entered the village, and we were ushered into a small shop that had a couple benches and a table. There was no soda for sale, but Chif bought some bread, which everyone eagerly gobbled down. We passed the night at the house of a local pastor, and he told us about a Canadian mining company that was active in the neighboring town of Rwinga.

The next morning we set out for Rwinga, where we hoped to find transportation to Bukavu. Although my medication seemed to be working, I was weakened by the previous day's ten-hour hike and the anemia caused by the malaria. As we passed the center of town, we could see a massive gold-mining operation at a small river adjacent to the village. Dozens of people had carved out ugly scars of trenches in the mud, and they were busy looking for gold. I wondered if any of them were unknowingly poisoning people downriver with the toxic, mercury-based reagents that are needed to obtain the gold. Overseeing the whole operation was a compound surrounded with barbed wire. Based on the presence of a satellite dish and a gleaming new truck, Chif said it was the headquarters for the Canadians.

Completely covered in mud from the thick, clay-like ooze on the road, we reached the edge of the town and found a large lorry loaded with crates of soda, beer, and about two dozen passengers on top of the load. After negotiating the team's passage and scraping copious amounts of mud off our boots, Chif and I climbed into the spacious cab with several other people, including the truck's teenage owner, who despite the mud was somehow wearing spotless new white tennis shoes. At last, we were able to leave the brutal conditions of Itombwe behind us. The journey was pleasant enough until I realized the truck's owner was much more childish than an eighteen-year-old should be. When he grew bored, he urged the driver to accelerate to a very dangerous speed and honk at the truck ahead of us. A woman perched on that truck looked back at us with a nervous smile, and the owner next to me cackled with delight as our heavily laden vehicle bounced up and down from the potholes we hit again and again. I told Chif that I thought we were going to die, and he did not argue with me. I heard him try to reason with the teenage owner to slow down, but the boy was having too much fun. But then we bounced off a particularly deep hole and I heard a loud pop from the side of our truck. I was actually thankful that we had a flat tire, and I could only hope that the loss of time and money would convince the owner to be more careful as we continued.

We enjoyed a beautiful view of the Mitumba Mountains in a small village as we waited for the truck to be repaired. Everything seemed to be all set for us to continue an hour later, and I climbed into the cab next to Chif. Just then a man appeared at the driver's side window with a stern look on his face. He seemed to be talking to the driver in a very serious tone, but the driver was dismissive and tried to wave him off. The conversation grew more heated as the driver fired up the truck and waited for the man to leave, but he did not take the hint and stubbornly continued what had become a full-blown argument. The driver put the truck into gear and started rolling down the road, but the man continued to cling to the side of the truck and was now shouting. At this moment the owner decided to hit the guy, and a fistfight broke out between the three of them as we continued to roll down the road. Alarmed, I looked at the road to see if there was a major drop-off on either end, and although I could see some sizable drainage ditches, we did not seem to be in danger of falling off a cliff. Somebody scored a direct hit on the man clinging to the side of the truck, and he finally released his grip on the driver side door and fell off. With a laugh, the driver hit the gas and we moved on. When I asked Chif what the argument was about, he mentioned that somebody owed the man about ten dollars for repairing a windshield. I could only shake my head in disbelief as we continued on our way, this time without any major interruption, all the way to Bukavu. Although the African Painted Frog had seemed to elude us, we had rediscovered

Phrynobatrachus asper, collected more specimens of the putative new species of *Adolfus* grass lizard, and found some other frogs and lizards that were quite rare. Itombwe's importance as a site for conservation of rare and threatened species was certainly confirmed. Happy with the discoveries we had made under difficult circumstances, I was looking forward to a much-needed rest, but unfortunately I would be laid up substantially longer than planned.

CONGOLIZATION

8 As chronicled in the movie *The Motorcycle Diaries*, Ernesto "Che" Guevara was trained as a doctor in Argentina in the 1950s, became aware of the plight of the poor during a trip through South America, and eventually joined Fidel Castro in the Cuban Revolution to overthrow a dictator who had been supported by the United States for decades. In the years following the success of that revolution, Che became increasingly restless. He felt that the American "Yankee imperialists" were continuing their practice of neocolonialism across the world, and as the only country to successfully rebuke this policy, Cuba had an obligation to assist and even fight for foreign revolutionary movements that were similarly trying to rid themselves of Western meddling.[1]

Because of the influence of the Americans, Cuba was shunned by other governments in Latin America, and as a consequence, Castro looked to Africa for friends. In the early 1960s, Africa was in turmoil from a wave of anticolonial feeling, which resulted in the independence of numerous countries, including Congo. In the power vacuum left by the departure of colonial administrations, various players jockeyed for influence, including the Soviets, China, South Africa, several European countries, and of course the United States.[2]

Che vowed to stop them, and in April 1965, he departed Cuba to assist a struggling rebel movement in Congo that was being led, at least ostensibly, by Laurent Kabila. Disguised as a shaved, bespectacled intellectual, Che's suitcase contained works of literature and numerous inhalers to combat his chronic asthma. With assistance from the government of Tanzania, Che and several other Cubans snuck across Lake Tanganyika and joined the rebel movement in the steep mountains just west of the lake. At the height of the operation, two hundred well-armed Cuban troops fought Mobutu's troops and his hired, white mercenaries in the region encompassing the Congolese towns of Baraka, Fizi, Lulimba, and Force Bendera. For over six months, Che and his Cuban *compañeros* struggled to motivate and lead the poorly planned Congolese rebel movement, and the putative leader Kabila, based in Tanzania, was almost never there. Living off of the monkeys, antelopes, and elephants that were common in the area, Che and his colleagues suffered from frequent attacks of malaria, dysentery, and other tropical diseases that they were poorly prepared to treat. A series of demoralizing military failures combined with a lack of focus, organization, and motivation created increasingly pessimistic attitudes among the Congolese, a mind-set that Che called *Congolization*. As the defeats mounted, Che remarked, "The soldier of the Congolese revolution [is] the worst example of a fighter I have encountered to date."[3] Toward the end of the operation, a mercenary force backed by the Congolese government delivered a heavy blow and scattered the rebels. Congolization seeped into the consciousness of all Che's men, including the Cubans. Disgusted with the Congolese soldiers' lack of leadership, professionalism, and idealism, Che and the remaining Cubans returned to Cuba. In a report to Castro that included Che's diary in Congo, he began by stating that his document was "the history of a failure."[4]

Shortly after returning from Itombwe on May 28 and finishing my anti-malarial medication, the symptoms returned with a vengeance. Bedridden for a week, I read a couple of books, including Mungo Park's *Travels in the Interior Districts of Africa*. My fevers and weakness were put into perspective when I read how Park, a Scottish explorer in West Africa, endured slavery and unimaginable hardship for two years in the late eighteenth century, when little medication was available. By June 5, weak or not, I could not bear to lie around any longer, and we prepared to leave the following day. I wanted to explore the Kabobo Plateau, a highland area just south of Itombwe, because Laurent had described several frogs from there in 1952,[5] and nobody had seen them since. Unlike Itombwe, where several members of the field crew had grown up, Kabobo was supposed to be uninhabited, and nobody we knew could give us reliable information about the integrity of the plateau's montane forests or the animals that might inhabit them. Assuming the forests were intact, I was also curious to know whether Kabobo's amphibian and reptile species would really be distinct from Itombwe's, as suggested by Laurent's brief research there. On June 6, Mululema picked us up and we traveled south to find out.

Dusk overtook us after passing through Uvira, and we stopped at a village called Nundu, where we were surprised to see a few small buildings with electric lights. After a quick investigation, Chif announced that an American surgeon was working at the town's hospital, and although he was out, we could stay in a building used for storage. The surgeon tried to stop by the next morning before dawn, but we were all asleep and I missed my opportunity to meet him. As we departed, I observed the vegetation around Nundu and realized we had crossed out of the remnants of rainforest that hugged the northwestern side of Lake Tanganyika. We had entered the yellow and lime-green Zambezi Miombo Woodlands Ecoregion,[6] a mixture of grassy savannas, spindly miombo trees in the genus *Brachystegia*, and umbrella-like acacia trees.[7] The trees were not very tall, perhaps only 20 feet (6 m) or so, and they did not occur so close together that they could be mistaken for a shady rainforest. A few granitic rock outcrops dotted the hills here and there, creating a quintessentially African landscape.

Soon after departing Nundu, we suddenly encountered a large line of vehicles sitting idly on the road. Chif and Aristote left to investigate, and when they returned, they said there was an enormous muddy pit ahead, and a heavily laden lorry had become stuck in it. The truck was so large that no other vehicles could get around it, and all we could do was sit and wait while a small group of men tried to use shovels, rocks, and logs to extract the vehicle. As we sat baking in the sun, a lone frog jumped out of the bushes on a hill overlooking the road and landed on the hood of our truck. I ran out and grabbed it, and discovered it was a *Ptychadena* rocket frog, the same genus we had encountered at Lwiro and Ruwenzori.

About three hours later, the truck was finally freed, and it rumbled

Wandege wanders through the miombo woodlands
looking for snakes on the road south of Nundu.

past us and the line of other vehicles impatiently waiting to move on. Several smaller cars were able to move through the obstacle and continued on their way, but as we grew close to the place where the truck had become stuck, I realized it would not be easy to get through. There was an enormous muddy pit at least 9 feet (3 m) deep, and fresh tracks showed where the truck had helplessly spun its wheels repeatedly. Surrounding the pit was a large area of thick mud, and surrounding that ring of mud was a low flat area with reeds—in fact, the road was actually passing through a flooded marsh. Recent rains had basically turned the "road" in this spot into a large muddy quagmire, and as the sun's heat slowly burned away the water, a thick goo of mud was left behind. I watched in amazement as several cars sped up to the muddy area and basically used their momentum to fishtail their way through the morass of sticky earth.

When it was our turn, I looked over at Mululema, said, "Bonne chance" (Good luck), and braced myself for a rough ride. After revving the engine and taking off at high speed, he did a valiant job trying to plow through the mud in the same way that several other cars had, but when we weaved to the side to avoid another truck that was stuck, the slippery mud took hold of our tires and did not let go. Mululema tried in vain to gun the engine several times in forward and reverse to get us out, and with a sigh, I stepped out and took a seat on the grassy hill next to the road. Three enterprising teenage boys with shovels and large rocks immediately offered to help us, and they started rapid arguments in Swahili over the best way to get us out.

I considered how the people of Congo could live this way. The government at that time was powerless to do anything to improve the roads, because there was no taxation system in place. Given the enormous problem of corruption in Congo, one could easily imagine that a significant portion of would-be revenue would disappear anyway. The people seemed to accept this impossible system as normal, and absolutely everything in the country was jerry-rigged as a result. There could be little hope for economic improvement in the absence of good roads, and little hope for better roads in the absence of economic improvement. As I watched the men toiling in the mud, I contemplated how our truck was an analogy for the country in general. It was a veritable patchwork of multiple shoddy repair jobs with substandard parts that somehow allowed it to lurch from one disaster to the next. The positive thing, however, was that no matter how difficult things got, the Congolese never gave up or lost faith in finding a solution, no matter how improbable it might seem at first. Even more impressive, they never lost their sense of humor. And in these respects, I will forever be in awe of their fortitude and patience.

As the hours wore on, my optimism began to wane. It was getting dark, and it would be absolutely miserable and dangerous to spend the night in the middle of a roadside marsh. A group of women lingering on the side of the road to sell grilled corn husks laughed at me, and with a jeer, they suggested that we would have to pass the night there. But then as sunset hit, Mululema managed to catch the truck's tires on a log that

Marcel stands barefoot in the foreground as Chifundera and Mululema crouch near a man trying to free our truck. The reeds of the surrounding marsh can be seen in the background.

had been laid underneath them, and he sped the battered vehicle onto a small hill leading away from the marsh. We were free.

At Aristote's suggestion I gave the boys ten dollars each for their tireless efforts to free us, and wide-eyed, they shouted with joy — they planned to have a party. With a parting, sarcastic wave to the corn-husk women, who were now cheering our victory, we continued on the pothole-ridden road as the darkness became complete. As it grew late, we finally approached a military roadblock at the entrance to the town of Fizi. Swahili for "hyena," Fizi is located at an interesting habitat intersection of the miombo woodland landscape we had entered at Nundu, and serpentine swaths of transitional rainforest. In the nineteenth century, Fizi was located along a major Arab slave route between the towns of Nyangwe and Baraka, where slaves where shipped in dhows to a large slave market at Ujiji on the east coast of Lake Tanganyika in modern-day

Tanzania. In the colonial era, Fizi was the headquarters for the regional territorial government, and the town had a sizable hospital.[8]

We passed the hospital and a few ancient Belgian houses, then reached a section of town with more recently constructed buildings and compounds, several of which were surrounded by great metal walls with barbed wire. We crammed into two tiny, spider-infested hotel rooms to rest for the night. I was surprised by the chilly air the following morning, but we had climbed to 4,265 feet (1,300 m) elevation, a noticeable increase from the hotter lowlands surrounding Lake Tanganyika. We stopped on our way out of town near the hospital so that Chif could acquire the requisite stamps from the local police chief, and I took a stroll near the old Belgian houses along the road. I could see chimneys sprouting from the top of each roof, and imagined how the Belgians must have kept warm during cold mornings like this. Most of the houses were very small, with perhaps only two rooms to each quaint structure, but many of them had withstood the weathering effects of time quite well. I could see that the Congolese had moved into the houses that were still in decent shape, and they had not removed any of the beautiful flowers, which might have been planted by the previous Belgian owners. I looked across the rolling grassy hills, which still had some remnants of forest. To the east, the hills steadily descended to the lake, whereas to the northwest, I could see the faint outline of Itombwe's misty mountains in the distance.

The landscape was still foggy when we departed Fizi to take the winding road south. We passed through beautiful hills, some covered with miombo trees, others with golden-brown grass, parched by a recent drought. Some of these hills had patches of gallery forest where small streams cascaded down from unknown sources in tiny little waterfalls. We stopped briefly to look for animals in a few of these picturesque places, but we found nothing. While we descended a hill during the hottest part of the day, the road seemed to be surrounded by vegetation resembling elephant grass. I suddenly saw an anachronism that would have been more common a century before. A barefoot, middle-aged man clad in rags clutched a long spear as he watched us go by. Three scrawny brown dogs with bells on their collars nervously scurried around him.

Chif said he was hunting antelope. I wondered how many hunters still utilized spears in the twenty-first century, but at the same time, I was very grateful for a glimpse of the quintessential Congolese hunter from a bygone era.

The road curved slightly as we crossed into the southeastern sliver of Maniema Province, so named for the man-eating tribes that once dominated the region. The sun had started to cast long shadows onto the road in front of us when we reached Lulimba, a hot and dusty town in the middle of a seemingly desolate stretch of the savanna/woodland mosaic. Within a few minutes of arriving, Chif had become friends with a local man who owned a hotel in the middle of the town. The dusty room was unusually hot because the tin roof had baked in the blazing sun all day and trapped the heat in the simple and poorly ventilated structure underneath. Reluctantly I set up my tent and prepared to deal with the hot temperatures, but when I awoke in the middle of the night hours later, I was unprepared for the sweat that had drenched my entire body. After taking my temperature, I realized that I was suffering from another fever, which was made all the more miserable by the hot and stuffy air surrounding me.

My temperature continued to rise even as the cool morning temperature finally made the room tolerable, and shortly after dawn I asked Aristote to see if the town had a clinic. He returned after an hour of reconnaissance to tell me that a German nongovernmental organization (NGO) had established a small clinic on the edge of town just a couple of years previously. Mululema drove us to the place, where a young Congolese doctor greeted us and ushered us into a small room. After explaining the problem, I allowed him to take a small blood sample, and within minutes of examining it under a microscope, he calmly pronounced I had malaria. I was dumbfounded. How could all the medication and rest I had taken only days before failed to cure me of the previous infection? Or could it be that I had been cured, but then immediately afterward I was infected again? And how could all of this happen while I was taking the most highly effective antimalarial prophylaxis medication on the market? Frustrated, feverish, and exhausted from my restless attempt at sleep the night before, I felt very demoralized.

The doctor tried to explain that no prophylaxis medication is 100 percent effective, and in Westerners, malaria can often persist after initial treatments. When I told him that I had used top-of-the-line artesunate medication from Europe (purchased in Bukavu) to treat the last infection, he commented that sometimes counterfeit or expired medication is sold in Congo. Could this be why the malaria had been knocked down, but not out? He suggested I switch to quinine pills, which he warned would be a harsh medication because of the side effects, but it promised to be more effective to kill the malaria once and for all. His pharmacist assistant appeared at that point and provided me with a small plastic bag full of large quinine pills. When I asked if it would be possible for me to work while taking the medication, he gestured that I was a big man and would not have any problem doing so. That said, he recommended I take plenty of vitamins and rest as much as possible, at least for the first few days, while the medication took effect. Satisfied that I had done all I could, I swallowed my first pill and we left the clinic to return to the hotel.

We returned to find that Wandege and Chif had been busy looking for frogs at a nearby swamp while I had been gone. In addition to a handful of common lizards, they found many puddle frogs, including some individuals with barred black-and-white lips that I had never seen before. I tried to ignore my fatigue as we photographed the animals for hours. I had just finished and cleaned up my laboratory for the day when a teenage boy brought us a harmless Olive Marsh Snake (*Natriciteres olivacea*) that he had killed near the village. I got back to work immediately so that the heat would not spoil the specimen, and by the time I finished and ate my dinner, it was dark. The quinine had given me a headache and made my ears ring, and I noticed a burning sensation when answering nature's call. I was also completely exhausted.

I woke up less during the night as the quinine started to kill off the parasite in my blood, and the next morning we decided to continue south. Late that afternoon, following another all-day drive through the beautiful miombo-woodland landscape, we arrived at the town of Force Bendera in the foothills of the Kabobo Plateau. I was surprised to see functional power lines supplying electricity to multiple houses in the area, many of which were adorned with satellite dishes. The plateau was impressive because it rose sharply from the flat savanna in rippled brown and green peaks, and the higher one's eyes looked at it, the more forest one could see. I knew the Belgians had built a road to extract mineral resources from the plateau in the colonial era, but I could see no evidence of it, nor could I make out any trace of human paths, settlements, or fires. It looked beautifully pristine, and I grew excited as I pondered what animals might be hiding within it.

I saw several colonial-era Belgian houses that still had working light bulbs over each doorway. I also spotted a large and modern-looking green canvas tent pitched next to one of the nicer houses, and a shiny new 4×4 truck near it. We soon learned that a white man was in the area. Still weak from my recovery, I pitched my own one-man tent on a concrete floor in one of the crumbling Belgian houses that one of the locals allowed us to rent. As usual, the toilet was missing its seat, the mirror over the sink had broken long ago, and there was no running water, but I noticed that the large bathtub was in good enough shape to afford a bath.

I rested well that night, and the next morning I was feeling well enough to photograph a White-lipped Herald Snake (*Crotaphopeltis hotamboeia*) that Wandege and Aristote found at a nearby river. With a maximum size of about 2.6 feet (80 cm), this nocturnal, rear-fanged snake is not dangerously venomous, but it bites readily when cornered and preys on frogs near water.[9] An invitation arrived from the white man to join him for afternoon tea, and I happily took a break from my work to meet him. Under the veranda of his rented house, I was introduced to a husky man named Pierre, who was working for a foreign mining company. I was treated to the rare luxury of a cold Sprite, and because of his gregarious nature, Chif joined us too. Pierre explained that he was directing logistics operations for the company because some of the locals had found gold on Kabobo and the company was investigating whether it would be worth mining. He had been in Congo for months, accompanied by African geologists and laborers. Over time he had become quite good at setting up little operations like this in the middle of nowhere, and he doled out a lot of advice about preventing mechanical breakdowns on

Congo's unforgiving roads, but all of his solutions required a fair bit of money that I did not have.

When I explained my work and asked him about Kabobo, he said he had climbed it only once and would never do it again because it was brutally difficult. He mentioned climbing at nearly 90-degree angles in small footholds carved out of the mountain's muddy slopes with machetes. It sounded like Itombwe, but much worse. However, he said there were almost no villages on the plateau, the forest was pristine, and he often heard chimpanzees hooting in the mornings. He offered to arrange for guides and porters to help us, and he suggested that we leave before dawn to avoid spending the hottest part of the day in the blisteringly hot savannas we would have to pass through before reaching the foot of the mountain. We marveled at the persistence of a working colonial-era generator at Force Bendera, and the conversation turned to Congo's history and the great tragedy that had occurred in recent decades.

But then almost imperceptibly, Pierre slowly drifted into an opinionated diatribe of the corruption that plagues Congo, and how it had ruined everything good that the Belgians did during the colonial era. I shifted uncomfortably in my seat. Chifundera wisely excused himself and left us, but Pierre did not catch the hint, and he continued bemoaning what he perceived as the shortcomings of the Congolese. When I broached the subject of his security, he scoffed at my concern. He was a former special-ops soldier, and he assured me that he could take care of himself. As the sun waned and a melodic chorus of birds gathered to pass the night in the surrounding trees, we watched in silence and enjoyed the orange glow cast along the rugged flanks of Kabobo. Pierre sipped on his beer, emitted a bored sigh, and said, "Ahhh, I miss killing people."

The following morning Marcel woke me before dawn with a cup of coffee and a putrid mix of sun-dried fish, greasy red sauce, and rice. Knowing that I would need all the energy I could muster, I ate as much of it as I could. In the grayish predawn haze, Mululema carefully maneuvered our truck down the decrepit road to the opposite edge of town, where we had arranged a rendezvous with Pierre and a handful of porters and guides. Wearing rags of faded T-shirts and shorts, none of them seemed to be older than eighteen, but Pierre assured me they were the best to be had. By the time the negotiations and salary advances were completed, the sun had risen high enough that I needed to apply sunblock. I thanked Pierre for his trouble, and with a final wave goodbye, we left on foot through a trail of thick and thorny bushes into the wild savanna. I could easily imagine how the habitat was full of elephants and antelope during Che Guevara's time there fifty years ago, but nothing stirred as we slowly walked through the quintessentially African landscape.

For two hours the thorny bushes and trees tore our clothes and scratched our arms and legs as we struggled to wind our way through the rough path in the bush. The vegetation had become so thick that I lost sight of the mountain, but our teenage guide looked confident as he strolled on and on. I was grateful when we entered a thick patch of gallery forest next to a river, because it afforded some shade from the increasingly hot sun, but then I saw we would have to cross through the river on foot. I tried not to dwell on the ghastly variety of waterborne parasites that surely dwelled in the water as I rolled up my pantlegs and walked through the murky brown water.

When I emerged from the forest patch on the opposite side of the river, I looked up to see a veritable wall of rock and mud that seemed to stretch to infinite heights above us. As Pierre warned, the angle of ascent was shockingly steep, and I realized I was in for the climb of my life. For endless hours, we scurried from one foothold to another in short bursts of energy that left us breathless from the exertion. Most of our ascent was on our hands and knees, and the blazing heat and rigorous exersion drenched me in sweat and made me gasp for air. More than once the loose soil collapsed under our feet, and we cursed as we slid down several feet after fighting so hard to ascend it the first time. In the late afternoon we finally reached a forested shelf adjacent to a stream, and I fought exhaustion long enough to pitch my tent. Nobody else had the energy to search for animals, but Aristote found a unique *Arthroleptis* squeaker frog in the leaf litter near the stream when he went to quench his thirst.

Hours of slogging up the steep mountainside continued the next morning shortly after dawn, but we were now over 6,500 feet (2,000 m) elevation, and the temperature was mercifully cooler than it had been during our ascent from the savannas. We emerged from the thick forest that clung to the side of the mountain and ascended a slippery trail that zigzagged through an open grassland on its way to the plateau. Breathing hard from the exertion and thin air, we finally reached the top of the mountain to find a beautiful patchwork of forest and grassland. Giant lobelia plants towered over our heads, and the montane trees were decorated with "old man's beard" moss. There was an enormous swamp in the middle of a depression in the grass, and not a single sign of human activity could be seen anywhere. The place looked absolutely prehistoric.

We shivered in the cold water as we spent some time with nets to look for tadpoles, which we found in good numbers. We searched the surrounding forests for a few hours, but they were bone dry, and we found nothing. As the afternoon wore on, we decided to set up camp and pass the night before continuing on to explore the rest of the plateau. It was eerily quiet, but I felt lucky to be in such a pristine place, because I had never seen anything like it anywhere else in Congo.

The next morning, Chif approached me with a concerned look on his face, and I knew trouble was brewing. After talking to the miners working for Pierre in a nearby camp, he was very concerned about security. He said in some parts of Kabobo there were some militia, and in others there were bandits that often robbed miners of their gold. If they learned of our presence, he warned, we could lose everything. None of our teenage guides were armed, and we would not be able to find armed escorts to help us now that we were on the isolated plateau. It was absolutely maddening that we were in the most pristine and poorly explored place we had ever seen in Congo, but we would not be able to stay long if we wanted the expedition to be successful. Reluctantly, I had to concede that he was right, and we would have to plan our return to Force Bendera. Not wanting to return the way we had come, and eager to explore just a little more before descending the plateau, I convinced him to find another way back. After a brief discussion with our guides, they said we could travel west to a large gold-mining village called Kilwemapante, and from there we could return to Force Bendera. Along the way there was nothing but forest, and we could look for animals en route.

For seven hours, we trudged through forest trails that had obviously not been used by many people. Vegetation swallowed the trail in many places, and within minutes of departing, our clothes were wet from the moist leaves that brushed our clothes as we passed through the jungle along a rarely used trail. Large trees had fallen over the trail in many places, and our clothes grew muddier each time we had to crawl over or under the enormous obstacles in our path. I dug around the base of trees, stuck my headlamp into every crevice, and peeled off bark looking for frogs, but I found nothing. Even when we encountered pristine streams in the middle of the forest, no frogs could be seen along the water or sheltering in the damp leaves nearby. Sometimes there is no rhyme or reason why animals are scarce in a given place at a given time, and unfortunately, we had come to Kabobo during a spell of exceptional dryness that had likely caused many of the animals to hide.

It was pitch dark when we descended an exceptionally steep hillside toward the village of Kilwemapante. At the bottom of the hill there was a large dropoff into a stream, and the only way across was an enormous tree that had either fallen by luck, or been cut down by someone who wanted it to serve as a bridge. Seeing that I would break a leg or worse if I slipped off, I slowly crossed over the tree on my hands and knees. I began to hear human voices on the other side, and I could smell smoke from the many fires burning in the village. Safely across but wet, muddy, and hungry, I greeted a few of the gold miners of Kilwemapante as the rest of the team slowly caught up to me. They were certainly shocked to see a white man emerge from the forest, but they greeted us warmly and provided an area in the village for us to spend the night.

I felt a little better the next morning, and I set out to explore the surrounding forest and grasslands with Wandege and Aristote. We finally had a little luck and found a handful of reed frogs and lizards, including a *Leptosiaphos* burrowing skink that had made the mistake of wiggling its way into Aristote's tent! Wandege also spotted a spectacular Johnston's Horned Chameleon (*Trioceros johnstoni*), so named for Sir Harry Johnston, the same British explorer who collected the first okapi specimens in Congo.

A day later during our return to Force Bendera, we were treated to a gorgeous hike through nearly pristine grasslands, and I listened to the wind rustling the grass as we slowly passed through several hills. At one point Wandege dropped his pack to dive for a lizard that proved to be a new species of *Trachylepis* skink. At least we now had one thing that promised to be interesting, but I vowed to return in the future so that I could explore the plateau more thoroughly. It was nearly noon when the grassy hills descended into a weathered, rocky trail that started a steep descent to the savannas below. I was feeling exceptionally weary as the afternoon sun caused us to sweat during the arduous hike, and I could see that more people had been in this area because I could see the remnants of many burned trees where patches of forest had once stood. I could not understand why someone had destroyed the forest here, because there was nothing left but barren soil and rock, and nobody had used the area of the cleared forest to plant crops or do anything else useful. I felt dizzy and dehydrated as the afternoon wore on, and the lower we descended through the barren landscape, the hotter it became. My pace had slowed to a crawl, and several times I had to stop in the small shade of a bush or tree to cool off and catch my breath. Impatient to return to Force Bendera and escape the blistering heat, everyone except Wandege left me behind. I drank copious amounts of the water, which was still somewhat chilly from our night in the mountains, but I ran out about an hour before leaving the mountain trail that ended at the edge of town. I knew I was tired from the long climb and hike through Kabobo, but I began to suspect something else was wrong.

I had just enough strength to set up my tent and lie down when I finally made it back to the house we had rented in the middle of town. I was startled when Marcel woke me after dark to offer me food, but I was too tired to eat and I fell back asleep immediately. Sometime in the middle of the night, I woke with a splitting headache. When I took my temperature, I discovered I was running a high fever yet again. Cursing my bad health luck, but grateful the problem had not surfaced in the middle of Kabobo, I went back to sleep and did not wake again until the late morning.

Aristote took me to a small clinic in the middle of town after I announced my fever in the morning. The dusty medical center was run by a single male nurse with no doctor, and the rusty equipment and beds seemed to date from the colonial era. He immediately suspected malaria when I told him about my recent medical history, but he did not have a microscope to examine a blood sample. Instead, he used a simple malaria antibody kit from India that was probably donated by a foreign NGO, but the test came up negative. Unable to do anything else, he suggested I start a two-day course of intravenous quinine, because the problem was probably linked to malaria or some other bloodborne parasite. The nearest semi-decent hospital was days away over difficult roads, so I decided to take his advice.

For five hours, I read a book or stared at the water stains in the leaky ceiling of the clinic as the warm fluid of the IV entered my arm. At one point two men carried a moaning teenage boy into the clinic, and the nurse sprang into action to care for him. As I marveled at his dedication, my fever and the afternoon heat made me sweat, and I was grateful when Pierre appeared with a cold bottle of soda. He urged me to take it easy for at least a week before continuing the rigorous schedule of mountain climbing I had been doing lately, and I assured him that I would take his advice. I repeated the unpleasant experience for ten hours the following day, and I was so weak and dizzy afterward that I had to lean against Wandege and take his hand like a child as he helped me back to the house.

Meanwhile, Chif and Aristote had been looking for animals in the swamp near Force Bendera, and a handful of interesting things turned up. In addition to some reed frogs and river frogs I did not recognize, someone had killed an olive-green Shreve's Tree Snake (Dipsadoboa shrevei), a nocturnal, rear-fanged, and secretive species that is not dangerously venomous.[10] Another brave person killed a puff adder near their house. One of Africa's largest (up to about 6.5 feet [2 m] long and weighing 13 pounds [6 kg]) and most widespread species of viper, the irascible puff adder (Bitis arietans) warns would-be predators by inflating its body and hissing loudly. Despite this warning, hundreds if not thousands are bitten every year, usually because the well-camouflaged, sit-and-wait ambush predator is not seen in tall grass when a hapless and barefoot person walks too close or steps on them. Although fatalities are not the norm, bites are extremely painful because of the long fangs and large venom glands with copious amounts of venom, which can lead to tissue necrosis, blistering, shock, heart damage, and kidney failure. If the fangs happen to pierce a vein and venom enters directly into the bloodstream, death can occur in thirty minutes.[11]

We had found a single specimen of a new species of lizard at Kabobo and obtained samples of some other rare species, including the tree snake, which proved helpful for a study of its evolutionary relationships years later. Satisfied that we had found enough interesting things under our unfortunate circumstances, I decided it was time to leave. I stopped by to say goodbye to Pierre and thanked him for his help and advice during my time in the area. He wished me well, but I noticed a slightly concerned tone to his voice when I explained my plans for the rest of the summer. After recovering in Bukavu, I would head north to the northern tip of the Albertine Rift Mountains, which were even more poorly known than Kabobo. From there, we would explore the Ituri rainforest to the west. Pierre shook his head and said that I should make sure my medivac insurance had plenty of coverage. Apparently I did not look so good, but I was determined to continue the expedition.

Several days later, I found myself back in Chif's house in Goma. The truck had blown out its brakes as we approached the city, and the team would have to wait several boring days for repairs. I decided to pass some of the time by interviewing Chif's ancient mother-in-law about the Congo of her youth, which she agreed to do in exchange for some beer. She told me that her name was Christiane Mwamudugiga and she was a member of the Bashi tribe. In her day, most girls in her tribe wore goatskin clothes, but her father worked for the Belgians, so she was able to wear white woman's clothes. She claimed that she was from a royal family and her father was king of a place called Nyangezi. Now known as Nya Ngezi, the town is located about 1.5 hours south of Bukavu on the road to Uvira. She had been born the same year the corkscrew road from Bukavu to Uvira had been completed by a white woman engineer sometime in the early twentieth century. Although there were no elephants or lions near the village during her childhood, the place used to be full of antelopes and warthogs. Girls were scarred on their nose and cheeks to protect them from disease, and spaces were carved between the teeth of girls to make them beautiful. She said life in the old days was good because there was peace, but there was occasional fighting to take territory of rival kingdoms, and wars with spears could break out at any time. She said that the Belgians were kind and had a good government, but people were afraid of them because they whipped people. Many people got married between age fifteen and seventeen, and the boy's family had to provide a substantial gift to the family of the girl. Sometimes friends would marry off each other's young children to solidify their friendship. Wedding ceremonies were fun — people from different villages would meet up and have a party with drinking and dancing. There were many masks used for different ceremonies, including weddings, funerals, birthdays, and so on. The king's mask was only for the king, and one could die or become sick if they touched it.

When I asked more about wild animals, she told me a story about an animal called *nyamungunga* in the Mashi tongue, which looked like a leopard but was much larger. Of course the magical monster was known to eat people, and everyone was terrified of it. Her parents and grandparents said that if she left the house at night, the animal would catch her and eat her. At night, everyone had to stay in their house, especially girls. She said an old wizard eventually captured the animal alive and attached a metal device that made noise to scare away the other animals. I was going to ask her why this was necessary, but the beer had made her drowsy, and the story trailed off to a whisper. Mesmerized by the tales of a vanished world, my mind swirled with thoughts of wildest Africa when I finally allowed the beer to lull me to sleep.

I was overjoyed in the morning when Mululema showed up with the truck (and a hefty repair bill), and everyone scrambled to pack up our gear and hit the road. As we headed north away from the bleak, lava-encrusted landscape of Goma, we passed an antirape sign erected by a Spanish NGO. I was reminded that on any given day in Congo, about eleven hundred women are raped.[12] This terrible association with rape and warfare is certainly not unique to Congo, but the problem is so pervasive that the country has been dubbed the "rape capital of the world" by

This roadside billboard is an antirape announcement. The Swahili is translated as follows: "Fighting Against Sexual Violence. What would you do if she was your wife? We must open our eyes and together fight against it."

UN Special Representative Margot Wallström. Filmmaker Fiona Lloyd-Davies documented a disturbing progression in the circumstances of rape in eastern Congo during the war and its aftermath in the first decade of the twenty-first century. Women told her they faced the terrible choice of staying in their huts and starving, or risking rape when they ventured to their fields for food. These horrifying attacks routinely involved multiple attackers, maiming sticks and bayonets, and even "rape camps" with daily roll calls. Often these rape victims were rejected by their families and communities and were forced into a brutal life of exile.[13]

Men and boys are also increasingly victimized by rape,[14] and multiple victims and eyewitnesses have documented "freelance cruelty" attacks from militias and soldiers (almost always young men with guns) who throw toddlers into open fires and force victims to rape, kill, and cannibalize their immediate relatives, spouses, and children.[15] Perhaps most disturbing of all, rape and violence against women outside conflict zones has increased substantially, suggesting that this behavior has become worryingly normal.[16] Eve Ensler, author of *The Vagina Monologues*, called this catastrophe "femicide," because the rape epidemic seems to be destroying women, literally, from the inside out. Because large parts of eastern Congo are effectively lawless, the vast majority of perpetrators are never brought to justice, although recent international efforts to bolster the country's judicial system have met with some limited success.[17]

Some writers who have documented this situation have been tempted to dehumanize the perpetrators of these horrific acts or to dismiss the violence as a manifestation of tribal rivalries that have been raging since time immemorial. But such classifications, which view Congo through an arguably colonial lens, have been called simplistic and racist. And how does our perspective change when we consider that many of the perpetrators and their families were victims of horrible violence as well? Two researchers asked, "If we recognize the humanity and suffering of those who rape, what then separates 'him' from us: are we more afraid of the 'rapist' or the 'human' who rapes, because 'he' could also be us?"[18]

As we passed through several towns heading north, I noticed another antirape billboard and watched stern-faced women balancing heavy loads of firewood, bananas, buckets of water, and other goods on their heads, often with babies strapped to their backs. I could not restrain myself from considering how many of them had endured personal attacks. How could the men of Congo not rise up in outrage against these atrocities? How horrified and powerless would I feel if my own mother or sister were attacked? Could it happen to me? A numbing chill crept into my body as I considered the reality of my violent surroundings. I did not yet realize that my biggest threat continued to thrive within me.

THIS MAN IS NOT RIGHT IN THE HEAD

9 For centuries the cause of malaria was a mystery. Linnaeus, the eighteenth-century biologist famous for inventing binomial nomenclature for scientific names, speculated that the disease was caused by particles of clay transported from drinking water into blocked capillaries.[1] Battles were won or lost in the US Civil War because of malaria, and it was also a big problem for US soldiers in the South Pacific during World War II.[2] Although malaria is currently most common in tropical areas of the world, it became so only recently. In the 1920s, an epidemic devastated a Russian town near the Arctic Circle, and poor sanitation allowed a few cases to pop up in Florida in 2003.[3]

We know now that malaria is a parasitic unicellular eukaryotic organism that, depending on the species, can infect many different kinds of animals, ranging from reptiles to humans. The parasite infects the salivary glands of about seventy of the world's thirty-five hundred species of mosquito, which are considered to be the deadliest animal in the world to humans, because they transmit several lethal illnesses. In the case of malaria, *Anopheles* mosquitoes transmit the parasite to red blood cells of vertebrate victims when they are bitten. The parasite alters the behavior of infected mosquitoes by retarding the enzyme apyrase, an anticlotting compound that allows the female insect (males do not bite) to feed on blood meals—without it, she cannot get enough blood and thus bites more victims, infecting more people each time. Once a human is infected, the shortage of functioning blood cells makes them fatigued and more likely to lie prone, allowing more mosquitoes to bite them and, in

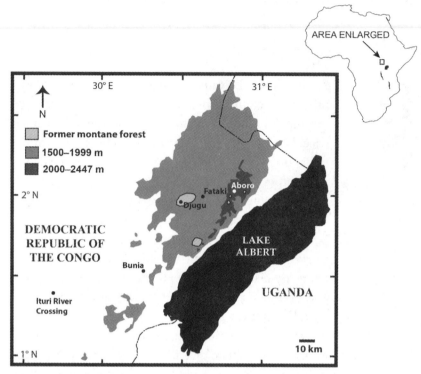

Map of the Lendu Plateau. Modified from Greenbaum et al. 2012b.

turn, become infected with malaria.[4] After a seven- to thirty-day incubation period in the human body, symptoms of fever, chills, malaise, body aches, nausea, vomiting, sweating, and terrible headaches commence. A roller coaster of sweating fevers and cold chills results from toxic substances that are released when the parasites cause the red blood cells to burst out their contents following an infection. *Plasmodium falciparum*, the most deadly species of malaria, is the most common form of the disease in Africa. In severe cases of *falciparum* malaria (about 2 percent), the parasite adheres to the walls of veins in the brain, and victims can die from neurological coma, severe anemia, hemolysis (red blood cell bursting) that turns urine black (known as blackwater fever), acute respiratory distress syndrome, low blood pressure, kidney failure, and complications from hypoglycemia (low blood sugar).[5]

The origins of P. *falciparum* are controversial,[6] but a recent study suggests that bats are the ancestral hosts of *Plasmodium* malaria parasites, which then switched hosts to other mammal species, including rodents and primates.[7] When scientists analyzed DNA samples obtained from malaria parasites in humans and wild apes in Central Africa, they found that human P. *falciparum* and malaria parasites in Western Lowland Gorillas (*Gorilla gorilla*) are nearly identical. Thus the origin of P. *falciparum* in humans seems linked to these gorillas, and the human form of the disease resulted from a "single cross-species transmission event" that likely occurred several hundred thousand to millions of years ago.[8] Multiple host-switching events probably occurred during the evolution of malaria in anthropoids (monkeys, apes, and human ancestors) as early as the Eocene epoch, 56–33.9 million years ago.[9]

Most deaths from malaria are from the *falciparum* form—a staggering three thousand African children die every day.[10] Worldwide, malaria infects 214 million people per year and kills about half a million.[11] In 2016, malaria was declared the leading cause of mortality in Congo, especially for children, because many parents cannot afford the prescription medication to treat the infections.[12] The Bill and Melinda Gates Foundation has spent hundreds of millions of dollars to combat malaria worldwide, and some progress has been made,[13] but unfortunately, the disease continues to do terrible damage because of short-term human benefits at the expense of the natural world.

Based on studies from the Amazon rainforest, mining and deforestation (to make way for farming or plantations) increase suitable breeding habitat for mosquitoes, allowing mosquito-borne illnesses to thrive, making malaria much worse than it would be otherwise. Because *Anopheles* mosquitoes prefer breeding ponds outside forests that are open and exposed to the sun, malaria infections increase 8 percent for every 1 percent increase in deforestation,[14] and the mosquitoes bite human hosts a whopping 278 times more;[15] presumably, similar figures hold true for Central Africa.[16] Gold mining is present in many areas of the Albertine Rift (in fact, about 1 percent of the world's gold supply originates from Congo),[17] and the use of mercury to isolate the gold has immunocompromising toxic effects, which can exacerbate malaria infections.[18] In nearly all parts of Central Africa, bushmeat (wild animal) hunting is a major problem that often follows new road construction associated with logging operations—the unsustainable annual illegal bushmeat trade in the Congo Basin is about 1 million metric tons, the equivalent of 4 million cattle.[19] Aside from the obvious loss of mammalian biodiversity, bushmeat hunting removes the mammalian hosts of mosquitoes and forces them to turn to humans.[20]

If that is not worrying enough, the risk of devastating new diseases will increase as deforestation continues. Most emerging infectious diseases originated from human contact with wild animals (i.e., zoonotic diseases), including the Ebola and Marburg viruses, HIV/AIDS virus, Zika, Nipah virus, Lassa fever virus, SARS, avian influenza, and many others. Such human-wildlife contact is most likely to happen at forest edges, where deforestation and human encroachment combine with dense human populations, and thus forest loss and fragmentation is likely to increase the emergence of zoonotic diseases in the future. The most likely place for this scenario to occur is in Central Africa (for example, Zika was first isolated in Uganda), because of the high levels of mammalian biodiversity and biomass, especially primates closely related to humans, which are hunted, transported, and eaten in massive quantities for the bushmeat industry.[21]

As all of these examples demonstrate, altering the natural environment disrupts the ecological balance between host and parasite and can have devastating consequences for malaria transmission rates, as well as many other tropical diseases.[22] Thus, as many people in the tropical world destroy the rainforest in an attempt to make a living or better their lives, they unknowingly make it worse by opening a Pandora's box of contagion.

There was little novelty on the drive from Goma through Virunga and beyond. Gradually the landscape changed from obviously denuded lowland rainforest and croplands near Beni to an increasingly dry woodland/savanna mosaic as the road headed north and then east toward Lake Albert. By the afternoon, the sun was oppressively hot, and the roads shimmered with heat as we pulled into the dusty town of Bunia. Like many other major towns in eastern Congo during the colonial era, Bunia served as a territorial headquarters for the Ituri region, and it also contained telephone, telegraph, banking, and business resources. Many of the Belgian settlers were in the coffee business, and Bunia was a major crossroads for trade.[23] The Alliance of Democratic Forces for the Liberation of Congo (AFDL) attacked Bunia during the First Congo War, undoubtedly damaging parts of the city.[24]

As we reached the center of the city, the distinctive white trucks of the UN seemed to be everywhere, because Bunia was a convenient staging ground for supplies arriving from the nearby border with Uganda and for ongoing operations in eastern Congo and the increasingly troubled South Sudan, which would be recognized as a new country exactly two years later, in July 2011. We drove around the city for over an hour looking for supplies, food, and a place to stay, finally settling on a decent hotel with its own restaurant near a major market in the city.

I wanted to explore the Blue Mountains west of Lake Albert, which were named by the nineteenth-century British explorer Samuel Baker, who glimpsed a blue haze in the foothills north of the Ruwenzori Mountains.[25] Although the Blue Mountains still appear on many maps of eastern Congo, the montane plateau is more commonly called the Lendu Plateau after the dominant tribe in the area. During the Second Congo War, also known as Africa's World War, the Lendu were engaged in fierce fighting with the Hema, a rival tribe in the region. In 1999, thirty thousand people fled the Ituri region during one of their clashes, and the following year, Lendu militia killed 425 Hema civilians near Bunia. More tit-for-tat killings occurred as the war dragged on.[26] During our visit to Lendu in 2009, the UN had recently convinced most of the Lendu to turn in their arms, and an uneasy peace was slowly returning to the region.

As a biologist, I was interested in the Lendu Plateau because twentieth-century studies of the region's birds suggested the area might harbor some endemic species.[27] Next to nothing had been published on the herpetofauna of Lendu, and with rumors of montane forest on the plateau's highest elevations, I was eager to collect where very few biologists had ever ventured before. Given the species that were endemic to other isolated highlands of the Albertine Rift, I was convinced that I would find new species at Lendu if I could reach its isolated montane forests.

On July 5, following yet another malarial fever in Bunia, I departed with the team for the town of Djugu, and as we approached I could see several brick buildings associated with an enormous church that must have been the center of a religious mission in the colonial era. Not sure how to proceed when we reached a fork in the road, Chif hailed a tall elderly man who was chatting with friends under the shade of a large tree. Trying to figure out where to go, we asked him whether the plateau had any forest left. My spirits rose as he smiled at me and gestured to a "grande forêt" (large forest) in the mountains. Apparently at the end of the road into the mountains there was an old Italian mission at the village of Aboro, just adjacent to the forest on the plateau.

Thrilled, we thanked the man and took the fork to Aboro. As the road became increasingly rocky, we paused at Fataki, the last town on my map. A few spindly Australian eucalyptus trees towered several feet above the town's colonial-era hotel. In the distance I could see endless rolling hills covered in tall grass and dotted with large granitic boulders and shrublike Erythrina and acacia trees. A passerby pointed us in the right direction for the road to Aboro, and suddenly the gravelly road became much better. In fact, it looked like it had been constructed just recently, and relatively new wooden bridges allowed us to pass with ease over small streams that meandered down the plateau. Then I spotted a sign nailed to a tree on the side of the road that explained what I was seeing: with an influx of American taxpayer funds during the presidency of George W. Bush, USAID had rehabilitated the road only four years before in 2005.

Many people are surprised to know that Bush did more for Africa during his time in power than any other previous American president, perhaps because the American media was more focused on the Iraq War than on good news in Africa. In 2003, Bush started the President's Emergency Plan for AIDS Relief, which provided free antiretroviral drugs to nearly 2 million HIV-positive Africans. In 2008, a third of the funds for the Global Fund to Fight AIDS, Tuberculosis and Malaria came from the United States, and he pledged another $350 million to fight other tropical diseases. By the time he left office, Bush had increased aid to the African continent by 640 percent. The Bush administration was also involved in peace negotiations between warring factions in Sudan in 2005.

Even after his presidency ended, Bush continued to promote initiatives in Africa, starting an anticancer campaign in Zambia during a visit there in 2012.[28] At an African summit in Washington, DC, in 2014, Bush optimistically predicted the "beginning of the end of AIDS" as he called for more support to fight disease in Africa.[29]

Although the former president's efforts are laudable by any standard, I wondered whether the economic benefit of the new road in Lendu came at the expense of its natural environment, including the virtually unknown fauna. From my observations, very few species of African animals can make a living in Australian eucalyptus tree plantations, and as we ascended the plateau, I could see no sign of any natural forest, but the eucalyptus was everywhere. Could the new road have been used to destroy the remaining natural forests to sell the hardwood? I began to worry that the forest described by the man in Djugu would be heavily damaged, but all I could do was wait and hope that Aboro would have some natural habitat left.

The road abruptly leveled off, and we found ourselves driving through hills on Lendu's highest plateau. We reached a marketplace where scores of people were busy selling vegetables, goats, and the usual cheap imported goods from India and China. A group of teenage boys pointed us in the direction of the Catholic mission where we hoped to find the forest, and we continued onto a long-neglected road that snaked its way through tall grass. We emerged from the thick vegetation onto a hill that ended with a tall European-style church, with nearby buildings that must have served as priest quarters during missions to Africa. A quick check of my GPS unit confirmed that we had reached an elevation of 7,874 feet (2,400 m), very close to the highest point of the plateau. I let Chif wander off to look for the person in charge as my eyes surveyed the eastern slope of the plateau, which gradually tapered down to an unseen Lake Albert in the distance. There was a steep mountain to the northeast, but in the last orangish-brown rays of the setting sun, I could not see anything that looked like forest. Perhaps the other side of the mountain could be forested, or maybe there was a patch somewhere within hours of walking, but the "large forest" described by the man from Djugu was nowhere in sight.

Within an hour, Chif became great friends with the caretaker of the abandoned priest quarters, and we were allowed to move into the dusty building. I could see crumbling calendars from the late twentieth century on one of the walls, suggesting that Italian missionaries had worked there until the waning days of the Mobutu regime. Spiderwebs and a healthy insect population prompted me to pitch my tent in one of the rooms to avoid bites while I slept.

I awoke to bad news the following morning. Chif had been talking to the locals and found out that the mountain I had seen nearby, also called Aboro, contained montane forest until a few years prior to our visit. The very last remnants had been destroyed only very recently. Apparently, we were too late and would only be able to sample the fauna endemic to the grasslands of the plateau. Sorely disappointed, I brooded as Marcel handed me a modest breakfast of rice, and I prepared myself for what I thought would be a long day of searching the grasslands. But before I could finish my meal, Aristote brought me some chameleons and a dusty African House Snake (genus *Boaedon*, so-called for their common occurrence around human habitations, where they feed on mice) that someone had dug up in the soil while tilling their fields. Realizing the chameleons were a species I had never seen before, I asked Wandege and Chif to return to the spot where they were found and look for more. I had only started to set up for photographs when a bonanza of frogs, lizards, and snakes started to roll in. First it was light brown and jet-black clawed frogs, then *Amietia* river frogs, *Ptychadena* rocket frogs, *Trachylepis* skinks, *Adolfus* lizards, a second species of chameleon, slug-eating snakes, house snakes, striped grass snakes, green snakes, and another species of *Hyperolius* reed frog with a beautiful red polka-dot pattern. Within hours, I was completely immersed in work, and Aristote and I photographed all the beautiful and novel creatures for many hours.

When the initial excitement of the enormous herpetological diversity started to subside, I began to scrutinize everything carefully to see if I could identify each species. Most of them looked familiar, but the second species of chameleon caught my eye because it resembled *Kinyongia adolfifriderici*, a poorly known species described a century ago from the Ituri lowland rainforest northwest of Beni. The chameleon I held in my hand resembled the lowland form, but it was much larger, and the crest around the back of its head ended in a sharp point instead of a subtle curve like K. *adolfifriderici*. I also thought about the fact that we were at least 4,900 feet (1,500 m) higher than Ituri, and Chif told me he had found the chameleons on bushes, not in rainforest. Could it be a new species?

I had to consider the possibility that the chameleons might be a sad example of extinction lag, which is a situation where a species loses its natural habitat and manages to hang on in a substitute habitat for a little while until eventually it succumbs and disappears. No other species of *Kinyongia* chameleon was known to survive outside forest habitats, and it could be that this putatively new species had lived in the forest at Aboro until the humans destroyed it. With nowhere else to go, perhaps they were eking out an existence in the bushes as refugees doomed to extinction. But then again, if the chameleon was really a new species, who could know for sure what kind of habitat it truly preferred? The animals seemed to be healthy, and as the day wore on and more animals were found, I realized they were quite common in the area. As I photographed an exceptionally colorful and energetic individual, I knew the answers to my questions would likely take years of careful research to answer. But if they did indeed prove to be a new species, a formal scientific description would let the world know that they are here and begin the process of affording them some kind of conservation protection and official status as threatened species.

As the team found more animals and my photography sessions continued into the next day, the children of Aboro squealed with delight as I picked up the harmless snakes to photograph them. Cautiously, they crowded around me and jockeyed for position to get a glimpse of the playback feature on my camera, chattering in their strange monosyllabic Sudanese dialect.[30] Aristote, who was fluent in five languages, seemed especially perplexed by their language, which was clearly very different from anything he had heard before. "What the hell kind of language is *that*?" he wondered out loud in English. I laughed, and when I pointed at him and smiled, the Lendu children laughed too. The children had a charming quality, and their boundless energy motivated me to work until

Lendu children crowd around the author as he photographs an animal
at the base of a tree. Note the snakeproof boots that protect the leg.
Photo by Mwenebatu M. Aristote.

I had forgotten about the lingering malaria infection that was fatiguing
my body.

As Aristote wandered off to look for more animals, I sent the remaining team to investigate the summit of Mt. Aboro while I worked on the
bounty of specimens in a makeshift laboratory in my bedroom. When
I opened the shutters to allow more light in, half a dozen teenage boys
approached to watch me from their convenient vantage point. I smiled
at them, but they grew a little annoying as they chatted away loudly, no
doubt speculating at the wizardry I was doing by taking DNA samples.
I picked up a squeeze bottle of water and, pointing the hook-like tip at
a right angle, bent down to look at a frog and then squeezed, ejecting a
strong stream of water into their unsuspecting faces. At first they were
shocked, but when I started laughing, they joined in, and they even
called more friends over to watch me, because the entertainment was
now interactive.

When Chif and the rest of the team returned from the summit of Aboro in the late afternoon, they had only a handful of *Adolfus* lizards, which were also quite common around the church. When I looked at the photographs they had taken, it was clear that the montane forest that had very recently covered Aboro was now damaged forever. With the exception of a few stumps and fallen lianas that would never again cling to towering trees, there was now little indication that the mountain had ever contained any forest at all. I felt slightly ill as I looked at the mountain and realized I was bearing witness to the extinction of an untold number of species. Based on vegetation maps of a Belgian ornithologist named Vrijdagh from 1949, the Lendu Plateau did not have much forest to begin with, it was never protected, and by the time of my team's visit in 2009, all of it had been destroyed. Those forests likely harbored several endemic species, which occur in a given area and nowhere else in the world, and they surely perished when the last forests were destroyed.[31]

We stayed very busy for several more days as the surprisingly diverse herpetofauna continued to roll in, including a slate-black Egg-eating Snake (*Dasypeltis atra*). During one particularly chilly morning, I shivered on the veranda of the priest quarters as Chif warmed his hands on a cup of coffee. As I started to eat my breakfast, I noticed two men staring at us from the path leading to the church. They were tall, dressed in rags, and there was something about their suspicious and calculating stare that unnerved me. With little danger they would understand our English, I ignored them and asked Chif if he knew who they were, and he replied that he had noticed them watching us for two days.

"This man was fighting in the war, and for him, maybe it isn't over. I think this man is not right in the head. Maybe they are planning to do something bad, and we should leave soon," he said. A familiar chill of fear crept up my spine.

Chif had explained to me before that it is dangerous to linger in remote places in Congo for too long, because would-be thieves can start looking for patterns in our daily activities and plan an attack to relieve us of supplies, money, and perhaps our lives. Somehow I could sense that Chif was right and that it would be a good idea to leave as soon as possible. At dawn the next day, we packed up our things, thanked the people who had been so kind to us, and left for Bunia.

Despite our frustratingly brief visit to Lendu, we had found a new species of chameleon, documented the most northern records for several other species endemic to the Albertine Rift, and sampled DNA from some interesting species we had not encountered before. It would take months of detailed laboratory investigations after the conclusion of the expedition to fully understand what we had found, and there was a surprise in store. When one of the DNA samples from the clawed frogs was analyzed by my colleague Ben Evans, it proved to be a new species, which we (along with Chifundera and several of Ben's students) named *Xenopus lenduensis* two years later.[32] Although it was clear the montane forest of Lendu was gone, the plateau seemed to harbor a healthy herpetofauna that needed conservation protection, and our work would bring these facts to the world's attention. If we could not work in Lendu anymore, we would travel west to the lowland Ituri rainforest at Epulu, where the bounty of interesting species promised to surpass anything we had experienced before.

FROGS IN ELEPHANT FOOTPRINTS

10 Once the team had safely escaped the precarious situation at Aboro, we spent the night in Bunia, and traveled west on July 10, stopping along the way to pick up a juvenile roadkilled puff adder. As the light brown forest-savanna landscape gradually transitioned into increasingly verdant croplands, we drove for hours before reaching the village of Ngalula at dusk, just as a thunderstorm forced us to seek shelter. Eager to reach Epulu, a village in the heart of the lowland Congo Basin rainforest, we broke camp early and saw an increasing amount of forest encroaching near the roadside. The diversity of emerald-colored vegetation was stunning, and it contrasted sharply with the reddish soil of the road. Slowly I could see an increasing number of dragonflies, butterflies, other insects, and birds, a bounty of biodiversity that suggested the forest was becoming more pristine as we drove west. The morning wore on and a light rain started to fall, reminding me that the rainforest can make its own weather.

In the final leg of the expedition, I wanted to assess the amphibian and reptile diversity of the Ituri rainforest, parts of which had actually been sampled reasonably well by two US biologists, James P. Chapin and Herbert Lang, exactly a century before during the American Museum Congo Expedition (1909–1915). However, because of its isolation and the danger from tropical diseases that are more numerous in the lowland jungles, very few herpetologists had visited the region since 1915, and some of the species discovered then had never been seen again. Moreover, DNA samples were not available from the vast majority of animals in the area, and the lack of recent biodiversity surveys suggested that many new species

Men loading illegally harvested wood from adjacent rainforest onto trucks at the Ituri River crossing, Congo.

awaited discovery. Most exciting of all, the hot, steamy climate was especially promising for snakes.

As I daydreamed of spectacular discoveries, I was shocked back into reality when we reached the Ituri River. Parked along the side of the road, I could see two large semitrailers, which were being loaded with wood from the neighboring forest. Dozens of men balanced thick planks of wood on their heads as they walked from the forest to the trucks — the beautiful trees were being destroyed for cheap building materials in front of our eyes. I felt a renewed sense of urgency for my work as I realized that, just like other areas of Congo, the Ituri rainforest was in danger of disappearing before scientists like me could assess its biodiversity.

Chainsaws screeched from somewhere in the distance, and we could see a huge crowd of people and vehicles at the edge of a bridge spanning the river, but nobody was crossing it. When I walked to the river to get a closer look, I could see that one section of the colonial-era bridge had collapsed, and the Congolese solution for getting across the river looked dangerous, chaotic, time consuming, and expensive. Large wooden rafts obviously made from the planks from the forest ferried people, supplies, and vehicles over the river. Small competing gangs of teenage boys pulled ropes to move the rafts to each side, demanding payment from everyone for their labors. Nobody seemed to be in charge, some of the barges were getting dangerously close to each other, and the scene of threatening shouts, arguing, haggling, and gesticulating immediately created a splitting headache. I wondered if crocodiles might be lurking in the vegetation near the riverbanks, waiting for an unlucky passenger to fall into the river, because just after World War II, Mary Akeley remarked that the river crossing was full of crocodiles.[1] However, I realized the prevalence of automatic weapons probably kept their populations in check, and quickly dismissed the thought.

Despite the racket of human traffic, a small troop of monkeys shrieked in the forest near the river. I knew it would take a long time and a lot of money to cross the river, so I stared at the growing crowd of people massing at the bank. Every walk of life seemed to brave the muddy banks to hop into the rickety and leaking barges. Women held up their colorful kitenge sarongs to prevent the mud from soiling the cloth, men in suits tried in vain to avoid mud splatters, and barefoot waifs in rags scuttled into dugout canoes when the ferries were too full. After paying one of the barge bosses about twenty dollars, Mululema slowly drove the truck onto two large wooden planks from the riverbank and climbed onto the rickety wooden raft that would allow us to cross the Ituri. A heavily loaded Chinese minibus was pushed into place behind our truck, and after a handful of passengers scurried onto the sides of the raft around the vehicles, several men started pulling us toward the opposite bank, shouting at people on other rafts and dugout canoes to get out of the way. I sat in the passenger seat of the truck and observed the scene of complete chaos and shouting as an enormous red bus was pulled in the opposite direction toward us. My eyes met with those of the bus driver, and he stuck his tongue out at me as he honked his horn, emitting an ear-splitting blast exactly like the General Lee horn from the television show *Dukes of*

Hazzard. He laughed at me as I instinctively raised my hands to cup my ears, which continued to ring for at least an hour afterward.

As we headed west, the canopy of the jungle encroached closer to the road until the 130-foot-tall (40 m) trees towered over us like leering giants. The diversity of vegetation was astonishing, and fleeting glimpses of colorful birds darting across the road added to the sense of untamed jungle and excitement about what we might find in its hidden depths. As we neared Epulu, we passed through some small roadside villages with people who were noticeably shorter and skinnier than the Congolese people I had observed previously, and their large eyes, light complexion, and homemade liana baskets were a dead giveaway that I was looking at an ancient race of hunter-gatherers known to the world as pygmies.

The first description of pygmies can be traced back to the Sixth Dynasty of Egypt (ca. 2,300 BCE) from the tomb inscriptions of a noble named Harkhuf, who had traveled in a caravan to Nubia (modern-day southern Egypt and Sudan). Harkhuf reported to Pharaoh Pepi II that a group of small people who liked to sing and dance lived in a great forest west of the modern-day Mountains of the Moon (i.e., the Ruwenzori Mountains). The word "pygmy" is derived from the Greek *pygmē*, meaning "fist," but was also used as a unit of measure for the distance between the elbow and knuckles.[2]

The Western world dismissed pygmies as mythical tales akin to fairies until a German botanist and explorer named Georg Schweinfurth provided an authoritative account in 1874. Shortly afterward, an Italian explorer named Giovanni Miani bought two pygmies from a Mangbetu king during his explorations in Central Africa, and they were sent to scientists in Sudan, Egypt, and eventually Europe, who were curious to see whether they possessed vestigial tails and might be a missing link between humans and apes.[3] Although this might seem ridiculous now, Ota Benga, a pygmy from Congo, was brought to the United States and displayed with an orangutan in the monkey house of the Bronx Zoo in 1906. Thanks to sensational newspaper headlines and keepers who encouraged him to bare his filed, fang-like teeth as he charged the bars of his cage, thousands flocked to the zoo to gawk at him; attendance peaked at forty thousand visitors in one day.[4]

During a three-year (1886–1889), ill-fated expedition to rescue Emin Pasha, an isolated European governor in Equatoria Province in modern-day South Sudan, the famous explorer Henry Stanley skirmished with pygmies through parts of the Ituri forest not far from Epulu. The pygmies were most likely defending themselves, because Stanley and his European counterparts were starving, and they often raided native villages in search of food to steal, shooting anyone they perceived as threatening or unhelpful.[5] As with many of the local Bantu tribes, it is likely that Stanley and his companions viewed the pygmies as subhuman or even animals—one British member of the expedition actually packed a murdered pygmy's head in salt so that his London taxidermist could stuff it.[6] Stanley sensationalized the battles with pygmies, who wielded bows with poisoned arrows, in his best-selling book *In Darkest Africa* (1890), which quickly sold 150,000 copies in England and the United States and was soon translated into ten languages.[7]

For decades afterward, scientists were mainly concerned with pygmy morphology, genetics, and origins, but in the late 1920s a wildly eccentric aspiring anthropologist named Patrick Putnam embarked on an unconventional academic journey that would eventually lead to a profound and intimate understanding of pygmy culture. Handsome, tall, and thin, with flaming red hair and a matching beard, he was hard to miss, and his eccentric personality made him the center of attention among all who met him. The spoiled and selfish son of a wealthy East Coast surgeon, Patrick had been inspired by the charismatic Harvard anthropologist Earnest A. Hooton to go off to remote places and study poorly known people. After starting a master's degree in anthropology at Harvard in 1927, Hooton obtained seven thousand dollars in research funds from the Rockefeller Foundation and sent Putnam and two other men on an expedition to West Africa. A yellow fever outbreak in Senegal forced them to change their plans at the last minute, and they diverted to Congo to study pygmy blood and skull morphology. Because of a cavalier attitude about the dangers of Africa and lax personal hygiene, Patrick repeatedly got sick and was nearly gored to death during an elephant hunt. The fallout from the attack was positive, because he fell in love with his caretaker—a Mboli woman named Abanzima—who successfully nursed him back to health.[8]

Despite his quirkiness, Patrick had found his calling interacting with pygmies in Congo, and for decades he lived in the Ituri forest, only occasionally traveling back to the United States for family visits when they would not come to visit him. Over the years he learned an enormous amount about the natural history of the Ituri rainforest flora and fauna, linguistics, and pygmy culture, but he published next to nothing, and his career as an anthropologist went nowhere. As a result, he had to find clever ways of making a living in Congo. At one point he worked as a medical officer for the Belgians at a small and isolated village named Penge in the Ituri forest, but his unashamed marriages to multiple African wives, disregard for authority, and flamboyant behavior (including smoking marijuana) soon brought that to an end. In the parlance of the colonial era, he had "gone native," suggesting a touch of madness as well.[9]

Unsure what to do next and suffering badly from seven bad teeth, Patrick decided to follow an old Arab slave path through the forest to get help from a missionary dentist. As he traveled east, Patrick passed through a picturesque spot with rocky cascades near the Epulu River, where the slightly higher elevation afforded an improved climate relative to Penge. Patrick's influential family secured the requisite permission from the Belgians, and he eventually settled in Epulu with his striking American wife Mary, who did not seem to mind that he was simultaneously married to three African women, including Abanzima. She adapted to Patrick's life in Epulu perfectly, and after the Belgians built a road nearby, the couple set up a popular tourist attraction with a small zoo, facilities for visiting scientists, and a rest house for travelers. Camp Putnam, as his station at Epulu was called, attracted adventurers and scholars from all over the world, including a young Scottish student named Colin Turnbull, who later wrote The Forest People, one of the most widely read accounts of pygmy ethos.[10]

Unlike many other white men in Congo, Putnam usually treated Africans with respect and fairness, and over time he became beloved by the pygmies of Epulu, serving as judge and doctor to them for years. Patrick remarried after Mary died from influenza during a visit to the United States in 1937, but his second American wife, Emilie, did not assimilate well to life in Africa, and after divorcing her, he married Anne Eisner, a painter from New York, whom he had met on a nude beach near the family home at Martha's Vineyard. She was not prepared to meet his African wife, Mada, and the fireworks that ensued led to Anne's nickname, "Madami ya Kaleli," or "the lady who makes a lot of noise." Heartbroken and humiliated, Anne spent long periods estranged from Patrick in the pygmy camps deep in the forest and eventually became a pygmy expert herself.[11]

Patrick smoked most of his life, and after a long battle with emphysema and a stiff leg damaged by polio, both of which severely limited his mobility, Putnam died in 1953 at the age of forty-nine.[12] Following his death in the waning years of the colonial era, a hotel was built near Epulu, and the zoological gardens, which included thirty captive okapi and a group of trained elephants, continued to attract visitors.[13] But in the aftermath of independence in the early 1960s, Simba rebels poisoned the European caretaker of the zoo and ate the remaining animals.[14] The so-called Simba Rebellion lasted until 1970, and during this time many villagers in Epulu were slaughtered in the internecine fighting between the rebels and government soldiers, but the pygmies saved the lives of many of their neighbors by helping them to flee into the forest.[15] Epulu fell into disrepair, but scientific endeavors did not end for long, and Americans would again make Epulu a home and base for research.

Husband-and-wife team John and Terese Hart met while protesting the Vietnam War and birdwatching at Carleton College in Minnesota in the early 1970s. In 1973, John traveled to Zaire to study pygmies in the Ituri forest, and a year later Terese joined the Peace Corps and worked in Nyankunde, near Bunia. After returning to Minnesota a couple of years later, the couple got married and had a child, and they pursued doctorates in biology—Terese focused on botany, while John worked on mammals hunted by the Mbuti pygmies. Toward the end of the 1970s they secured funding for their doctoral dissertations' fieldwork and took up residence at Epulu with their three-year-old daughter Sarah. Kenge, a pygmy who had worked extensively with Turnbull, became indispensable for their work, and he helped them build a new house on the site where Putnam had lived. In 1982, with little break from the couple's forest research, Terese gave birth to a second daughter, Rebekah, at Epulu. Following a brief return to the United States to finish their doctoral dissertations in the mid-1980s, the Harts returned to Epulu under the auspices of their new employer, the New York Zoological Society, which eventually became the internationally recognized Wildlife Conservation Society (WCS). Over the years, the Americans continued to focus on scientific endeavors at Epulu, and during this time, a third daughter named Eleanor (nicknamed Jojo) joined the family.[16]

The Harts, sometimes accompanied by their daughters, returned to Epulu several times a year in the 1990s while the war raged in nearby parts of eastern Congo. Every time, another one of their friends or acquaintances had gone missing, and in the chaos that accompanied the war, poaching and illegal mining increased at Epulu.[17] Over time, the Harts' scientific focus shifted from ecology to conservation biology, and as the decades passed and their influence grew, they became increasingly determined to save as many of the wild areas of Congo as they could. In 2007, with their children grown and pursuing lives in the United States, John and Terese set their sights on an ambitious new goal—they would move their scientific and conservation-based operations to the TL2 Conservation Landscape (so-called for the Tshuapa, Lomami, and Lualaba Rivers that form a triangle in the region, but now known as Lomami National Park), which is mostly located northwest of Kindu in Maniema Province. The huge swath of lowland rainforest was among the most poorly explored in Congo, and it contained healthy populations of bonobos (a relative of the chimpanzee), forest elephants, Congo peafowl, and other rare and endangered species.[18] They would continue to monitor Epulu from afar, but when I arrived at the town in 2009, they had been immersed somewhere in TL2[19] for at least a year.

As we pulled into Epulu, Chifundera greeted some rangers manning a road barrier. He pointed to several small buildings near the side of the road that were used as ranger headquarters and research facilities, including fenced-in areas for captive okapi. When we reached the center of town, shadows from the late-afternoon light were rapidly transitioning from long, dark sinews in the orangish light to ephemeral grayish pools in the dusk. Hungry and with little hope of finding supplies for Marcel to cook anytime soon, we stopped at a restaurant with a festive mural of forest animals in a rock band—a chimpanzee was playing guitar, a colobus monkey was on the drums, and the lead singer seemed to be a howling leopard. A dour teenage girl with a flashlight led us to some grimy tables, and following a brief conversation, Aristote explained that the only thing they could offer was bushmeat from monkeys or antelopes. I immediately rejected that menu, and we decided to find the Hart house and look for supplies afterward. Someone pointed us in the right direction, and after a short drive along a pretty forested road with a few small buildings on the sides, we emerged into a small clearing with a prominent large house at its end. A caretaker had heard we were coming, and we negotiated a modest fee to set up our base camp in and around the house, which was within sight of the Epulu River and impressive forest.

The house was remarkable for its organization and cleanliness; several bookshelves were stocked with paperbacks, mostly in English, and the furniture was modest but comfortable. A well-constructed outhouse was just a few feet away from the house, and I could see adjacent facilities for showers and cooking. There was also a screened porch, where I imagined the Harts must have spent many hours listening to the forest while working on their research and caring for their daughters. Compared to other places I had stayed in during my Congo trips, the house might as well have been a four-star hotel.

Excited to be in the heart of Ituri, I couldn't wait to explore the nearby forest with Wandege. We started hearing *Leptopelis* treefrogs, and within minutes we tracked down one calling from a tree about 9 feet (3 m) above a stream. I was delighted to see that it was an exceptionally large and green species with cream flecks, and the underside of its legs seemed to have been dipped in golden yellow paint. It was a good omen.

I awoke in the morning to Aristote's soft knocking on the bedroom door. "Hello, my boss," he said plaintively. I groaned as my exhausted body emerged from the mosquito net to open the door, but he was bearing gifts. "Look," he said as he held up a plastic bag of bread. "Verrrrry good!" After trying a sample, I bought the whole bag for the team's breakfast, and guessed at his real motive when he mentioned that the girl selling the bread was very beautiful. "I think she can bring some more tomorrow, no problem," he said with a sly grin.

Aristote also told me that he was planning to work with local pygmies to look for animals, and within hours, they started to trickle in. They found a rugose species of forest toad that I did not recognize, a curious *Hyperolius* reed frog with a flaming orange belly, and Chifundera chased down a very rare Flat Wolf Snake (*Lycophidion laterale*) that happened to cross the road in front of him near the ranger station. In the evening after a meal of rice and beans, we decided to explore the forest edge near the Epulu River, and Mululema drove us to a spot suggested by Musa, one of our pygmy guides, who was less than 5 feet (1.5 m) tall. Aristote and I wandered into a swath of forest by ourselves, and we used our snake tongs to pull down the leaf of a plant where a treefrog sat at least 9 feet (3 m) above our heads. Something on another branch caught my eye, and I spotted a skinny snake creeping along it in search of food. When I used my snake tongs to gently pluck it from the branch, I alerted some ants on the branch too, and they swarmed onto the stick and bit my hands as I carefully restrained the snake to ascertain whether it was venomous. It turned out to be a rare and harmless Yellow Forest Snake (*Hormonotus modestus*), and I marveled at its tan body, mustard-yellow belly, and brownish, catlike eyes.

Delighted with the catch, I decided to nurse my burning ant bites in the truck while Mululema and Aristote wandered off to search for the rest of the team. I listened to the buzzing of insects and strange shrieks from nocturnal mammals as the pain from the ant venom subsided, and I turned off my headlamp to soak in the prehistoric chorus of animals. The moon was illuminating the road, and as my eyes adjusted to the darkness, I noticed a small cat prowling along the edge of the forest. At first I thought I was looking at a serval because of the spotted pattern on the stocky animal, but given its relatively small size (only slightly larger than a housecat) and the rainforest habitat, I realized I was observing the rarely seen African Golden Cat (*Caracal aurata*). The golden cat, endemic to the equatorial forest zone, is Africa's only forest-dependent cat, although it sometimes wanders into gallery forests in savannas and woodlands. Like medium-sized cats in other parts of the world, golden cats prey on small birds and mammals, but they will also go after medium-sized duiker antelope and monkeys. Little is known about their reproduction or behavior, but they seem to have a complex vocal repertoire for social interactions, and captive animals have litters of two kittens. In many parts of Africa golden cats are hunted for their skins, which are used for traditional ceremonies or good-luck charms for hunting, and as a result of this practice and deforestation, they are considered vulnerable to extinction.[20]

Aristote returned with Mululema to say that Chifundera and Wandege had found a handful of common species of frogs but would continue to look on their own and return to the house shortly. When we drove down the road to return to the Hart house, my heart stopped as I noticed a lime-green snake slowly moving across the road—a Green Bush Viper (*Atheris squamigera*)! I rushed out of the truck when Mululema hit the brakes, and I gently plucked the venomous snake off the road with my snake tongs and deposited it into a container that Aristote had placed at my feet. Rarely exceeding 2.5 feet (80 cm) in length, the Green Bush Viper actually ranges in color from orange to gray, but the most common phase is light green with yellow cross bands. Sometimes when cornered they will contort their body into C-shaped coils and rub their scales against each other in opposite directions, producing a hissing sound similar to droplets of water falling on a boiling-hot pan. Almost nothing is known about the venom, but a snakebite victim in neighboring Central African Republic did not improve with antivenom treatment and blood transfusions, and died six days later.[21]

When I returned to the Hart house, I searched the bookcases to look for an interesting read to relax. Anne Frank's *Diary of a Young Girl* caught my eye, probably because I had heard about it in high school but had never had a chance to read it. The back cover summarized her clandestine life under the noses of Nazis in the Netherlands until she was discovered and transferred to a concentration camp, where she likely suffered from malnutrition until she died of typhus along with countless other victims of the Holocaust. Spellbound, I read late into the night.

On July 15, Aristote and I spent most of the day photographing all the animals I had collected with the team the previous night. In the evening, we decided to search for animals in the forest west of town, and Musa brought along another pygmy friend named Makelele to help us. We found many more frogs, and on the return, I spotted another Flat Wolf Snake crossing the road. Immediately realizing it was harmless, I jumped out of the truck and picked it off the road with my hands. Musa screamed from the back of the truck like a teenage girl at a horror film, surely convinced I was going to die. Everyone had a good laugh about this, and Wandege took the snake from me to show Musa that he too had wizard-like powers to "charm" snakes. We ended the evening next to the river where Aristote and I had found the Yellow Forest Snake the night before. This time we saw no snakes, but I heard a very unusual buzzing sound that resembled the flapping wings of a dragonfly emanating from a reed frog. Eventually I figured out that it was *Hyperolius bolifambae*, which was originally described from Mount Cameroon. The females were especially decorative, with a yellowish cream dorsum, large patches of chocolate brown on their legs, bright white spots on a black background on their legs and belly, and bright orange fingertips and toes. It had certainly been a productive and interesting night, but unfortunately, it would take a turn for the worse.

A couple of hours after turning in for the night, I awoke from a fitful sleep. I suddenly felt very weak, my GI tract was a mess, and an excessive amount of heat seemed to be emanating from my legs. I had a fever, but somehow it did not quite feel like the attacks of malaria I had experienced before. I tossed, turned, and sweated profusely until dawn, when I got out of bed to finish *Diary of a Young Girl*. When Aristote showed up, I told him I was sick again, and he responded that there was a small clinic in town. Within hours I had the diagnosis of typhoid fever, and because of my poor nutrition and recent attacks of malaria, my immune system was too weak to fight it off. I was told to take copious amounts of ciprofloxacin antibiotics, but I thought of Anne Frank and shuddered in fear. What exactly was this infection, and could it be dangerous?

I took the medication and worked until the afternoon, when I was sure it would not be too early to call the United States to have someone google typhoid fever. It turned out that typhus and typhoid fever are often

A female Bolifamba Reed Frog (*Hyperolius bolifambae*) displaying
the striking pattern on its legs and belly.

confused, but they are actually caused by different genera of bacteria.
Typhus infections are from *Rickettsia* bacteria spread by ticks, fleas, and
lice, whereas typhoid is caused by ingestion of food contaminated with
Salmonella typhi, which is not the same species that causes common food
poisoning. But the thing that got my attention was the fatality rate—at
least 20 percent without treatment.[22] I winced and wisely decided to take
it easy for the rest of the day while my antibiotics took effect.

I did not feel much better when I awoke the next day, but by then Aristote, Wandege, and Chifundera had befriended many pygmies in Epulu,
and they caught several interesting snakes that had to be photographed
and measured to the best of my ability. My body swayed from dizziness
when I stood up to work, but I took my time, and it helped me keep my
mind off the microscopic invader ravaging my body. I ate very little, but
my fever made me thirsty, and I drank plenty of water as the droplets of
sweat incessantly tickled my skin for hours.

Following a long night of rest, I started to feel better, but a relentless
downpour discouraged the team from working, and I read for most of
the day. By the late afternoon, I was feeling restless and bored, and the

rain started to taper off—perfect conditions for frogs. I decided to join the team to look for frogs near the Epulu River, and we climbed into Mululema's truck with Musa and Makelele so that I would not have to tire myself on a long walk to the site. Shortly after entering the forest, we fanned out in search of animals, and I let out a hoot when I discovered a harmless file snake sleeping on a bush. I grabbed the purplish-gray serpent and proudly showed my catch to the rest of the team when they came running to see what I had found. Aristote commented that I was lucky, but the best find of the night was still ahead of us.

I recorded the call of some common Christy's forest treefrogs (*Leptopelis*) and Aristote grabbed a couple of White-lipped frogs (*Amnirana*) near a stream, but for the better part of an hour we found nothing. And then something caught the eye of Musa near some large depressions on the forest floor. In the rapid and excited exchange of Swahili between him and the rest of the team, I could make out one word: *tembo* (elephant). As I drew near to the place where they were hunched over, I saw Musa dipping twigs into elephant footprints that had filled with rainwater, and Wandege suddenly swiped at something wiggling at the edge of the depression. He smiled as a small grayish frog got trapped between his fingers, and he brought it over to me for a closer look. It was a *Hymenochirus*, commonly known as the Dwarf Clawed Frog. Remarkably thin and rugose (warty looking), it looked like someone had taken a normal-looking brownish frog and flattened it into an oval-shaped pancake, with two rows of orange-yellow tubercles following along the flanks of its body onto its hind legs. The frog turned out to be *Hymenochirus boettgeri*, a species described in the late nineteenth century from Ituri. Based on observations of captive specimens that have been very popular in the freshwater aquarium hobby circle for decades, the species is known for its elaborate ballet of aquatic amplexus (the mating embrace of frogs) that culminates with a series of rapid somersaults and upside-down egg laying and fertilization at the surface of the water.[23]

Along with the widespread Clawed frogs (*Xenopus*) and the West African endemic Merlin's Clawed Frog (*Pseudhymenochirus*), Dwarf Clawed Frogs are the African members of the ancient Pipidae family, which originated in the Jurassic. Back then they probably made their homes in the footprints of enormous herbivorous dinosaurs like *Brontosaurus*. The African and South American members of the Pipidae were separated from each other about 100 million years ago when the ancient supercontinent Pangaea broke up into the southern continents we recognize today, including South America and Africa.[24] The relatively primitive morphology of the frogs is highlighted by the retention of a lateral-line system in adults, which is the same string of sensory organs used by fish to detect movement and vibrations in water. In fact, the barbels that dangle off the sides of the mouth of Pipidae tadpoles have always reminded me of the "whiskers" on catfish.

Excited by the interesting find, I focused the team's attention on the other footprints, and eventually we found one more example of the *Hymenochirus* frog and a couple common Pygmy Clawed Frogs (*Xenopus pygmaeus*). Sensing that I had overdone it, I started feeling tired and dizzy, and we returned to the Hart house with our satisfying catch. As I rested my ailing body and listened to the sounds of the nearby rainforest in my bed, I wondered if the frogs we had found were dependent on elephant footprints for their survival. If that was the case, would they go extinct as the elephant population was poached to annihilation in Central Africa? There still seemed to be a healthy population of elephants around Epulu, but how long could that last? I had no definitive answers as I drifted off to sleep, and I dreamed of pink elephants in some kind of bizarre, nightmarish recollection of my childhood.

My health continued to improve in the morning, and after finishing the usual work with the animals, I accepted an invitation from Musa and Makelele to do a walking tour of Epulu. At the research headquarters, we visited two young American men who were doing short-term projects with WCS and USAID. We saw several captive okapi in nearby pens, and I marveled at their graceful strides as they wandered around their enclosures in search of the fresh leaves their pygmy caretakers brought for them daily. After we took a few photos by the Epulu River, I looked at them and noticed the loose clothes dangling over my body. I realized that the repeated attacks of malaria and now the typhoid fever had reduced

From left to right, Wandege, Musa, the author, and Makelele stand near the Epulu River. Photo by Mwenebatu M. Aristote.

me to a frail toothpick. I had been in the wilds of Congo for over two months, and it was definitely time to wrap up the work and return home for some desperately needed rest.

The journey back to Bukavu took several days of travel over brutally decrepit roads, but along the way, there was one more surprise waiting for us in Virunga. We were slowly passing along the pockmarked roads in the middle of the park when I noticed several rangers waving at us to get our attention. "Tembo!" (Elephant!), they yelled, with enthusiastic gestures to the side of the road. As quickly as I could, I switched the lens on my camera to telephoto, assuming that the herd would be relatively far away. Mululema hit the brakes, and we ran to the small ranger station to find a couple elephants browsing on small trees only 25 feet (7.6 m) away. One of them seemed to be a teenager, and it was standing in full view of everyone, completely unconcerned about the humans nearby. The adrenaline and excitement of seeing a wild elephant from close quarters made my body shake, but then one of the rangers grabbed my arm and pulled me to a small, wall-less shelter only 10 feet (3 m) away from the animal. The pachyderm flared its ears in a subtle warning that we were getting a little too close, but as I snapped off a few photos with little noise and movement, it lost interest and went right back to feeding. Cracks of branches snapping from the animals' browsing, low grumbles of communication among the herd, and the crunching noise as they ate the rough twigs and small branches were the only sounds I could hear as my heart pounded. When the elephants wandered off into the bush and we walked back to the truck, I felt almost giddy from the unexpected and intense encounter. When we were ready to continue our journey, I looked back at everyone and asked, "Did that *really* just happen?"

We were incredibly lucky to have seen the largest living terrestrial animal on the planet, and as the violent impacts of the potholes jerked my body back into reality, I wondered how long the roughly four hundred elephants of Virunga could hold out from the surrounding poachers who coveted their ivory. In the late 1940s when Mary Akeley visited Virunga, she remarked that the Belgians had estimated twenty-five thousand elephants were being killed every year in Congo (mostly with their blessing), but she still managed to photograph a herd of forty animals in the park.[25]

The most recent conservation assessment of elephants by the International Union for the Conservation of Nature in 2008 considered African elephants to be only a Vulnerable species, one step below the more worrying status of Endangered. The assessment conceded that some elephant populations were declining, especially in West Africa, but in some areas of East and South Africa with competent law enforcement, populations were actually increasing. However, there is some evidence to suggest the West African populations might be a distinct species (and if so, they would surely be classified as Endangered or even Critically Endangered), and an increasing number of sources now distinguish between distinct forest and savanna elephants species in other parts of Africa.[26] In fact, a 2016 study published in *Nature* used the genome of an extinct, 120,000-year-old European straight-tusked elephant species to demonstrate that African forest elephants are more closely related to it than they are to African savanna elephants, bolstering substantial evidence that there are two species of African elephants.[27]

But the living African elephants are on track to join their close relatives in extinction soon. Between 2002 and 2011, the effect of poaching on the Central African forest elephant was absolutely devastating—their numbers declined by 62 percent, and in Congo, the country that contained the largest numbers of forest elephants in the twentieth century (estimated at five hundred thousand in 1937), 99 percent have been wiped out. Why was Congo hit so hard? The main correlations point to absence of law enforcement, poor governance, and corruption.[28] Some sources, including a provocative animated video from Oscar-winning director Kathryn Bigelow,[29] claimed that black-market sales in ivory and other endangered species products are a major source of income for terrorists,[30] but this statistic has been challenged, at least for the African terrorist groups Boko Haram (which pledged allegiance to ISIS in 2015) and Al Shabab, the infamous Al Qaeda affiliate in Somalia.[31] However, nobody contests that Ugandan warlord Joseph Kony's Lord's Resistance Army (LRA) and Sudan's Janjaweed (responsible for the ongoing genocide in Darfur) are benefiting from illegal sales of ivory. A daring experiment by National Geographic used a fake elephant tusk with a GPS tracking device to prove that the LRA is indeed smuggling ivory north to Sudan.[32]

But who is *really* fueling the demand for this illegal ivory? Although the United States has become the second-largest market in the world for illegal wildlife products,[33] the vast majority of the world's poached ivory ends up in China, where a pair of carved chopsticks can sell for hundreds of dollars and intricately carved tusks sell for hundreds of thousands of dollars.[34] Chinese culture has coveted ivory for centuries, valuing its aesthetic, economic, social, religious, and putative medical aspects. In a recent study that examined the legal and illegal trade of ivory in China, sellers lauded ivory as an "inflation-proof" investment, and they are probably right—as the commodity becomes increasingly rare, its value will only go up in time. Another benefit to buyers is the social value, because it is a way to bestow a sense of prestige among the wealthy elite who can afford to possess beautifully carved ivory works of art. Ivory powder is used in traditional Chinese medicine, along with rhino horn and many other endangered species products with unproven medical benefits, and ivory trinkets are believed to ward off evil spirits and bring good luck. As the Chinese economy surged in the early twenty-first century, trends in the Chinese ivory auction market from 2002 to 2013 closely mirrored the slaughter of elephants in Africa. The Chinese government started enforcing wildlife laws in late 2011 and ivory auction sales plummeted, but lobbying efforts to lift the ivory auction ban are on-going, and the illegal ivory trade likely continues.[35] Some have called for a controlled legal trade, but this will not work. Widespread corruption among governmental officials who are supposed to enforce wildlife laws in Africa helps to funnel illegal ivory into potentially legal markets, and once that happens, it is nearly impossible to identify ivory from poached elephants.[36]

What is the good news? In 2015, Chinese president Xi Jinping pledged a "nearly complete" ban on ivory imports and exports, and at a meeting of the Forum on China-Africa Cooperation (Focac), his officials said they would support Africa's efforts to support wildlife.[37] At the end of 2016, China went a step further by announcing it would halt its commercial ivory trade by the end of 2017.[38] A new $200 million hydroelectric dam project is being built just outside Virunga's park boundary, at least one of eight planned power plants is operational, and by 2025 it will supply enough electricity to generate up to one hundred thousand jobs. In May 2016, Chifundera told me that there will even be enough power to supply the city of Goma. With luck, this desperately needed economic windfall will generate widespread support for conservation of the park and its wildlife, including elephants.[39]

The situation for Africa's elephants and its wildlife in general is in-deed very dire, but it is not too late to act. What we have been doing in Central African conservation up to this critical point in time is insuffi-cient, and the global community has a narrow window of opportunity to reverse course. What factor is most crucial? Multiple studies from around the world point to the same thing: law enforcement.[40] If the law is not being enforced because of corruption, lack of resources, weak gov-ernance, or other related factors, exploitation of wildlife and their habi-tats is unpunished and unstoppable.[41] Against all odds, Virunga's park rangers and wardens have managed to save the most important habitats of the park and its iconic inhabitants from certain annihilation, but their success came with a heavy price. Over 150 of Virunga's rangers have died protecting the park since 1996, and in April 2014 the park's incorruptible director (who is also a Belgian prince), Emmanuel de Merode, was ambushed and shot four times in the chest and stomach.[42] Amazingly, when I passed through Virunga's headquarters at Rumangabo at the end of an expedition in July 2014, de Merode was back at work! The future of Africa's wild places depends on the continued commitment of brave men and women like this, and we must do everything in our power to support them. However, we should not ignore the importance of financial and infrastructure benefits to people who live near national parks, because the success of conservation efforts is linked to local support. Many Congolese people who live near national parks and reserves are in desperate need of improved roads, hospitals, schools, clean water, and electricity. If wealthy nations can support more projects like Virunga's hydroelectric power plants, local people and conservation efforts will succeed, which will be a win-win for every person, plant, and animal involved. All of us should have a vested interest in seeing conservation efforts in Congo succeed, because as global climate change worsens, the world will need tropical rainforests to mitigate the damage to our planet.

THE DEATH OF ASUKULU

11 A few weeks after returning from my expedition in 2009, I received news from Chifundera that his promising protégé Asukulu M'Mema, our guide through Itombwe during two grueling ascents, was dead. As with most unpleasant events in Congo, the initial details were foggy and shrouded in intrigue. At first, the story went that Asukulu had been investigating the poaching of some gorillas in Itombwe, but the Interahamwe resented his efforts to conserve the animals they considered bushmeat, and they tied him to a tree, where they supposedly tortured and killed him to discourage similar efforts in the future. I shuddered as I considered what the militia might have done to us if things had not gone so well with Commander Kifo at Muhuzi. In 2010, Asukulu's efforts were even awarded the Abraham Prize for Nature Conservation by the World Wildlife Fund (renowned as the conservation organization with the giant panda as its icon). During a subsequent expedition while the team was working around Fizi, we bumped into Asukulu's widow and I gave her some money, because she was struggling to buy medicine for her ailing son. According to her, Asukulu was poised to become chief of his village, but the relative who was next in line decided to stab him to death so that he could claim the position for himself. Whatever the truth might have been, I decided then and there that one of the new species we had discovered through the tireless efforts of our guide should be named after him so that he would never be forgotten.

As my students and I meticulously went through the specimens that had been collected during the expeditions to Itombwe, several new species were identified, but I began to focus my attention on the *Adolfus* grass lizard that the team had first stumbled across during our return from Miki in 2008. I had immediately recognized something different about these lizards, because they were in a completely different habitat and higher elevation from *Adolfus vauereselli*, the common and widespread species we had encountered in many areas of the Albertine Rift from Itombwe all the way to the Lendu Plateau. The coloration was noticeably different too, because the Itombwe lizards had a distinctive black stripe that ran down the middle of their backs, and they lacked the latter species' copper coloration. Because I had series of specimens available for comparison in the laboratory, I was able to take detailed measurements and count scales from different areas of their bodies, and make statistical comparisons with these data. I noticed that the Itombwe population had several significant differences from *A. vauereselli*. In the twentieth century, this combined evidence would have been enough to describe the Itombwe population as a new species of *Adolfus*, but as an evolutionary geneticist in the twenty-first century, I wanted to take things a step further by analyzing DNA from all the closely related genera in the entire Equatorial African group of these lacertid lizards to bolster my hunch that I had indeed discovered a new species. When I used the DNA data to construct a phylogenetic tree, analogous to a branch-like pedigree diagram for species instead of people, I noticed that the Itombwe samples were on a distinct branch from, but closely related (i.e., sister) to, *A. vauereselli*, providing additional, powerful evidence that the Itombwe lizards were indeed a new species. But there was something else. The branch containing the new species and *A. vauereselli* was distinct from the one containing the other species in the genus, including *A. africanus*, *A. alleni*, and *A. jacksoni*. Moreover, the length of these branches was comparable to those leading to other distinct genera in the Lacertidae family, suggesting that two major lineages were currently contained within the single genus *Adolfus*. In a DNA-based phylogenetic tree, the length of the branches is determined by the number of random mutations that have accumulated in a given lineage over time; the longer the branch, the longer that lineage has been on its own independent evolutionary path. This evidence suggested that we had discovered not only a new species of *Adolfus*, but a new genus as well.

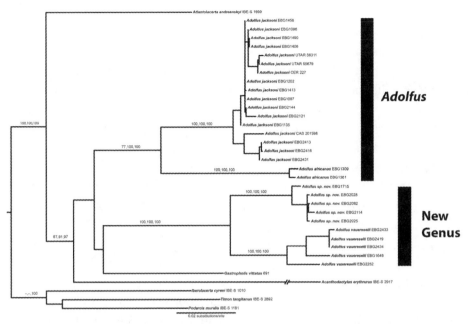

A phylogenetic tree of Equatorial African Lacertidae, showing two distinct lineages for the genus *Adolfus*, one of which includes a new species (*Adolfus* sp. nov.) from Itombwe that belongs in a new genus. Modified from Greenbaum et al. 2011, which has additional details of numerical support values.

I began to dig deeper to see if I could back up the molecular results of a new genus with morphological evidence. I reexamined photos I had taken of the animals in the wild, took X-rays of the specimens, and scoured the literature, finding a seminal paper from the late 1980s that mentioned some skeletal differences between *Adolfus vauereselli* and other species recognized in the genus at that time. It turned out that the new Itombwe species and *Adolfus vauereselli* had multiple morphological differences from the other lineage of *Adolfus* species, including a distinctive shape of the ribs and clavicle, features of the genitals in both sexes, and coloration of the belly. Once I was convinced two genera were involved, I had to determine which lineage was the bona fide *Adolfus* and which was new. The taxonomic principles of type species and priority made this easy, because whichever species had been assigned to the genus first was attributable to *Adolfus*, and in this case it turned out to be A. *africanus*.

In my taxonomic action I transferred *Adolfus vauereselli* to a new genus I named *Congolacerta* (*lacerta* is Latin for "lizard"), and the new Itombwe species was named *Congolacerta asukului*.[1]

With time and help from my students and collaborators, other specimens collected during the expeditions divulged their secrets as well. Itombwe, we found, was especially rich in numbers of unrecognized new species, probably because it served as one of the largest forest "refugia" in Central Africa by remaining ecologically stable millions of years ago during the Miocene and Pliocene, when shifts in climate caused forests in neighboring areas of the Albertine Rift and Congo Basin to retract. This long-term ecological stability likely minimized extinction, allowing ancient relicts such as *Callixalus* and *Laurentophryne* to persist, while simultaneously increasing speciation rates to allow many genera to diversify into recently evolved, endemic species that we are just now discovering.[2] Some of the new species include *Leptopelis mtoewaate* (the species name means "treefrog" in Kibembe), named from specimens collected by the team from Kiandjo and Miki in 2008.[3] The toad Aristote and I found hopping in the forest near Miki is a new species, along with the *Amietia* we found in multiple places in Itombwe. The mystery frog we found at Lake Lungwe in 2009 turned out to be an unknown color variant of *Chrysobatrachus cupreonitens*, a species last recorded in 1951 by Laurent. But Itombwe does not have a monopoly on new species—the colorful chameleon the team found on the Lendu Plateau in 2009 was described as *Kinyongia gyrolepis*,[4] and many additional new species have been identified from several other areas of the Albertine Rift and Congo Basin. I will be very busy describing all of them in the coming years. Chifundera tells me that the team's published research is supporting recent efforts to expand national parks and forest reserves in Congo, but I am absolutely sure that some of the species I am encountering will be extinct by the end of the century.

Unfortunately, the stunningly beautiful forests of Congo are disappearing much faster than research programs can unlock their secrets, and I fear that someday soon the time will come when there is nothing left to discover. If this sad day comes to pass, we will also lose something of ourselves. Given the proximity of many human ancestor fossils to Central Africa, and the presence of our closest living relatives (chimps, bonobos, and gorillas) in Congo, it is obvious that these forests are our ancestral home. The world's tropical forests, including those in Congo, serve as the "green lungs" of the planet by soaking up greenhouse gases and other pollutants from the environment, providing oxygen as the end product of photosynthesis, contributing to local and global weather patterns, and serving as a home to the majority of the planet's terrestrial biodiversity, which is linked together in a poorly understood but crucially important global ecosystem. If we allow these forests to disappear—and many of them are on track to do so within our lifetimes—the domino effects will likely threaten much, if not all, of the remaining natural space on our planet, and perhaps wipe us out in the process. The threat is not a Chicken Little exaggeration, a worst-case scenario, a far-off possibility, a hoax, or a conspiracy by scientists to scare politicians into funding more of their research. It is now our last chance to take decisive action to save what is left of the natural world. I am optimistic that it is not too late, the forests still have time to recover, and the lives of people in Congo and other developing nations can benefit immensely if the rest of the world is willing to acknowledge that our standard of living will be diminished or even destroyed without tropical forests.

As I write these words, the birds outside my window are still singing. For how long depends on us.

Starting with Charles Darwin in the nineteenth century, one of the central tenets of evolutionary biology is the concept of fitness, also known as reproductive success—individuals that escape death from natural selection (e.g., predators, disease, etc.) leave more offspring with their advantageous genes in the next generation. In the overall scheme of things, she or he who lives and reproduces the most wins. Of course this idea is relevant to human beings, even if it is occurring at the subconscious level, and there are numerous worldwide examples of men's social status and wealth being measured by the number of children they possess. In Congo, this sentiment applies to women as well. Terese Hart noted that "in Epulu, as in any Congolese village, a woman's worth is seen in the children she produces and a man has not lived until he has assured the next generation."[5]

But there is a sinister aspect to reproductive success and natural selection in Congo. Given the country's poor medical facilities and the deadly scourge of malaria and other tropical diseases on African children, several Congolese men I have met told me they had many children because "maybe not all of them would survive" to adulthood. But after multiple generations of this mentality, Africa's human population is rapidly reaching a critical threshold where the environment will no longer sustain them all, and this is already leading to unrest in Congo and its crowded neighbors in Rwanda and Burundi. Parts of eastern Congo experienced 4 percent population growth from 1950 to 1984, and by the mid-1990s it contained one of the highest human population densities in Central Africa, with over three hundred individuals per square kilometer.[6]

About two centuries ago, the world's human population had not yet reached 1 billion, and it had taken countless millennia to reach that point. At that time, a minority of the planet's humans lived in tropical regions. In 2011, the world population spiked to 7 billion, largely as a consequence of improved agricultural yields, hygienic infrastructure (i.e., water treatment and sewers), and medical care in the twentieth century.[7] Today over 80 percent of the human population lives in developing countries, including the tropics, and another billion people will join our planet in less than a decade. In sub-Saharan Africa, the human population has reached about 1 billion, and another half billion people will join them by 2025.[8] At current rates, a million people are added to the global population every four and a half days, but back-of-the-envelope calculations from Paul Ehrlich and colleagues estimated that only 2 billion people, the global population in 1930, can occupy our planet without destroying the ecosystems we all rely on, and the scientific community agrees that we are already using more resources and producing more waste than our planet can handle. It is clear that the human population growth on Earth must slow down to ensure humanity has a future, but how can this be done without violating ethics, cultural sensitivities, religion, and other related social concerns? Empowering women is key, and obviously, access to birth control is a first step. A 2011 study by the Vienna Institute of Demography suggested that if every country in the world invested heavily in girls' education, an endeavor that should be supported regardless of the population problem, there would be a billion fewer people on the planet in 2050—apparently, educated women want smaller families.[9]

Given Earth's ballooning human population, and despite the best possible outcome from conservation efforts, illegal poaching and habitat destruction will continue in many places with insurmountable challenges. And this brings me to the second major action (after habitat conservation) we must take to avoid extinction. Zoos, aquariums, and other "ex-situ" captive-breeding programs have been heavily criticized, especially in the wake of an incident at the Cincinnati Zoo in 2016, in which a boy fell into a gorilla enclosure and zoo officials made the difficult decision to kill Harambe, a young silverback, to save the boy's life. The ensuing public outrage was visceral and emotional. When discussing captive animals in general, critics point out, rightfully so in some cases, that not all zoos are accredited, people and profit often come first, and animals are kept in poor conditions that can be physically and mentally draconian. More unrealistic and controversially, some have argued for nonhuman personhood with associated legal rights, the abolition of zoos in favor of sanctuaries, and the diversion of all money associated with zoos into conservation programs instead. This assumes, of course, that big donors would prefer to fund a project in a faraway land instead of their own backyard, where their sponsorship can be prominently displayed and acknowledged by their community.[10]

I agree that poorly monitored zoos should have better oversight, and nobody likes to see animals, especially large and intelligent ones, behind bars or in small enclosures. Sanctuaries allow former zoo, circus, and abused animals to roam around in relatively large spaces, but because they generally have limited to no contact with paying visitors, long-term financial sustainability is a concern, and the number of sanctuaries is low—in the United States there are only two that accommodate elephants.[11] A common misconception is that American institutions that display live animals frequently remove them from the wild, and indeed some do take a limited number of rescue animals that can no longer survive on their own, but the majority of animals in zoos today were actually born in zoos. If we focus on the accredited, public institutions, zoos are the only opportunity for millions of people to see living examples of species that they would never see otherwise, because visits to national parks and foreign travel are not possible for many people for a variety of reasons. Partnerships with schools and educational media have improved in recent years, and zoo visitors learn about the plight of endangered species and related environmental issues, and even inspire people to seek careers that involve animals, as the Buffalo Zoo did for me. Zoos also raise tens of millions of dollars every year for an ever-increasing number of research and conservation programs of animals in the wild (known as in-situ conservation), frequently via proceeds from paying visitors, who often consider their visits to be family entertainment, recreation, and educational outings.[12] This category of the public's disposable income does not compete with independent fundraising efforts by conservation organizations, which people consider to be charitable and tax-deductible donations. Thus the argument that money spent on zoos could automatically be diverted to conservation programs in the wild is dubious.[13]

And in any case, what exactly do we mean by "the wild" in the twenty-first century? My colleague Danté Fenolio, vice president of conservation and research at the San Antonio Zoo, has spent most of the last decade working on field projects with wildlife in foreign countries. "When people say 'put everything back in the wild,' what are they talking about?" he asks.[14] The natural world has already sustained heavy damage, few areas of true wilderness remain, remote areas are still affected by human pollution (including via global climate change), populations of many animals are fragmented and isolated, and many protected areas are powerless to stop corruption, poaching, habitat damage, and other biodiversity loss. Can we really be surprised by the modestly paid park ranger who helps poachers kill an animal to obtain enough money for ten years of honest work?

For example, rhinos are getting hit hard right now — thousands have been poached over the last decade, and three of the world's five species are critically endangered, the most serious threat level before extinction. The Javan Rhinoceros (*Dicerorhinus sumatrensis*), unique for its coat of reddish brown hair, has only a couple hundred remaining individuals.[15] Chinese art and antique collectors regard rhino horn products as an investment, and this seems to be driving most of the current pressure for poaching.[16] Another factor across larger areas of Asia is the mistaken belief that rhino horn is a cure-all for everything from AIDS to cancer. Fenolio points out that it will take generations of hard work and millions of dollars in public awareness campaigns to significantly change these attitudes about wildlife. But rhinos will not last that long. Unless zoos and captive-breeding facilities are involved, Fenolio is convinced that rhinos will disappear, and given the catastrophic and ongoing rates of poaching in Africa and Asia, it is hard to argue otherwise. Equally clear is that if we are really serious about saving species from extinction, the importance of zoos will only increase with time.

Large, charismatic animals come to mind in a discussion of zoos and captive-breeding programs, but are they relevant to smaller animals like amphibians and reptiles? Ten years ago, in a widely read paper in the journal *Science*, my colleague Joseph R. Mendelson III and several other eminent herpetologists called for the formation of the Amphibian Survival Alliance (ASA), with an initial five-year budget of $400 million. The money would be focused on regional centers of disease research (mainly chytrid fungus) and captive-breeding programs,[17] which I agree are urgently needed. Another group of herpetologists pointed out the limitations of the "Noah's Ark" captive-breeding strategy. How many of the limited number of species that could be included in the captive-breeding initiative of the ASA, they asked, could survive and have a home worth returning to? Instead of focusing on captive breeding, they argued, the world should wage "an international war on environmental deterioration."[18] In response, Mendelson and colleagues clarified that captive-breeding programs are currently the only tool available to forestall extinctions in populations of amphibians that are highly susceptible to chytrid fungus infections. Control of chytrid infection in the wild is not currently possible, and while captive-breeding programs should be considered an action of last resort, it is the only hope for many species that will be wiped out without such measures. Obviously efforts to mitigate the effects of global climate change, deforestation, and other human-induced environmental changes, all of which are threats to amphibians and other animals, should not be abandoned while captive-breeding programs are under way. But even under the best-case (and sadly unrealistic) outcome of a rapid turnaround in environmental deterioration, improvements would take decades to accomplish, and meanwhile many more species of amphibians would go extinct.[19] The Amphibian Ark (AArk), a partner of the ASA, is helping to raise awareness and develop more captive-breeding programs. But when I checked the ASA website[20] in August 2016, I saw that the organization had spent only $1.6 million on various projects. If we want amphibians, an integral part of the global ecosystem, to be around in the future, we obviously have to do much better.

It turns out that with more funding, more critically endangered species of amphibians are likely to be saved with captive-breeding and reintroduction programs. Compared to birds and mammals, many (but not all) species of amphibians have multiple advantages, including multiple economic benefits because of small body size, limited space and maintenance requirements, and cost-effective programs; sexual maturity is reached quickly; fertility is high (e.g., American bullfrogs and some toads lay tens of thousands of eggs); and there is often no parental care. Many amphibians retain "hardwired" behavior and physiology from the wild after multiple generations in captivity, and remarkably, some new avenues of research are showing that amphibians can actually be trained to avoid predators while still in captivity, potentially increasing success rates of reintroductions. With more funding, many zoos, aquariums, and captive-breeding programs (including those run by the private sector) will have the capacity to expand the number of species that can be included in captive-breeding programs.[21] Although some invasive-species removal, habitat-restoration, translocation, and reintroduction programs have had mixed results to restore threatened amphibians to their native habitats for a variety of reasons, many had some degree of success, and several of these have been enormously successful.[22] Many challenges remain: not all amphibian species are amenable to captive-breeding programs, and in general, reintroduction success rates drop as the amount of time between capture and subsequent release of captive-bred animals increases. But as technology improves and we learn more about the breeding requirements for species that have never been in captivity before, success rates will likely increase with time.[23] New genetic-engineering technologies (e.g., CRISPR-Cas9) might allow scientists of the future to tweak the genomes of endangered amphibians to make them immune to chytrid fungus infections, allowing reintroductions to areas where the fungus cannot be eliminated.

Many of the attributes that make amphibians an excellent fit for conservation programs are also shared by reptiles. In a great example of a successful reptile captive-breeding and reintroduction program, we can look to the Galápagos Islands, where Charles Darwin's observations of the local fauna led to the greatest epiphany of the nineteenth century, the theory of evolution via natural selection. We now know that during Darwin's visit there were fifteen species of giant tortoises on the islands, each with a unique shell morphology, but annihilation due first to traveling whalers looking for food, and later to destructive feral goats, resulted in the eventual extinction of four of the tortoises (one lone survivor, Lonesome George, died in 2012). Eight of the remaining ones are threatened with extinction. One of these critically endangered species, the Española Giant Tortoise (*Chelonoidis hoodensis*), once numbered in the thousands. It is endemic to the island of Española, and compared to its neighbors, the tortoise is small, with a saddle-shaped shell, which in males is highest at the upward-turned flair behind the neck. By 1971, the global population had been reduced to a paltry twelve females and three males, including one precious male who was transported to the newly established breeding program at the Galápagos National Park's headquarters after a worldwide search found him at the San Diego Zoo. Under most circumstances, such a small number of breeding individuals would not be enough to bring a species back from the brink of extinction, because tiny populations like these often suffer from a loss of genetic diversity that leads to inbreeding depression, a very serious problem for the sustainability of a species. But somehow, over the course of forty years, these fifteen virile survivors produced over seventeen hundred offspring, which were reintroduced to the island. One-quarter of the tortoises living on the island in 2007 were offspring of repatriates, and this heartening number is growing.[24] The moral of this story is that it is never too late to take action to prevent extinction, and zoos and captive-breeding programs have a crucial role to play in the triage of the increasing number of critically endangered species that are being wiped out across the planet.

Unfortunately, all of these valiant efforts might be undone by the juggernaut of global climate change, which is a growing threat that could eventually wipe out the natural areas that remain in the twenty-first century. We have all heard the basic idea before — greenhouse gases such as carbon dioxide and methane that are belched out from automobiles, power plants, agriculture, cattle ranching, industry, and even deforestation accumulate in Earth's atmosphere and trap solar radiation and heat, slowly warming the planet's temperature and causing climate patterns to change. In fact, because of massive deforestation and the associated release of stored carbon, Indonesia is the third largest emitter of greenhouse gases, behind China and the United States.[25] Large climatic fluctuations have occurred many times in Earth's past, including extremes such as "snowball" Earth over half a billion years ago, and hot and dry climates in the Triassic during the first appearance of the dinosaurs, and life moved on. The reason that the current climate change scenario is so devastating is the rapidity of the change (decades now vs. millennia or more earlier) and the fact that plants and animals can no longer move through human-dominated landscapes to try to adapt to the changes. For example, the climate at the end of the last ice age warmed 5 degrees Celsius in seven thousand years, but current predictions put us on track to warm 3 degrees Celsius in a century. Most animals cannot shift their range that quickly, and as a result, many species will die out.[26] As climatic variables such as temperature and precipitation change in the twenty-first century, species must respond by moving to more suitable habitats, shifting their phenology (timing of life cycle events, including flowering, seasonal migration, etc.) or adapting their internal physiology and/or behavior to deal with the new environmental conditions. Many species that live within a narrow range of environmental conditions will not be able to adapt, and in cases where some adaptation is possible, there is a limit to how much an organism can change itself or shift to another environment or time frame. Other threats including deforestation, invasive species (e.g., Asian pythons introduced to Florida), and disease will become more destructive as the climate worsens. Consequentially, the more the climate changes, the more species will die out, with catastrophic consequences for the world's ecosystems.[27] Species that are endemic to the highest elevations of mountains, including *Congolacerta asukului*, *Chrysobatrachus*, *Callixalus*, and many others, are likely to be pushed to extinction first, because as the climate becomes warmer, they will have nowhere to go to escape warming temperatures and shifting rainfall patterns.[28]

It is difficult to predict how Central African rainforests will fare as global temperatures rise and rainfall patterns change in this century, because the region has very few meteorological stations (only three stations in Congo reported to the Global Telecommunication System in 2013), although satellite data are beginning to fill in the gaps. The Congo Basin seems to play a crucial role in water circulation to the atmosphere, which affects many drier regions of the continent.[29] A study of Central African satellite data taken since 1983 suggested that rainfall has decreased by 20 percent during the rainy season of west-central Uganda in the Albertine Rift and Congo Basin.[30]

The good news is that compared to those in the Amazon, African rainforests have experienced a more variable climate over the last ten thousand years and are thus more adaptable to future climate change.[31] Tree biomass of African rainforests seems to be increasing over time, suggesting that increased carbon dioxide levels might be "fertilizing" them.[32] This general trend was confirmed in the New World as well. A very encouraging 2016 study from the prestigious journal *Nature* suggested that regenerating secondary forests of the Amazon and other areas of the Neotropics soak up an astonishing eleven times more greenhouse gases than old-growth primary forests.[33] If this finding is extrapolated globally, it provides unprecedented hope that tropical forests will be an integral part of the solution to mitigate the impending, catastrophic effects of global climate change, if only we can establish worldwide policies to reverse deforestation. Such policies are likely to cost developed nations dearly in political capital and treasure, but if we do nothing, the projected economic devastation of trillions of dollars from runaway global climate change will eclipse the funds we invest to avert disaster now. There is no time to lose, because as global climate change with concomitant droughts worsen, tropical forests will almost certainly sustain enough damage to convert them from "carbon sinks," which soak up greenhouse gases and store them in soil and living and dead biomass, to the opposite, where they die off, burn, and become carbon sources.[34] That critical shift will signal the endgame for the planet.

If we fail to act to avert increasingly rapid global climate change, as we have for decades now, the consequences will be irreversible, economically crippling, and extremely damaging to humanity. Many of the predictions of the Fifth Assessment Report of the Intergovernmental Panel on Climate Change are not surprising given recent record-breaking headlines — cold days and nights will become less frequent and the frequency of heat waves will increase, as will heavy precipitation events, but overall precipitation amounts will decrease in the subtropics (including a southern band of the United States from Virginia to California), and areas affected by drought will expand. The oceans have already soaked up about half of the carbon dioxide from fossil fuels and deforestation that have been released into the atmosphere, and as this gas is naturally converted to carbonic acid, it increases the acidity of the oceans, which, together with warming water temperatures, is wiping out the planet's biodiverse coral reefs and contributing to sea level rise.[35] In 2016, the real estate website Zillow.com used data from the National Oceanic Atmospheric Administration to publish a report about the likely effects of six feet of sea level rise on the US home market, especially in coastal cities like Miami, New York, and Boston, and their conservative projections suggest that 2 million homes worth about a trillion dollars will be damaged or destroyed.[36] Our guilty pleasures are beginning to suffer as well. Eating shellfish is becoming a game of Russian roulette, because warming oceans are already increasing potentially deadly *Vibrio* bacterial infections in our food.[37] Most horrifying to me personally, climate change will alter the required conditions for wine making in many of the best vineyards in the world, including those in California and France, and the same thing is likely to happen to coffee.[38]

Worrying studies are being published almost daily, and many of them are challenging older models that suggested serious effects will occur decades into the future. For example, a study based on satellite data from 2016 demonstrated that low-level cloud cover over tropical areas is thinning, allowing more sunlight to warm the surface and create a positive feedback loop, which is likely to speed up the pace of global warming faster than anyone thought in the past.[39] There are likely to be global climate tipping points that we have not conceived of yet, with unknown but possibly catastrophic and irreversible consequences. Damage to the United States will be bad, but the worst effects of climate change are likely to be felt in tropical regions of the developing world, which has the fewest resources to deal with them. Africa and, surprisingly, China are the least adaptable economies to climate change, and with billions of people involved, one can easily imagine a conflagration of conflict as they compete with their neighbors for dwindling resources. Because of poor water supplies and rudimentary or nonexistent sanitation infrastructure in many areas of Africa, increased precipitation events and flooding will lead to an increase in disease.[40]

The COP21 climate conference in Paris in 2015 committed the United States to reducing its carbon dioxide emissions up to 28 percent below 2005 levels by 2025, which would have allowed the country to make the largest absolute reduction of energy-related carbon dioxide emissions of any country in the world. However, implementation of the Paris commitment will be extremely difficult given the Trump administration's withdrawal from it in 2017, and regardless, it probably would not have diverted us from the dangerous path we are on. A 2016 study modeled the most likely effects of the Paris agreement and all other major climate policy proposals from around the world that are (or were) on the table to take action by 2030, and even with optimistic assumptions, it found that the agreements will do almost nothing to stabilize the climate.[41] Because of "thermal inertia" from warming oceans and the tendency of greenhouse gases to linger in the atmosphere for many decades, and even if we were able to magically stop burning fossil fuels and halt deforestation tomorrow, the amount of greenhouse gases that have already accumulated in the atmosphere is enough to continue global climate change for many years. Many scientists from around the world, including myself, are exasperated that the issue is not being treated as an emergency by global leaders, and I fear that we will inflict a deep and lasting wound upon ourselves and future generations before appropriate and decisive action is taken. With such grim prospects ahead, what are we to do? We must certainly adopt a combination of mitigation and abatement (halting the release of greenhouse gases to the best of our ability) and adaptation (accepting the reality of some climate change and adjusting our way of life to cope) with the guidance of technology and additional research.[42]

But surely someone will think of something before we burn to a crisp, right? Geoengineering, the idea of large-scale tinkering with the Earth's climate, would be both a quick fix and our only hope if things get really bad, but the best and brightest minds behind it warn that many of the ideas for implementing it are very risky. One popular idea is to dump large amounts of iron into targeted areas of the ocean to stimulate photosynthetic phytoplankton, microscopic organisms that produce the vast majority of oxygen for the planet, to bloom in greater numbers and remove more carbon dioxide from the atmosphere. But nobody knows how changing the nutrient balance will affect the oceans and its life, especially at the scale that would be required to change the global climate. Other schemes, including a fleet of three hundred massive boats that can spray tiny saltwater particles from the ocean into clouds to brighten them, may fail or create other problems.[43] In an assessment of the science, risks, feasibility, cost effectiveness, ethics, and public acceptance of climate engineering ideas, a 2014 study panned these risky options but suggested that some geoengineering will probably be needed to accompany abatement as climate change worsens, and forest and soil management policies are the most promising way to do this.[44]

And thus, we return to the importance of reversing deforestation to save the majority of the planet's biodiversity and mitigate the effects of dangerous climate change. Obviously huge challenges lie ahead, but despite the advantage of powerful corporate interests to keep business-as-usual exploitation on track, I am optimistic that we can reverse course. Costa Rica, for example, experienced rapid deforestation in the past, and many conservation challenges remain, but its people have reaped the socioeconomic benefits of ecotourism, and as a result many of the country's forests are regenerating and the importance of biodiversity is part of the national psyche, a "win-win" that can serve as a model for other tropical countries.[45] In 2015, the Obama administration announced that it will use American intelligence agencies to combat illegal wildlife trafficking, which the president called an "international crisis."[46] Recent droughts, fires, floods, and heat waves are creating a tangible feeling among the public at large that something is indeed wrong with the climate, which is moving polls of global climate change perceptions in the right direction.[47]

As the climate continues to worsen and our dire predicament sets in, it will be tempting to blame previous generations for the problem, and indeed, many of the greenhouse gases that are lingering in the atmosphere did originate from their wasteful activities. But during much of the twentieth century, the idea of global climate change was unknown, and our ancestors can hardly be blamed for the world's scientific ignorance at that time. But we know better now, and it is certainly time to demand meaningful action from our leaders to fight humanity's common enemy. Someone *will* think of something to get us out of this mess, but the United States and other governments need to increase funding to their equivalent national science foundations immediately so that more scientists can start testing new ideas and technology by running relevant experiments now. The longer we wait to figure out how to repair the looming crisis, the more we will lose in the long run. I am confident that we will spring into action before we risk dooming ourselves, but probably not before a significant portion of the planet's biodiversity is wiped out. It is already too late for many species, and in June 2016, the Australian rodent *Melomys rubicola* became the first known mammal species to be driven to extinction by climate change when rising sea levels swamped its habitat on the tiny island of Bramble Cay.[48] Unfortunately, this species will not be the last to disappear in the coming years from climate change, and the pace of extinction will undoubtedly increase as the human population swells. This is precisely why we need to immediately and substantially increase our financial and political support for biodiversity exploration and conservation of the natural world via natural history museums, zoos and aquariums, universities, conservation organizations, and taxonomists all over the world. Such efforts should begin in Congo, because its stunningly beautiful forests are relatively intact and we have much to learn from its poorly known biodiversity. Given the developed world's historic and continued resource exploitation of the country, we owe it to the people of Congo to improve their lives while they enter a partnership with the rest of the world to achieve these noble and urgent goals.

If we rise to this challenge, future generations will surely herald our actions for centuries to come, because by then humanity will understand that we narrowly avoided oblivion when we saved much of the Earth's biodiversity in the eleventh hour. If we do not, evolution will start over from scratch, and an intelligent organism that has little resemblance to us will study our remains in the fossil record tens of millions of years from now. It will wonder, with awe, why the age of humans came to an end so abruptly.

ACKNOWLEDGMENTS

I am grateful to the people and organizations who supported my expeditions to Congo and the science that occurred when I returned, all of which is explained in this book. My benefactors included the Department of Biology at Villanova University, specifically Russell Gardner, Aaron Bauer, and Todd Jackman, who reluctantly gave me their blessing to run off to Africa when I should have been consummating my postdoctoral marriage to a DNA sequencer, which only briefly ceased to churn out gecko data during my four-week absence. That first trip was also funded by an IUCN/SSC Amphibian Specialist Group Seed Grant.

When I did not embarrass them by getting killed in some ghastly manner, Villanova funded me again the following year, this time for a ten-week expedition in the happy interim between the end of my postdoctoral work and beginning of my career as an assistant professor at the University of Texas at El Paso (UTEP). I also convinced Kurt Reed, MD, MGIS, a potential collaborator I had never met in person, to contribute finances to this trip. Using the momentum I gained from the first trip, I scored a grant from the Percy Sladen Memorial Fund, a trust fund set up by the widow of a marine biologist in England, which coincidentally funded the British Museum Expedition to the Ruwenzori Mountains almost exactly a century before my trip.[1] That early twentieth-century expedition documented several new species of vertebrates on the Ugandan side of the glacier-capped "Mountains of the Moon," whereas mine did the same on the Congolese side.

While returning from the latter trip and moving to El Paso, I learned that I would be able to combine funds from my new employer with those from the National Geographic Society, which funded my proposal to survey the stunningly beautiful Itombwe Plateau. This resulted in another ten-week expedition across eastern DRC in the summer of 2009, which was by far the most grueling trip for several reasons, not the least of which was a putative case of malaria that repeatedly stymied my efforts. This book is essentially the story of these two ten-week expeditions in

2008 and 2009. Much of the book was researched or written during downtime on subsequent expeditions to Congo, which occurred annually from 2010 to 2015.

For putting up with my wanderlust in isolated places, I am grateful to my family, who never questioned my purpose or sanity, at least in my presence, and demonstrated incredible fortitude and patience while I disappeared from all modern contact for weeks at a time. The lion's share of my gratitude goes to my wife, Wendy Rivera Greenbaum, who married me despite my penchant for running off to Africa every year. Our late dog Jolie motivated me by providing plenty of affection during countless hours of research and writing. Wendy and several other family members read early drafts of some chapters and provided excellent feedback from the nonacademic viewpoint.

Of course none of my work would have been possible without the incredible dedication, generosity, and motivation of my Congolese friends, colleagues, and collaborators. It is impossible for me to express the enormous amount of respect and gratitude I have for my fellow herpetologist Chifundera "Zacherie" Kusamba. Chief or Chif, as he is affectionately called by our team, has an incredible understanding of the history, politics, and culture of Congo's national parks and governmental institutions, and a political charisma that has allowed us to work in places where few other scientists have been able to penetrate. I owe my entire professional career in Congo to the lasting collaboration we formed in 2006, and his wisdom has certainly protected me from serious harm on several occasions. Mwenebatu M. Aristote is another indispensable member of the team. Intelligent and charismatic, Aristote lifted my spirits when the realities of Congo had stolen all my hope, he shielded me from a panoply of threats, and his loyalty is unparalleled. Wandege Mastaki Muninga is a gentle and happy soul who rarely complained during the worst of circumstances, his catlike reflexes in the jungle resulted in many rare animal captures, and he never seemed to run out of energy when everyone else (especially me) lay prostrate with exhaustion. Mululema Zigabe was an excellent driver and mechanic, and he performed several miracles on our battered Toyota to prevent us from being stranded on several occasions. Angalikiana Mulamba Marcel is a jovial grandfatherly figure who constantly managed to provide the team with nourishment and entertaining stories in the most remote places. I am also indebted to Maurice Luhumyo, John and Felix Akuku, and the late Asukulu M'Mema, who guided the team during our most difficult work in Itombwe. Baluku Bajope and Muhimanyi Manunu of the Centre de Recherche en Sciences Naturelles provided project support and permits, and we all thank the Institut Congolais pour la Conservation de la Nature for permits to work in protected areas. As of this writing, I have been extremely fortunate to have worked in Congo nine times (and Burundi and Uganda one and two times, respectively), and hope that the collaborations I have fostered can continue to flourish in the future.

As a white man working in Africa, and considering the shameful history of other white men in Africa, I fear it is impossible to convince every reader of this book that I have made every effort to be fair to the amazing Congolese people I have worked with over the years, but as imperfect as my efforts may have been, that was my goal. It is my sincere hope that my actions have improved the lives of the people (and their families) I have worked with, and that my work will be a great benefit to the country I have been privileged to know and love. Funds from my recent grant (DEB-1145459) from the US National Science Foundation (NSF) were used to obtain a dissecting microscope and other scientific materials for my African colleagues and students at their research center in Lwiro. Specimens we collected together were shared with the research and teaching collections at Lwiro, I participated in a training workshop for African park rangers, students and scientists in 2014, and we have published two dozen scientific papers together—so far. The results of these studies are helping stakeholders prioritize conservation efforts in Congo and elsewhere in Central Africa. The latter point is the biggest benefit to Congo and the world, because conservation efforts are ineffective unless the stakeholders know *which* species they are conserving and *where* the threatened and endemic species occur. Chifundera has benefited from our successful research program in other ways—the international recognition of our publications has allowed him to acquire his own grants for conservation projects, and he recently obtained a position as director of the Itombwe Forest Conservation Initiative. As a testament to our friendship and collaboration, Aristote named his first son Eli, who was born on New Year's Day in 2011 in the middle of our expedition to the mountains of Katanga. Despite these strong partnerships, I have never forgotten that I am a guest when I visit Congo, and I am grateful to the scientists, administrators, and government officials who have continuously invited me back year after year.

My thinking about the Central African fauna has benefited immensely from discussions with fellow herpetologists Ben Evans, David Blackburn, William R. Branch, Jos Kielgast, Zoltán Nagy, Danny Meirte, Michele Menegon, J. Maximilian Dehling, Alan Channing, and Kate Jackson. Kate is by far the toughest field biologist on the planet, and her book *Mean and Lowly Things* partially inspired me to write this narrative. Terese Hart, John Hart, and Julian Kerbis Peterhans provided help as my career in Congo started, and selflessly shared invaluable information about their decades of experience in the country. I would be remiss if I failed to acknowledge the time and dedication of my mentors: Larry Radford at the Buffalo Zoological Gardens, John L. Carr during my master's degree work with turtles at the University of Louisiana at Monroe, Frank Pezold (Texas A&M Corpus Christi) who invited me to Africa for the first time in 2001 and repeated the experience the following year, Christopher Raxworthy (American Museum of Natural History) who advised me during my first year of doctoral work with vipers at the University of Kansas, and Linda Trueb, William Duellman, Ed Wiley, Rafe Brown, and several graduate student colleagues, who guided me to the completion of my graduate work with microhylid frogs at the latter institution. Rafael O. de Sá (University of Richmond) provided crucial resources and time for my dissertation work as well. Many other excellent biologists, too numerous to name here, helped me along the way, or when necessary, kicked me toward the completion of difficult goals. I am also grateful to the numerous curators, collection managers, and curatorial assistants from several natural history museums in the United States, Europe, and Africa, who allowed me to examine important specimens under their care. Many of the scientific findings reported herein would not have been possible without their collaboration and assistance.

I would like to thank my colleagues at UTEP for taking the risk to hire and support me, especially Robert Kirken, Carl Lieb, Elizabeth Walsh, Bruce Cushing, and Diana Natalicio. Several other UTEP colleagues commented on parts of this book, including Arshad Khan, Sid Das, William Mackay, Art Harris, Teresa Mayfield, Charles Ambler, Brian Yothers, and Robert Gunn. Other people who have contributed comments or crucial information include Danté Fenolio (San Antonio Zoo), Joseph Mendelson III (Atlanta Zoo), David Blackburn, Edward Stanley and Greg Jongsma (University of Florida), Aaron Bauer (Villanova University), John Simmons (Museologica, Pennsylvania), Andy Plumptre (Wildlife Conservation Society, Uganda and United Kingdom), Jenny Pramuk (Woodland Park Zoo, Seattle), and my Congolese colleagues Chifundera Kusamba and Mwenebatu M. Aristote. I believe the manuscript benefited greatly from all of their input, but I alone am responsible for any errors.

My students at UTEP helped me analyze the data that allowed me to understand the evolutionary biology and taxonomy of the animals I sampled in 2008 and 2009. I thank undergraduate students Nancy Conkey, Cesar Villanueva, Cesar Barron, Delilah Castro, Rachel Romero, Federico Valdez, Waleeja Rashid, Samantha Stewart, Aaron Robbins, and Morgan Newton; master's students Katrina Dash, Christopher G. Anderson, Maria "Fernie" Medina, Thornton Larson, and J. Adan Lara; and PhD students Frank Portillo, Daniel F. Hughes, and Mark Teshera. Discussions with numerous students in my graduate-level Herpetology and Biodiversity classes informed some of the conservation issues discussed in this book.

Finally, I would like to thank Jill Marsal and Stephen Hull (and many others at the University Press of New England) for their efforts to make this book a reality.

CONGOLESE SWAHILI GLOSSARY

Note that Congolese Swahili differs in word usage and phraseology from Swahili spoken in Tanzania and others countries in East Africa. Many commonly used Swahili dictionaries are based on these East African countries.

ange: take care, watch out!
bangi: marijuana
bongo: a great liar; also a word to accuse someone of lying
habari gani: hello, how's it going?
hapana: no
jambo: hello, greetings
kadogo: tiny
kifo: death
matatizo: big problem
muzungu: white man
ndiyo: yes
pombe: potable alcohol, usually beer but sometimes
    the equivalent of Congolese moonshine
siafu: ants
sumu: poison, witchcraft
tembo: elephant

HOW CAN I HELP?

These organizations are doing great work in Congo and across the world. Your donations will make a difference.[1]

Virunga National Park, Congo: http://www.virunga.org
Terese Hart's field notes for Lomami National Park and other areas
    of conservation concern in Congo: http://www.bonoboincongo.com
The Dian Fossey Gorilla Fund International: www.gorillafund.org
Jane Goodall Institute for chimpanzees: http://www.janegoodall.org
African Wildlife Foundation: https://secure.awf.org
Wildlife Conservation Society: https://www.wcs.org
World Wildlife Fund: http://www.worldwildlife.org
Conservation International: http://www.conservation.org
Amphibian Ark: www.amphibianark.org
Amphibian Survival Alliance: http://www.amphibians.org
Stop the trade in ivory: http://www.lastdaysofivory.com
Forest Stewardship Council: https://us.fsc.org/en-us
Eastern Congo Initiative: http://www.easterncongo.org
Camfed (supporting African girls' education): www.camfed.org

NOTES

PREFACE

1. "Emerald Abyss," YouTube video, April 27, 2016, https://www.youtube.com
/channel/UCLYpN_mMfSJWbXaeE5iPQdg.

2. From a July 2, 2012, PBS *Newshour* story titled "Alan Alda's 'Flame Challenge'
Illuminates Importance of Communicating Science," www.pbs.org. In 2007, Tyson was noted as one of the hundred most influential people in the world by editors at *Time* magazine.

CHAPTER 1. NO JOY IN THE BRILLIANCE OF SUNSHINE

1. Prigogine 1973; Fry, Keith, and Urban 1988.

2. Lippens and Wille 1976; Fry, Fry, and Harris 1999; Sinclair and Ryan 2003.

3. IUCN 2017.

4. Edgerton 2002. For a different version of this legend, see Grann (2010).

5. Also known as Diego Cam, as used in Emerson 1979.

6. Edgerton 2002.

7. Conrad 1980; Hochschild 1999; Novaresio 2006.

8. Conrad 1980, 50.

9. Hochschild 1999; Flügel, Eckardt, and Cotterill 2015.

10. Novaresio 2006.

11. Edgerton 2002.

12. Hochschild 1999.

13. Emerson 1979; Vansina 1990.

14. Adler 1989; Bocage 1895; Tuckey 2006.

15. Tuckey 2006.

16. Rice 2001.

17. Edgerton 2002.

18. Chifundera pointed out to me that Babembe is the correct, plural term for this tribe, Mubembe is singular, and Kabembe or Kibembe are acceptable names for the language. Some sources refer to the tribe as Wabembe, perhaps because the prefix *wa-* in Swahili is used to make a word plural.

19. Dickerson 2006; Eddleston et al. 2010; Oldstone 2010.

20. Anonymous 1956; Rorison 2008.

21. Hallet 1967.

22. Anonymous 1956, 453.

23. Bobb 1999.

24. Rorison 2008.

25. Schaller 1964; Lambrecht 1991.

26. Tilbury 2010.

27. Pianka and Vitt 2003.

28. Edgerton 2002.

29. MacDonnell 1970; Emerson 1979.

30. Emerson 1979; Hochschild 1999.

31. Hochschild 1999, 36.

32. MacDonnell 1970, 10–11.

33. Emerson 1979; Hochschild 1999.

34. Dugard 2003.

35. Emerson 1979; Hochschild 1999; Edgerton 2002; Dugard 2003.

36. Emerson 1979; Hochschild 1999; Dugard 2003.

37. Emerson 1979; Hochschild 1999.

38. Emerson 1979; Hochschild 1999.

39. Hochschild 1999.

40. Emerson 1979, 183.

41. Edgerton 2002.

42. Reports of cannibalism among Congo's tribes continued into the twentieth century. In the 1910s, a young ornithologist named James P. Chapin was deep in the Ituri Forest of northeastern Congo as a member of the American Museum Congo Expedition (1909–1915). Chapin remarked that local Africans came from surrounding villages to stare at him, and they would wait for hours to shake his hand and stroke his arm during the greeting. Many of them remarked in Swahili, "Nyama mingi! Nyama nzuri!" Chapin was horrified when the words were translated to mean "lots of good meat." The Africans laughed and said they would not kill Chapin and his white colleague, because their meat was considered a delicacy, ostensibly because the salt in their diet made them tastier, and they would be obliged to send all of it to their chiefs (Lindsey, Green, and Bennett 1999). As in other tropical areas of the world, such as Papua New Guinea, cannibalism likely arose in Congo as a response to protein starvation (Hallet 1967; Diamond 1999). I hypothesize that cannibalism arose in Central Africa because game availability fluctuates with the seasons and rainfall in equatorial rainforests of Africa (Breuer and Breuer-Ndoundou Hockemba 2012), thus creating cycles of protein feast and famine. As for Chapin, he continued to work as an ornithologist in Congo for decades, eventually describing the spectacular Congo peafowl (*Afropavo congensis*) in 1936 (Chapin 1948). During World War II the US Office of Strategic Services, the predecessor of the CIA, recruited Chapin (codename CRISP) as a spy to sup-

port covert operations to export uranium from the Belgian Congo for the atomic bombs that were detonated in Japan. Chapin was a poor spy, and his failures provoked a nervous breakdown, but after being recalled to the United States to receive electroshock therapy, Chapin recovered and continued to work as an ornithologist for two more decades, in both Congo and the United States (Akeley 1961; American Museum of Natural History 2003; Williams 2016).

43. Hochschild 1999.
44. Hochschild 1999; Edgerton 2002.
45. Hochschild 1999.
46. Twain 1970, 72.
47. Ibid., 13.
48. Hochschild 1999.
49. Emerson 1979, 254.
50. Hochschild 1999, 250.
51. Hochschild 1999.
52. Edgerton 2002.
53. Hochschild 1999.
54. Sodhi, Brook, and Bradshaw 2007.
55. Greenbaum et al. 2013.
56. IUCN 2017.
57. Minteer et al. 2014.
58. Rocha et al. 2014.
59. Krell and Wheeler 2014.
60. Ceríaco et al. 2016.
61. Tobin 2004.
62. Greenbaum and Rasmussen 2004.
63. Caruso et al. 2014.
64. J. Gardner et al. 2011.
65. J. Simmons, pers. comm., August 2016.
66. Conniff 2016.
67. For example, see Jaeger and Cherel 2011.
68. Hykin, Bi, and McGuire 2015.
69. Greenbaum et al. 2012a.
70. Skerratt et al. 2007, 125.
71. Whittaker and Vredenburg 2011.
72. Lips 2014; Rodriguez et al. 2014; Pough et al. 2016.
73. Krajick 2006.
74. IUCN 2017.
75. J. Pramuk, pers. comm., August 2016.

76. Penner et al. 2013.

77. Doherty-Bone et al. 2013.

78. Greenbaum et al. 2008.

79. Greenbaum et al. 2015.

80. Seimon et al. 2015.

81. Wake and Vredenburg 2008.

82. Jenkins, Pimm, and Joppa 2013.

83. Moore 2014.

84. Jørgensen 2013.

85. Callaway 2016.

86. Vaidyanathan 2011.

87. Mora et al. 2011.

88. Locey and Lennon 2016.

89. Kolbert 2014, 3.

90. Ibid.

91. E. O. Wilson 2016.

92. Collins and Crump 2009; E. O. Wilson 2016.

93. Martins 2013.

94. Newbold et al. 2016.

95. E. O. Wilson 2016, 206.

96. Weisman 2013, 81.

97. Newbold et al. 2016.

98. Conniff 2016.

99. Agnarsson and Kuntner 2007.

CHAPTER 2. KING KONG OF KAHUZI VOLCANO

1. The name "gorilla" is possibly related to the West African Fulani word *gorel*, meaning "little men," or pygmies (Conniff 2011, 233).

2. Groves 2003.

3. Brokken 1997; Howgego 2008, 249–250.

4. Du Chaillu 1861, 457.

5. Du Chaillu 1861; Brokken 1997.

6. Brokken 1997; Howgego 2008, 249–250.

7. Du Chaillu 1861, 322.

8. Ibid., 487.

9. Schaller 1963; Boy and Allan 1989; Groves 2003; Van Schuylenbergh 2009.

10. Schaller 1963; Howgego 2008.

11. Groves 2003.

12. Schwarz 1927.

13. Groves 2003; Tuttle 2003.
14. J. Kirk 2010.
15. Ibid.
16. Roosevelt 1987, 67.
17. Quinn 2006, 47.
18. J. Kirk 2010.
19. Quinn 2006.
20. Mitman 1993.
21. J. Kirk 2010.
22. Quinn 2006, 27.
23. J. Kirk 2010.
24. Schaller 1963; Fossey 1983.
25. Fossey 1983.
26. Ghazoul and Sheil 2010.
27. J. Kirk 2010.
28. Fossey 1983.
29. Quinn 2006.
30. Schaller 1964.
31. Schaller 1963.
32. Ibid.
33. Ibid.
34. Schaller 1964, 104.
35. Schaller 2007.
36. Mowat 1987.
37. Ibid.
38. Ibid.
39. Ibid., 365.
40. Ibid.
41. Briggs and Booth 2006.
42. Walsh 2006, 192.
43. Nielsen 2008.
44. Thalmann et al. 2011.
45. Draper 2016.
46. Ibid.
47. M. Jenkins 2008.
48. Lovgren 2011.
49. Dranginis 2016.
50. Chifundera and Jean Claude Kyungu (see chapter 5) explained that Tshiaber-imu is one of many examples of African names transliterated incorrectly to French

by the Belgians. The correct name should be spelled Kyavirimu, which is the name in Kinande, a locally spoken dialect of Nande. He told me the name means "mountain of spirit." To avoid confusion and facilitate comparisons to historic and recent scientific literature, however, I maintain the spelling Tshiaberimu herein.

51. Hall et al. 1998.

52. C. Kusamba, pers. comm., October 2015.

53. Plumptre et al. 2015; IUCN 2017.

54. R. A. Wilson 1999.

55. Anthony et al. 2007.

56. Steinhauer-Burkart, Mühlenberg, and Slowik 1995.

57. Kasereka et al. 2006.

58. Mitani 2011.

59. Ibid.

60. Vande weghe 2004.

61. Roberts et al. 2012.

62. Steinhauer-Burkart, Mühlenberg, and Slowik 1995.

63. Iyatshi and Schuler 2005.

64. Conniff 2015.

65. Adler 2007, 156–157.

66. Roelke et al. 2011.

CHAPTER 3. THE WRONG PLACE AT THE WRONG TIME

1. Edgerton 2002.

2. Hallet 1967; Edgerton 2002; Chrétien 2003.

3. Edgerton 2002, 180–181.

4. Hepburn 1987, 119.

5. Edgerton 2002.

6. Ibid., 184.

7. Ibid.

8. Ibid., 192.

9. Years later, in the aftermath of the Nixon Watergate scandal, the US Senate held a series of hearings into abuses by the CIA. The secretive organization had worked with scientists at Fort Detrick to develop biological weapons to assassinate several unwanted people, including Lumumba (codename Stinky), whom they planned to kill with botulism (Dickerson 2006). Larry Devlin, the CIA station chief in Leopoldville, refused to carry out the poisoned-toothpaste plot, but additional US actions ensured that this would not be necessary (Webb 2009).

10. Edgerton 2002; Devlin 2007.

11. Ibid.

12. Edgerton 2002; Hochschild 1999.
13. Wrong 2002, 99.
14. Marriage 2013, 2.
15. Edgerton 2002.
16. Ibid., 218.
17. Van Reybrouck 2014.
18. Edgerton 2002; Wrong 2002.
19. Anonymous 1956.
20. Stearns 2011.
21. Mentis 1972.
22. IUCN 2017.
23. Gourevitch 1998.
24. Ibid.
25. Gourevitch 1998; Chrétien 2003; Van Reybrouck 2014.
26. Gourevitch 1998; Van Reybrouck 2014.
27. Gourevitch 1998.

CHAPTER 4. THE RATS OF MIKI
1. Anonymous 1956.
2. Burton 2010.
3. Wollaston 1908.
4. Anonymous 1956.
5. Chrétien 2003.
6. Anonymous 1956.
7. Rorison 2008.
8. See also Doumenge 1998.
9. Chrétien 2003; Lemarchand 2009; Van Reybrouck 2014.
10. Lawrence and Vandecar 2015.
11. Mongabay homepage, www.mongabay.com, accessed August 15, 2016.
12. A. Kirk 2016.
13. Mongabay homepage, www.mongabay.com, accessed August 15, 2016.
14. T. Gardner et al. 2010.
15. Vijay et al. 2016.
16. Sodhi, Brook, and Bradshaw 2007.
17. Lenzen et al. 2012.
18. Mapping the Global Footprint, www.worldmrio.com/biodivmap/, accessed August 15, 2016.
19. Deforestation Free Funds: Palm Oil, www.deforestationfreefunds.org/, accessed August 15, 2016.

20. Vijay et al. 2016; Milman 2016.

21. Plumptre et al. 2007.

22. Draper 2011.

23. Plumptre et al. 2007; Greenbaum and Kusamba 2012.

24. A. Plumptre, in litt., August 2016.

25. Malhi et al. 2013.

26. Newbold et al. 2016.

27. Moore 2014.

28. Butsic et al. 2015.

29. Laporte et al. 2007; Potapov et al. 2012.

30. Potapov et al. 2012; Hansen et al. 2013.

31. Laporte et al. 2007; Butsic et al. 2015.

32. Malhi et al. 2013.

33. Avissar, Ramos da Silva, and Werth 2006.

34. Lawrence and Vandecar 2015.

35. Sukumar 2003.

36. Ghazoul and Sheil 2010.

37. Fortey 2008, 33.

38. Bonal et al. 2016.

39. Sodhi, Brook, and Bradshaw 2007; Ghazoul and Sheil 2010.

40. Holland 2013.

41. Yang et al. 2015.

42. Pough et al. 2016.

43. Chivian and Bernstein 2008.

44. Laurance et al. 2012.

45. R. Harrison 2011.

46. Greenbaum and Kusamba 2012.

47. Kelvin S.-H. Peh of the University of Cambridge concluded, "Governments that ignore the sheer scale of corruption in their countries are ultimately devoured by it" (Peh 2013, 224).

48. Omari et al. 1999; IUCN 2017.

49. Nest 2011.

50. Wrong 2002, 315.

51. Adler 2007.

52. A scientific study that examined the evolutionary genetics of the introduced rat species *Rattus rattus* in Congo had a surprising conclusion: the genetic lineages of rats in the eastern and western parts of Congo mirror the country's tragic history with slavery. Rats in western Congo are of western European origin, whereas

those in the east are derived from "Arab" stock in the Middle East and Southeast Asia (Kaleme et al. 2011).

53. Du Chaillu 1861.

54. Schaller 1964, 86.

CHAPTER 5. A VAMPIRE IN VIRUNGA

1. Van Schuylenbergh 2009.

2. De Witte 1941.

3. Languy and de Merode 2009; Van Schuylenbergh 2009.

4. Boy and Allan 1989; Rorison 2008; Languy and de Merode 2009.

5. The Ugandan side of the Ruwenzori Massif, a former British territory, is now spelled Rwenzori to more accurately reflect the English translation of the local language. However, because the Congolese side is Francophone, most publications focused on the Congolese mountains continue to use the original spelling Ruwenzori, which I use here to avoid confusion.

6. Languy and de Merode 2009.

7. IUCN 2017.

8. Languy 2009.

9. Potapov et al. 2012.

10. Verschuren 2009; Rorison 2008.

11. De Witte 1941. This taxon is now considered to be a synonym of *Polemon christyi*, which was described from Uganda nearly four decades earlier.

12. Laurent 1972.

13. Hallet 1967.

14. Schaller 1964.

15. If you are not familiar with the nimble dance moves of this young musician, you don't know what you're missing. A video from his popular song "Waka Waka" is on YouTube: www.youtube.com/watch?v=gcy7VPAnxIk&list=PLEozUb8NNWA cgwp6khoaLI-GL4SRpBdP4, posted July 16, 2009.

16. T. Hart and J. Hart 1992; Lindsey, Green, and Bennett 1999.

17. Johnston 1923; Lindsey, Green, and Bennett 1999.

18. Burgess et al. 2004.

19. Schaller 1964.

20. Mitani 2011.

21. Crevecoeur et al. 2014.

22. Leder 2009; Eddleston et al. 2010; Andrew Thompson and Monis 2011.

23. Spawls et al. 2004.

24. Sinclair and Ryan 2003.

25. Stauffer and Smith 2004.

26. E. O. Wilson 2014.

27. Ibid.

28. Keller and Gordon 2010; Moffett 2010.

29. Duellman and Trueb 1994.

30. Spawls et al. 2004.

31. Laurent 1972.

32. See chapter 10 for a vague but much earlier account by the Egyptian noble Harkhuf.

33. Boy and Allan 1989.

34. Rice 2001.

35. Boy and Allan 1989.

36. Languy and de Merode 2009.

37. Roberts et al. 2012.

38. Boy and Allan 1989.

39. Languy and de Merode 2009.

40. Wollaston 1908, 139–140.

41. Rorison 2008.

42. White 2000.

CHAPTER 6. WANDEGE'S EYE

1. Some of these published details by Wrong (2002) are contested by Chifundera. According to him, the monument was erected to celebrate the victory of the ANC (Armée Nationale Congolaise) commanded by then Lt. General Mobutu over the Mulele rebels in 1963.

2. Wrong 2002.

3. C. Kusamba, pers. comm., February 2014.

4. Greene 1997.

5. Wüster et al. 2007; Greene 2013.

6. This story has become legend among the veteran members of my field team, and it is retold every year to the accompaniment of howls of laughter.

7. According to Chifundera, the plant is known as *katumbanyi* in the local Lega dialect, and it belongs to the family Euphorbiaceae. In collaboration with the University of Copenhagen, he is studying the antivenomous activity of the extract.

CHAPTER 7. THE MURDERER OF MUGEGEMA

1. Gourevitch 1998; Chrétien 2003; Van Reybrouck 2014.

2. Gourevitch 1998.

3. Wrong 2002; Stearns 2011; Van Reybrouck 2014.

4. Prunier 2009; Van Reybrouck 2014.

5. Umutesi 2004.

6. Stearns 2011; Van Reybrouck 2014.

7. Stearns 2011, 188.

8. Stearns 2011; Van Reybrouck 2014.

9. Van Reybrouck 2014.

10. Marriage 2013; Van Reybrouck 2014.

11. Prunier 2009.

12. Laurent 1964.

13. Greenbaum and Kusamba 2012.

14. Ghazoul and Sheil 2010.

15. Pough et al. 2016, 83.

CHAPTER 8. CONGOLIZATION

1. Guevara 2000.

2. Ibid.

3. Guevara 2011, 221.

4. Guevara 2000, 1.

5. Laurent 1952.

6. As used in Burgess et al. 2004.

7. Technically, this iconic African tree is now a misnomer, because the genus *Acacia* in Africa is now attributable to either *Vachellia* or *Senegalia* (Miller, Seigler, and Mishler 2014).

8. Anonymous 1956.

9. Spawls et al. 2004.

10. Ibid.

11. Meier and White 1995; Mallow, Ludwig, and Nilson 2003; Marais 2004.

12. Streib 2011.

13. Lloyd-Davies 2011.

14. Gettleman 2009, 2011.

15. Gettleman 2007, 2009, 2012.

16. Gettleman 2007.

17. Gettleman 2008.

18. Eriksson Baaz and Stern 2013, 39.

CHAPTER 9. THIS MAN IS NOT RIGHT IN THE HEAD

1. Conniff 2011.

2. Knox 2011.

3. Packard 2007.

4. Shah 2010.

5. Centers for Disease Control and Prevention 2015; Shah 2010.

6. Packard 2007.

7. Lutz et al. 2016.

8. Liu et al. 2010; Andreína Pacheco et al. 2011.

9. Andreína Pacheco et al. 2011.

10. Shah 2010.

11. A. Baker 2016.

12. Migiro 2016.

13. *New York Times* 2013; Sifferlin 2014.

14. Pearson 2003.

15. Vittor et al. 2006.

16. Patz et al. 2000.

17. What is the largest gold retailer in the United States? Walmart.

18. Silbergeld, Sacci, and Azad 2000; Granatstein and Young 2009.

19. Peh 2013.

20. Cunningham, Daszak, and Patel 2006.

21. Cunningham, Daszak, and Patel 2006; Sifferlin 2016.

22. Patz et al. 2000.

23. Anonymous 1956.

24. Van Reybrouck 2014.

25. Akeley 1961.

26. Prunier 2009.

27. Fishpool and Collar 2006.

28. Geldof 2008; Hughes 2013.

29. P. Baker 2014.

30. Anonymous 1956.

31. Greenbaum et al. 2012b.

32. Evans et al. 2011.

CHAPTER 10. FROGS IN ELEPHANT FOOTPRINTS

1. Akeley 1961.

2. Mark 1995.

3. Ibid.

4. Bradford and Blume 1992.

5. Liebowitz and Pearson 2005.

6. Hochschild 1999.

7. Liebowitz and Pearson 2005.

8. Mark 1995.

9. Ibid.

10. Turnbull 1968; Mark 1995; Hahn 2011.

11. Mark 1995.

12. Ibid.

13. Anonymous 1956.

14. Mark 1995.

15. J. Hart and T. Hart 1984.

16. Root 1991; T. Hart 2014.

17. T. Hart 2014.

18. Searching for Bonobo in Congo: Field Notes from Dr Terese Hart, www.bonoboincongo.com, accessed August 15, 2016.

19. When I had an opportunity to visit TL2 in 2015, I learned that efforts were well under way to upgrade the "conservation landscape" to Lomami National Park. See Terese Hart's YouTube channel for footage of elephants, leopard, Congo peafowl, bonobos, and the recently discovered lesula monkey: e.g., Terese Hart, "Lesula at Okulu," YouTube video, December 14, 2014, https://www.youtube.com/watch?v=SBG7mM3Yokw.

20. Kingdon and Hoffmann 2013; IUCN 2017.

21. Spawls et al. 2004.

22. Eddleston et al. 2010.

23. Rabb and Rabb 1963.

24. Roelants and Bossuyt 2005.

25. Akeley 1961.

26. Maisels et al. 2013; IUCN 2017.

27. Callaway 2016.

28. Maisels et al. 2013.

29. End Ivory-Funded Terrorism, December 7, 2014, www.lastdaysofivory.com.

30. Beardsley 2014.

31. McConnell 2015.

32. Christy 2015.

33. Nixon 2015.

34. Levin 2013.

35. Gao and Clark 2014.

36. Bennett 2014.

37. Huang 2016.

38. *New York Times* 2017.

39. Damon and Swails 2015.

40. Sodhi, Brook, and Bradshaw 2007; M. Harrison et al. 2015.
41. Cronin et al. 2015.
42. Howard 2014; Damon and Swails 2015; Draper 2016.

CHAPTER 11. THE DEATH OF ASUKULU
1. Greenbaum et al. 2011.
2. Greenbaum and Kusamba 2012.
3. Portillo and Greenbaum 2014.
4. Greenbaum et al. 2012b.
5. T. Hart 2014.
6. Hall et al. 1998.
7. Kunzig 2011.
8. Gibson and Raven 2013.
9. Weisman 2013.
10. Nolan 2015; Tullis 2015; Revkin 2016.
11. Tullis 2015.
12. Zimmermann et al. 2007.
13. Revkin 2016; interview with Danté Fenolio, August 23, 2016.
14. Interview with Danté Fenolio, August 23, 2016.
15. IUCN 2017.
16. Gao et al. 2016.
17. Mendelson et al. 2006b.
18. Pounds et al. 2006, 1541.
19. Mendelson et al. 2006a.
20. Amphibian Survival Alliance hompepage, www.amphibians.org, accessed August 15, 2016.
21. Griffiths and Pavajeau 2008; Tapley et al. 2015.
22. Smith and Sutherland 2014; Tapley et al. 2015.
23. Tapley et al. 2015.
24. Milinkovitch et al. 2013.
25. Information obtained from the PBS *NewsHour* for February 17, 2014, www.pbs.org.
26. Sodhi, Brook, and Bradshaw 2007.
27. Bellard et al. 2012.
28. La Sorte and Jetz 2010.
29. Malhi et al. 2013.
30. Diem et al. 2014.
31. Kinver 2012.
32. Malhi et al. 2013.

33. Poorter et al. 2016.

34. Bonal et al. 2016.

35. Mann and Kump 2015.

36. Clark 2016.

37. McKenna 2016.

38. Goodell 2010; Mann and Kump 2015.

39. Brient and Schneider 2016.

40. Mann and Kump 2015.

41. Lomborg 2016.

42. Goodell 2010.

43. Ibid.

44. Cusack et al. 2014.

45. Broadbent et al. 2012.

46. Nixon 2015.

47. Saad and Jones 2016.

48. Innis 2016.

ACKNOWLEDGMENTS
1. Wollaston 1908.

HOW CAN I HELP?
1. For a great article that explains ways to reduce your carbon footprint, see Katz and Daniel 2015.

REFERENCES

Adler, Kraig, ed. 1989. *Contributions to the History of Herpetology.* Oxford: Society for the Study of Amphibians and Reptiles.

———, ed. 2007. *Contributions to the History of Herpetology.* Vol. 2. Saint Louis: Society for the Study of Amphibians and Reptiles.

Agnarsson, Ingi, and Matjaž Kuntner. 2007. "Taxonomy in a Changing World: Seeking Solutions for a Science in Crisis." *Systematic Biology* 56 (3): 531–539.

Akeley, Mary L. J. 1961. *Congo Eden: A Comprehensive Portrayal of the Historical Background and Scientific Aspects of the Great Game Sanctuaries of the Belgian Congo with the Story of a Six Months Pilgrimage Throughout that Most Primitive Region in the Heart of the African Continent.* New York: Dodd, Mead & Company.

American Museum of Natural History. 2003. American Museum Congo Expedition 1909–1915. January. http://diglib1.amnh.org.

Andreína Pacheco, M., Fabia U. Battistuzzi, Randall E. Junge, Omar E. Cornejo, Cathy V. Williams, Irene Landau, Lydia Rabetafika, et al. 2011. "Timing the Origin of Human Malarias: The Lemur Puzzle." *BMC Evolutionary Biology* 11: 299.

Andrew Thompson, R. C., and Paul T. Monis. 2011. "Taxonomy of *Giardia* Species." In *Giardia: A Model Organism*, edited by Hugo D. Luján and Staffan Svärd, 3–15. Vienna: SpringerWienNewYork.

Anonymous. 1956. *Traveler's Guide to the Belgian Congo and the Ruanda Urundi.* 2nd ed. Brussels: Tourist Bureau for the Belgian Congo & Ruanda-Urundi.

Anthony, Nicola M., Mireille Johnson-Bawe, Kathryn Jeffery, Stephen L. Clifford, Kate A. Abernethy, Caroline E. Tutin, Sally A. Lahm, et al. 2007. "The Role of Pleistocene Refugia and Rivers in Shaping Gorilla Genetic Diversity in Central Africa." *Proceedings of the National Academy of Sciences (USA)* 104 (51): 20432–20436.

Avissar, Roni, Renato Ramos da Silva, and David Werth. 2006. "Impacts of Tropical Deforestation on Regional and Global Hydroclimatology." In *Emerging Threats to Tropical Forests*, edited by William F. Laurance and Carlos A. Peres, 67–86. Chicago: University of Chicago Press.

Baker, Aryn. 2016. "Should We Just Kill Them All?" *Time* 187 (18): 39–41.

Baker, Peter. 2014. "Bush Urges Renewed Fight against Deadly Diseases in Africa." *New York Times*, August 6, www.nytimes.com.

Beardsley, Eleanor. 2014. "France Takes a Stand, Crushing Ivory beneath the Eiffel Tower." *Weekend Edition*, NPR, February 9, www.npr.org.

Bellard, Céline, Cleo Bertelsmeier, Paul Leadley, Wilfried Thuiller, and Franck Courchamp. 2012. "Impacts of Climate Change on the Future of Biodiversity." *Ecology Letters* 15 (4): 365–377.

Bennett, Elizabeth L. 2014. "Legal Ivory Trade in a Corrupt World and Its Impact on African Elephant Populations." *Conservation Biology* 29 (1): 54–60.

Bobb, F. S. 1999. *Historical Dictionary of Democratic Republic of the Congo (Zaire).* Revised edition of Historical Dictionary of Zaire. African Historical Dictionaries, no. 76. Lanham, MD: Scarecrow.

Bocage, J. V. Barboza du. 1895. *Herpétologie d'Angola et du Congo.* Lisbonne: Impremerie Nationale.

Bonal, Damien, Benoit Burban, Clément Stahl, Fabien Wagner, and Bruno Hérault. 2016. "The Response of Tropical Rainforests to Drought—Lessons from Recent Research and Future Prospects." *Annals of Forest Science* 73 (1): 27–44.

Boy, Gordon, and Iain Allan. 1989. *Snowcaps on the Equator: The Fabled Mountains of Kenya, Tanzania, Uganda and Zaire.* London: Bodley Head.

Bradford, Phillips V., and Harvey Blume. 1992. *Ota: The Pygmy in the Zoo.* New York: St. Martin's.

Breuer, Thomas, and Mireille Breuer-Ndoundou Hockemba. 2012. "Intrasite Variation in the Ability to Detect Tropical Forest Mammals." *African Journal of Ecology* 50 (3): 335–342.

Brient, Florent, and Tapio Schneider. 2016. "Constraints on Climate Sensitivity from Space-Based Measurements of Low-Cloud Reflection." *Journal of Climate* 29: 5821–5835.

Briggs, Philip, and Janice Booth. 2006. *Bradt Travel Guide Rwanda.* 3rd ed. Guilford: Globe Pequot.

Broadbent, Eben N., Angélica M. Almeyda Zambrano, Rodolfo Dirzo, William H. Durham, Laura Driscoll, Patrick Gallagher, Rosalyn Salters, et al. 2012. "The Effect of Land Use Change and Ecotourism on Biodiversity: A Case Study of Manuel Antonio, Costa Rica, from 1985 to 2008." *Landscape Ecology* 27 (5): 731–744.

Brokken, Jan. 1997. *The Rainbird: A Central African Journey.* Translated by Sam Garrett. Melbourne: Lonely Planet.

Burgess, Neil, Jennifer D. Hales, Emma Underwood, Eric Dinerstein, David Olson, Illanga Itoua, Jan Schipper, et al. 2004. *Terrestrial Ecoregions of Africa and Madagascar: A Conservation Assessment.* Washington: World Wildlife Fund, Island Press.

Burton, Richard F. 2010. *The Lake Regions of Central Africa*. New York: Cosimo Classics.

Butsic, Van, Matthias Baumann, Anja Shortland, Sarah Walker, and Tobias Kuemmerle. 2015. "Conservation and Conflict in the Democratic Republic of Congo: The Impacts of Warfare, Mining, and Protected Areas on Deforestation." *Biological Conservation* 191: 266–273.

Callaway, Ewen. 2016. "Elephant History Rewritten by Ancient Genomes." *Nature News*, September 16, www.nature.com/news.

Caruso, Nicholas M., Michael W. Sears, Dean C. Adams, and Karen R. Lips. 2014. "Widespread Rapid Reductions in Body Size of Adult Salamanders in Response to Climate Change." *Global Change Biology* 20 (6): 1751–1759.

Centers for Disease Control and Prevention. 2015. "Malaria: Disease." CDC, www.cdc.gov, accessed October 7.

Ceríaco, Luis M. P., Eliécer E. Gutiérrez, Alain Dubois, et al. 2016. "Photography-Based Taxonomy Is Inadequate, Unnecessary, and Potentially Harmful for Biological Sciences." *Zootaxa* 4196 (3): 435–445.

Chapin, James P. 1948. "How the Congo Peacock Was Discovered." *Animal Kingdom* 51: 67–75.

Chivian, Eric, and Aaron Bernstein, ed. 2008. *Sustaining Life: How Human Health Depends on Biodiversity*. Oxford: Oxford University Press.

Chrétien, Jean-Pierre. 2003. *The Great Lakes of Africa: Two Thousand Years of History*. New York: Zone Books.

Christy, Bryan. 2015. "How Killing Elephants Finances Terror in Africa." *National Geographic*, August 12, www.nationalgeographic.com.

Clark, Patrick. 2016. "Rising Sea Levels Could Cost U.S. Homeowners Close to $1 Trillion." Bloomberg, August 2, http://www.bloomberg.com.

Collins, James P., and Martha L. Crump. 2009. *Extinction in Our Times: Global Amphibian Decline*. New York: Oxford University Press.

Conniff, Richard. 2011. *The Species Seekers: Heroes, Fools, and the Mad Pursuit of Life on Earth*. New York: W. W. Norton & Company.

———. 2015. "Out of the Shadows." *National Geographic* 228 (6): 120–139.

———. 2016. "Our Natural History, Endangered." *New York Times*, April 1, www.nytimes.com.

Conrad, Joseph. 1980. *Heart of Darkness*. Norwalk, CT: Easton.

Crevecoeur, Isabelle, Matthew M. Skinner, Shara E. Bailey, Philipp Gunz, Silvia Bortoluzzi, Alison S. Brooks, Christian Burlet, et al. 2014. "First Early Hominin from Central Africa (Ishango, Democractic Republic of Congo)." *PLoS ONE* 9: e84652.

Cronin, Drew T., Stephen Woloszynek, Wayne A. Morra, Shaya Honarvar, Joshua M. Linder, Mary Katherine Gonder, Michael P. O'Connor, et al. 2015. "Long-Term Urban Market Dynamics Reveal Increased Bushmeat Carcass Volume Despite Economic Growth and Proactive Environmental Legislation on Bioko Island, Equatorial Guinea." *PLoS ONE* 10: e0134464.

Cunningham, Andrew A., Peter Daszak, and Nikkita G. Patel. 2006. "Emerging Infectious-Disease Threats to Tropical Forest Ecosystems." In *Emerging Threats to Tropical Forests*, edited by William F. Laurance and Carlos A. Peres, 149–164. Chicago: University of Chicago Press.

Cusack, Daniela F., Jonn Axsen, Rachael Shwom, Lauren Hartzell-Nichols, Sam White, and Katherine R. M. Mackey. 2014. "An Interdisciplinary Assessment of Climate Engineering Strategies." *Frontiers in Ecology and the Environment* 12 (5): 280–287.

Damon, Arwa, and Brent Swails. 2015. "Can Clean Energy Save the Gorillas of Virunga National Park?" CNN, December 1, www.cnn.com.

Devlin, Larry. 2007. *Chief of Station, Congo: A Memoir of 1960–67*. New York: PublicAffairs.

de Witte, Gaston F. 1941. *Exploration du Parc National Albert: Mission G. F. de Witte (1933–1935): Batraciens et Reptiles*. Brussels: Institut des Parcs Nationaux du Congo Belge.

Diamond, Jared. 1999. *Guns, Germs, and Steel: The Fates of Human Societies*. New York: W. W. Norton & Company.

Dickerson, James L. 2006. *Yellow Fever: A Deadly Disease Poised to Kill Again*. Amherst, MA: Prometheus Books.

Diem, Jeremy E., Sadie J. Ryan, Joel Hartter, and Michael W. Palace. 2014. "Satellite-Based Rainfall Data Reveal a Recent Drying Trend in Central Equatorial Africa." *Climatic Change* 126 (1): 263–272.

Doherty-Bone, T. M., N. L. Gonwouo, M. Hirschfeld, T. Ohst, C. Weldon, M. Perkins, M. T. Kouete, et al. 2013. "*Batrachochytrium dendrobatidis* in Amphibians of Cameroon, including First Records for Caecilians." *Diseases of Aquatic Organisms* 102: 187–194.

Doumenge, C. 1998. "Forest Diversity, Distribution, and Dynamique in the Itombwe Mountains, South-Kivu, Congo Democratic Republic." *Mountain Research and Development* 18 (3): 249–264.

Dranginis, Holly. 2016. "The Mafia in the Park: A Charcoal Syndicate Is Threatening Virunga, Africa's Oldest National Park." Enough Project, June 20, www.enoughproject.org.

Draper, Robert. 2011. "Rift in Paradise: Africa's Albertine Rift." *National Geographic* 220 (5): 82–117.

———. 2016. "The Battle for Virunga: Saving One of the World's Most Dangerous Parks." *National Geographic* 230 (1): 56–83.

du Chaillu, Paul B. 1861. *Explorations and Adventures in Equatorial Africa; With Accounts of the Manners and Customs of the People, and of the Chase of the Gorilla, the Crocodile, Leopard, Elephant, Hippopotamus, and Other Animals.* New York: Harper & Brothers.

Duellman, William E., and Linda Trueb. 1994. *Biology of Amphibians.* Baltimore: Johns Hopkins University Press.

Dugard, Martin. 2003. *Into Africa: The Epic Adventures of Stanley & Livingstone.* New York: Broadway Books.

Eddleston, Michael, Robert Davidson, Andrew Brent, and Robert Wilkinson. 2010. *Oxford Handbook of Tropical Medicine.* 3rd ed. Oxford: Oxford University Press.

Edgerton, Robert B. 2002. *The Troubled Heart of Africa: A History of the Congo.* New York: St. Martin's.

Emerson, Barbara. 1979. *Leopold II of the Belgians: King of Colonialism.* New York: St. Martin's.

Eriksson Baaz, Maria, and Maria Stern. 2013. *Sexual Violence as a Weapon of War? Perceptions, Prescriptions, Problems in the Congo and Beyond.* London: Zed Books.

Evans, Ben J., Eli Greenbaum, Chifundera Kusamba, Timothy F. Carter, Martha L. Tobias, Simone A. Mendel, and Darcy B. Kelley. 2011. "Description of a New Octoploid Frog Species (Anura: Pipidae: *Xenopus*) from the Democratic Republic of the Congo, with a Discussion of the Biogeography of African Clawed Frogs in the Albertine Rift." *Journal of Zoology, London* 283: 276–290.

Fishpool, L. D. C., and N. J. Collar. 2006. "The Taxonomic and Conservation Status of Chapin's Crombec *Sylvietta (leucophrys) chapini.*" *Bulletin of the African Bird Club* 13 (1): 17–22.

Flügel, Tyrel J., Frank D. Eckardt, and Fenton P. D. Cotterill. 2015. "The Present Day Drainage Patterns of the Congo River System and Their Neogene Evolution." In *Geology and Resource Potential of the Congo Basin,* edited by Maarten J. de Wit, François Guillocheau, and Michiel C. J. de Wit, 315–337. Regional Geology Reviews. Berlin: Springer-Verlag.

Fortey, Richard. 2008. *Dry Storeroom No. 1: The Secret Life of the Natural History Museum.* New York: Vintage.

Fossey, Dian. 1983. *Gorillas in the Mist.* Boston: Houghton Mifflin.

Fry, C. H., Kathie Fry, and Alan Harris. 1999. *Kingfishers Bee-Eaters and Rollers: A Handbook.* London: Christopher Helm.

Fry, C. H., Stuart Keith, and Emil K. Urban. 1988. *The Birds of Africa.* Vol. 3. San Diego: Academic Press.

Gao, Yufang, and Susan G. Clark. 2014. "Elephant Ivory Trade in China: Trends and Drivers." *Biological Conservation* 180: 23–30.

Gao, Yufang, Kelly J. Stoner, Andy T. L. Lee, and Susan G. Clark. 2016. "Rhino Horn Trade in China: An Analysis of the Art and Antiques Market." *Biological Conservation* 201: 343–347.

Gardner, Janet L., Anne Peters, Michael R. Kearney, Leo Joseph, and Robert Heinsohn. 2011. "Declining Body Size: A Third Universal Response to Warming?" *Trends in Ecology and Evolution* 26 (6): 285–291.

Gardner, Toby A., Jos Barlow, Navjot S. Sodhi, and Carlos A. Peres. 2010. "A Multi-Region Assessment of Tropical Forest Biodiversity in a Human-Modified World." *Biological Conservation* 143: 2293–2300.

Geldof, Bob. 2008. "Geldof and Bush: Diary from the Road." *Time*, February 28, http://content.time.com.

Gettleman, Jeffrey. 2007. "Rape Epidemic Raises Trauma of Congo War." *New York Times*, October 7, www.nytimes.com.

———. 2008. "Rape Victims' Words Help Jolt Congo Into Change." *New York Times*, October 17, www.nytimes.com.

———. 2009. "Symbol of Unhealed Congo: Male Rape Victims." *New York Times*, August 4, www.nytimes.com.

———. 2011. "Congo Study Sets Estimate for Rapes Much Higher." *New York Times*, May 11, www.nytimes.com.

———. 2012. "The World's Worst War." *New York Times*, December 15, www.nytimes.com.

Ghazoul, Jaboury, and Douglas Sheil. 2010. *Tropical Rain Forest Ecology, Diversity, and Conservation*. Oxford: Oxford University Press.

Gibson, Luke, and Peter H. Raven. 2013. "Introduction: Giving a Voice to the Tropics." In *Conservation Biology: Voices from the Tropics*, edited by Navjot S. Sodhi, Luke Gibson, and Peter H. Raven, 1–3. West Sussex: Wiley Blackwell.

Goodell, Jeff. 2010. *How to Cool the Planet: Geoengineering and the Audacious Quest to Fix Earth's Climate*. Boston: Houghton Mifflin Harcourt.

Gourevitch, Philip. 1998. *We Wish to Inform You That Tomorrow We Will Be Killed with Our Families: Stories from Rwanda*. New York: Picador; Farrar, Straus and Giroux.

Granatstein, Solly, and Nicole Young (Producers). 2009. "Congo's Gold." CBS News, November 29, www.cbsnews.com.

Grann, David. 2010. *The Lost City of Z: A Tale of Deadly Obsession in the Amazon*. New York: Vintage Departures.

Greenbaum, Eli, and Chifundera Kusamba. 2012. "Conservation Implications Following the Rediscovery of Four Frog Species from the Itombwe Natural

Reserve, Eastern Democratic Republic of the Congo." *Herpetological Review* 43 (2): 253–259.

Greenbaum, Eli, Chifundera Kusamba, Mwenebatu Aristote, and Kurt D. Reed. 2008. "Amphibian Chytrid Fungus Infections in *Hyperolius* (Anura: Hyperoliidae) from Eastern Democratic Republic of Congo." *Herpetological Review* 39 (1): 70–73.

Greenbaum, Eli, Jennifer Meece, Kurt Reed, and Chifundera Kusamba. 2015. "Extensive Occurrence of the Amphibian Chytrid Fungus in the Albertine Rift, a Central African Amphibian Hotspot." *Herpetological Journal* 25: 91–100.

Greenbaum, Eli, and Jens B. Rasmussen. 2004. *"Chalcides thierryi pulchellus* (Cylindrical skink): Attempted Predation." *Herpetological Review* 35 (2): 166–167.

Greenbaum, Eli, Ulrich Sinsch, Edgar Lehr, Federico Valdez, and Chifundera Kusamba. 2013. "Phylogeography of the Reed Frog *Hyperolius castaneus* (Anura: Hyperoliidae) from the Albertine Rift of Central Africa: Implications for Taxonomy, Biogeography and Conservation." *Zootaxa* 3731 (4): 473–494.

Greenbaum, Eli, Edward L. Stanley, Chifundera Kusamba, Wandege M. Moninga [sic], Stephen R. Goldberg, and Charles R. Bursey. 2012a. "A New Species of *Cordylus* (Squamata: Cordylidae) from the Marungu Plateau of South-Eastern Democratic Republic of the Congo." *African Journal of Herpetology* 61 (1): 14–39.

Greenbaum, Eli, Krystal A. Tolley, Abdulmeneem Joma, and Chifundera Kusamba. 2012b. "A New Species of Chameleon (Sauria: Chamaeleonidae: *Kinyongia*) from the Northern Albertine Rift, Central Africa." *Herpetologica* 68 (1): 60–75.

Greenbaum, Eli, Cesar O. Villanueva, Chifundera Kusamba, Mwenebatu M. Aristote, and William R. Branch. 2011. "A Molecular Phylogeny of Equatorial African Lacertidae, with the Description of a New Genus and Species from Eastern Democratic Republic of the Congo." *Zoological Journal of the Linnean Society* 163: 913–942.

Greene, Harry W. 1997. *Snakes: The Evolution of Mystery in Nature.* Berkeley: University of California Press.

Greene, Harry W. 2013. *Tracks and Shadows: Field Biology as Art.* Berkeley: University of California Press.

Griffiths, Richard A., and Lissette Pavajeau. 2008. "Captive Breeding, Reintroduction, and the Conservation of Amphibians." *Conservation Biology* 22 (4): 852–861.

Groves, Colin P. 2003. "A History of Gorilla Taxonomy." In *Gorilla Biology: A Multidisciplinary Perspective,* edited by Andrew B. Taylor and Michelle L. Goldsmith, 15–34. Cambridge: Cambridge University Press.

Guevara, Ernesto C. 2000. *The African Dream: The Diaries of the Revolutionary War in the Congo*. New York: Grove.

──────. 2011. *Congo Diary: Episodes of the Revolutionary War in the Congo*. Melbourne: Ocean Press.

Hahn, Emily. 2011. *Congo Solo: Misadventures Two Degrees North*. Edited and with an introduction by Ken Cuthbertson. Montreal: McGill-Queen's University Press.

Hall, Jefferson S., Kristin Saltonstall, Bila-Isia Inogwabini, and Ilambu Omari. 1998. "Distribution, Abundance and Conservation of Grauer's Gorilla." *Oryx* 32 (2): 122–130.

Hallet, Jean-Pierre. 1967. *Congo Kitabu*. Greenwich, CT: Fawcett.

Hansen, M. C., P. V. Potapov, R. Moore, M. Hancher, S. A. Turubanova, A. Tyukavina, D. Thau, et al. 2013. "High-Resolution Global Maps of 21st-Century Forest Cover Change." *Science (Washington)* 342 (6160): 850–853.

Harrison, Mariel, Julia Baker, Medard Twinamatsiko, and E. J. Milner-Gulland. 2015. "Profiling Unauthorized Natural Resource Users for Better Targeting of Conservation Interventions." *Conservation Biology* 29 (6): 1636–1646.

Harrison, Rhett D. 2011. "Emptying the Forest: Hunting and the Extirpation of Wildlife from Tropical Nature Reserves." *BioScience* 61 (11): 919–924.

Hart, John A., and Terese B. Hart. 1984. "The Mbuti of Zaire." *Cultural Survival Quarterly* 8: 18–20.

Hart, Terese B. 2014. "Ituri Story." *Searching for Bonobo in Congo: Field Notes from Dr Terese Hart* (blog), June 14, www.bonoboincongo.com.

Hart, Terese B., and John A. Hart. 1992. "Between Sun and Shadow." *Natural History* 101: 28–35.

Hepburn, Katharine. 1987. *The Making of The African Queen or How I Went to Africa with Bogart, Bacall and Huston and Almost Lost My Mind*. New York: Alfred A. Knopf.

Hochschild, Adam. 1999. *King Leopold's Ghost: A Story of Greed, Terror, and Heroism in Colonial Africa*. New York: Houghton Mifflin.

Holland, Jennifer S. 2013. "The Bite That Heals." *National Geographic* 223 (2): 64–83.

Howard, Brian C. 2014. "Chief Warden Shot in Africa's Oldest National Park." *National Geographic*, April 17, http://news.nationalgeographic.com.

Howgego, Raymond J. 2008. *Encyclopedia of Exploration 1850 to 1940: Continental Exploration*. Potts Point, Australia: Hordern House.

Huang, Shaojie. 2016. "Q. and A.: Patrick Bergin on China's Role in Protecting Africa's Wildlife." *New York Times*, May 17, www.nytimes.com.

Hughes, Dana. 2013. "George W. Bush's Legacy on Africa Wins Praise, Even from Foes." ABC News, April 26, www.abcnews.go.com.

Hykin, Sarah M., Ke Bi, and Jimmy A. McGuire. 2015. "Fixing Formalin: A Method to Recover Genomic-Scale DNA Sequence Data from Formalin-Fixed Museum Specimens Using High-Throughput Sequencing." *PLoS ONE* 10: e0141579.

Innis, Michelle. 2016. "Australian Rodent Is First Mammal Made Extinct by Human-Driven Climate Change, Scientists Say." *New York Times*, June 14, www.nytimes.com.

IUCN. 2017. "The IUCN Red List of Threatened Species." Version 2016-3. IUCN Red List, www.iucnredlist.org, accessed February 4.

Iyatshi, Bernard I., and Carlos Schuler. 2005. "News from Kahuzi-Biega: May–October 2005." *Gorilla Journal* (31): 3–4.

Jaeger, Audrey, and Yves Cherel. 2011. "Isotopic Investigation of Contemporary and Historic Changes in Penguin Trophic Niches and Carrying Capacity of the Southern Indian Ocean." *PLoS ONE* 6: e16484.

Jenkins, Clinton N., Stuart L. Pimm, and Lucas N. Joppa. 2013. "Global Patterns of Terrestrial Vertebrate Diversity and Conservation." *Proceedings of the National Academy of Sciences (USA)* 110 (28): E2602–E2610.

Jenkins, Mark. 2008. "Who Murdered the Virunga Gorillas?" *National Geographic* 214 (1): 34–65.

Johnston, Harry H. 1923. *The Story of My Life*. Garden City, NJ: Garden City Publishing.

Jørgensen, Dolly. 2013. "Reintroduction and De-extinction." *Bioscience* 63 (9): 719–720.

Kaleme, P. K., J. M. Bates, H. K. Belesi, R. C. K. Bowie, M. Gambalemoke, J. Kerbis-Peterhans, J. Michaux, J. M. Mwanga, B. R. Ndara, P. J. Taylor, and B. Jansen van Vuuren. 2011. "Origin and Putative Colonization Routes for Invasive Rodent Taxa in the Democratic Republic of Congo." *African Zoology* 46: 133–145.

Kasereka, Bishikwabo, Jean-Berckmans B. Muhigwa, Chantal Shalukoma, and John M. Kahekwa. 2006. "Vulnerability of Habituated Grauer's Gorilla to Poaching in the Kahuzi-Biega National Park, DRC." *African Study Monographs* 27 (1): 15–26.

Katz, Josh, and Jennifer Daniel. 2015. "What You Can Do about Climate Change." *New York Times*, December 2, www.nytimes.com.

Keller, Laurent, and Elisabeth Gordon. 2010. *The Lives of Ants*. New York: Oxford University Press.

Kingdon, Jonathan, and Michael Hoffmann, eds. 2013. *Mammals of Africa*, vol. 5: *Carnivores, Pangolins, Equids and Rhioceroses*. London: Bloomsbury.

Kinver, Mark. 2012. "Africa's Rainforests 'More Resilient' to Climate Change." *BBC News*, January 6, www.bbc.com.

Kirk, Ashley. 2016. "Deforestation: Where Is the World Losing the Most Trees?" *The Telegraph*, March 23, www.telegraph.co.uk.

Kirk, Jay. 2010. *Kingdom under Glass: A Tale of Obsession, Adventure, and One Man's Quest to Preserve the World's Great Animals*. New York: Henry Holt and Company.

Knox, Richard. 2011. "Military Medicine's Long War against Malaria." *All Things Considered*, NPR, September 1, www.npr.org.

Kolbert, Elizabeth. 2014. *The Sixth Extinction: An Unnatural History*. New York: Picador.

Krajick, Kevin. 2006. "NewsFocus: The Lost World of the Kihansi Toad." *Science (Washington)* 311 (5765): 1230–1232.

Krell, Frank-T., and Quentin D. Wheeler. 2014. "Specimen Collection: Plan for the Future." *Science (Washington)* 344 (6186): 815–816.

Kunzig, Robert. 2011. "Population 7 Billion." *National Geographic* 219 (1): 32–63.

Lambrecht, Frank L. 1991. *In the Shade of an Acacia Tree: Memoirs of a Health Officer in Africa, 1945–1959*. Vol. 194. Philadelphia: Memoirs of the American Philosophical Society.

Languy, Marc. 2009. "Dynamics of the Large Mammal Populations." In *Virunga: The Survival of Africa's First National Park*, edited by Marc Languy and Emmanuel de Merode, 141–151. Tielt, Belgium: Lannoo.

Languy, Marc, and Emmanuel de Merode. 2009. "A Brief Overview of Virunga National Park." In *Virunga: The Survival of Africa's First National Park*, edited by Marc Languy and Emmanuel de Merode, 20–63. Tielt, Belgium: Lannoo.

Laporte, Nadine T., Jared A. Stabach, Robert Grosch, Tiffany S. Lin, and Scott J. Goetz. 2007. "Expansion of Industrial Logging in Central Africa." *Science (Washington)* 316 (5830): 1451.

La Sorte, Frank A., and Walter Jetz. 2010. "Projected Range Contractions of Montane Biodiversity under Global Warming." *Proceedings of the Royal Society, B* 277: 3401–3410.

Laurance, William F., D. Carolina Useche, Julio Rendeiro, Margareta Kalka, Corey J. A. Bradshaw, Sean P. Sloan, Susan G. Laurance, et al. 2012. "Averting Biodiversity Collapse in Tropical Forest Protected Areas." *Nature (London)* 489 (7415): 290–294.

Laurent, Raymond F. 1952. "Reptiles et Batraciens Nouveaux du Massif du Mont Kabobo et du Plateau des Marungu." *Revue de Zoologie et de Botanique Africaines* 46: 18–34.

————. 1964. "Adaptive Modifications in Frogs of an Isolated Highland Fauna in Central Africa." *Evolution* 18 (3): 458–467.

————. 1972. "*Amphibiens.*" *Exploration du Parc National des Virunga. Deuxième Série, Bruxelles* 22: 1–125.

Lawrence, Deborah, and Karen Vandecar. 2015. "Effects of Tropical Deforestation on Climate and Agriculture." *Nature Climate Change* 5: 27–36.

Leder, Karin. 2009. "Intestinal Protozoa: *Giardia, Amebiasis, Cyclospora, Blastocystis hominis, Dientamoeba fragilis*, and *Cryptosporidium parvum*." In *Tropical Disease in Travelers*, edited by Eli Schwartz, 294–302. West Sussex, UK: Wiley-Blackwell.

Lemarchand, René. 2009. *The Dynamics of Violence in Central Africa*. Philadelphia: University of Pennsylvania Press.

Lenzen, M., D. Moran, K. Kanemoto, B. Foran, L. Lobefaro, and A. Geschke. 2012. "International Trade Drives Biodiversity Threats in Developing Nations." *Nature (London)* 486 (7401): 109–112.

Levin, Dan. 2013. "From Elephants' Mouths, an Illicit Trail to China." *New York Times*, March 1, www.nytimes.com.

Liebowitz, Daniel, and Charles Pearson. 2005. *The Last Expedition: Stanley's Mad Journey through the Congo*. New York: W. W. Norton & Company.

Lindsey, Susan L., Mary N. Green, and Cynthia L. Bennett. 1999. *The Okapi: Mysterious Animal of Congo-Zaire*. Austin: University of Texas Press.

Lippens, Léon, and Henri Wille. 1976. *Les Oiseaux du Zaïre*. Tielt, Belgium: Lannoo.

Lips, Karen. 2014. "A Tale of Two Lineages: Unexpected, Long-Term Persistence of the Amphibian-Killing Fungus in Brazil." *Molecular Ecology* 23 (4): 747–749.

Liu, Weimin, Yingying Li, Gerald H. Learn, Rebecca S. Rudicell, Joel D. Robertson, Brandon F. Keele, Jean-Bosco N. Ndjango, et al. 2010. "Origin of the Human Malaria Parasite *Plasmodium falciparum* in Gorillas." *Nature (London)* 467 (7314): 420–427.

Lloyd-Davies, Fiona. 2011. "Why Eastern DR Congo Is 'Rape Capital of the World.'" CNN, November 25, www.cnn.com.

Locey, Kenneth J., and Jay T. Lennon. 2016. "Scaling Laws Predict Global Microbial Diversity." *Proceedings of the National Academy of Sciences (USA)* 113 (21): 5970–5975.

Lomborg, Bjorn. 2016. "Impact of Current Climate Proposals." *Global Policy* 7 (1): 109–118.

Lovgren, Stefan. 2011. "Marijuana Trade Threatens African Gorilla Refuge." *National Geographic*, April 29, http://news.nationalgeographic.com.

Lutz, Holly L., Bruce D. Patterson, Julian C. Kerbis Peterhans, William T.

Stanley, Paul W. Webala, Thomas P. Gnoske, Shannon J. Hackett, et al. 2016. "Diverse Sampling of East African Haemosporidians Reveals Chiropteran Origin of Malaria Parasites in Primates and Rodents." *Molecular Phylogenetics and Evolution* 99: 7–15.

MacDonnell, John de Courcy. 1970. *King Leopold II: His Rule in Belgium and the Congo*. New York: Argosy Antiquarian.

Maisels, Fiona, Samantha Strindberg, Stephen Blake, George Wittemyer, John Hart, Elizabeth A. Williamson, Rostand Aba'a, et al. 2013. "Devastating Decline of Forest Elephants in Central Africa." *PLoS ONE* 8: e59469.

Malhi, Yadvinder, Stephen Adu-Bredu, Rebecca A. Asare, Simon L. Lewis, and Philippe Mayaux. 2013. "African Rainforests: Past, Present and Future." *Philosophical Transactions of the Royal Society, B* 368 (1625): 20120312.

Mallow, David, David Ludwig, and Goran Nilson. 2003. *True Vipers: Natural History and Toxinology of Old World Vipers*. Malabar, FL: Krieger.

Mann, Michael E., and Lee R. Kump. 2015. *Dire Predictions: Understanding Climate Change*. 2nd ed. New York: DK.

Marais, Johan. 2004. *A Complete Guide to the Snakes of Southern Africa*. 2nd ed. Cape Town: Struik Nature.

Mark, Joan. 1995. *The King of the World in the Land of the Pygmies*. Lincoln: University of Nebraska Press.

Marriage, Zoë. 2013. *Formal Peace and Informal War: Security and Development in Congo*. Routledge Explorations in Development Series. London: Routledge.

Martins, Dino J. 2013. "People, Plants and Pollinators: Uniting Conservation, Food Security, and Sustainable Agriculture in East Africa." In *Conservation Biology: Voices from the Tropics*, edited by Navjot S. Sodhi, Luke Gibson, and Peter H. Raven, 232–238. West Sussex, UK: Wiley Blackwell.

McConnell, Tristan. 2015. "The Ivory-Funded Terrorism Myth." *New York Times*, October 29, www.nytimes.com.

McKenna, Maryn. 2016. "Climate Change May Make Shellfish (and Us) Sick." *National Geographic*, April 18, www.nationalgeographic.com.

Meier, Jürg, and Julian White. 1995. *Handbook of Clinical Toxicology of Animal Venoms and Poisons*. Boca Raton: CRC.

Mendelson, Joseph R., III, Karen R. Lips, James E. Diffendorfer, Ronald W. Gagliardo, George B. Rabb, James P. Collins, Peter Daszak, et al. 2006a. "Response." *Science (Washington)* 314 (5805): 1541–1542.

Mendelson, Joseph R., III, Karen R. Lips, Ronald W. Gagliardo, George B. Rabb, James P. Collins, James E. Diffendorfer, Peter Daszak, et al. 2006b. "Confronting Amphibian Declines and Extinctions." *Science (Washington)* 313 (5783): 48.

Mentis, Michael T. 1972. "A Review of Some Life History Features of the Large Herbivores of Africa." *The Lammergeyer* (16): 1–89.

Migiro, Katy. 2016. "Malaria 'Out of Control' in Congo with Sick Children Dying at Home—Charity." Thomson Reuters Foundation News, June 9, www.news.trust.org.

Milinkovitch, Michel C., Ricardo Kanitz, Ralph Tiedemann, Washington Tapia, Fasuto Llerena, Adalgisa Caccone, James P. Gibbs, et al. 2013. "Recovery of a Nearly Extinct Galápagos Tortoise despite Minimal Genetic Variation." *Evolutionary Applications* 6 (2): 377–383.

Miller, Joseph T., David Seigler, and Brent D. Mishler. 2014. "A Phylogenetic Solution to the *Acacia* Problem." *Taxon* 63 (3): 653–658.

Milman, Oliver. 2016. "US Investors Ploughing Billions into Palm Oil, Claims Report." *The Guardian*, July 26, www.theguardian.com.

Minteer, Ben A., James P. Collins, Karen E. Love, and Robert Puschendorf. 2014. "Avoiding (Re)extinction." *Science (Washington)* 344 (6181): 260–261.

Mitani, John C. 2011. "Fearing a Planet without Apes." *New York Times*, August 20, www.nytimes.com.

Mitman, Gregg. 1993. "Cinematic Nature: Hollywood Technology, Popular Culture, and the American Museum of Natural History." *Isis* 84 (4): 637–661.

Moffett, Mark W. 2010. *Adventures among Ants: A Global Safari with a Cast of Trillions.* Los Angeles: University of California Press.

Moore, Robin. 2014. *In Search of Lost Frogs: The Quest to Find the World's Rarest Amphibians.* Buffalo, New York: Firefly Books.

Mora, Camilo, Derek P. Tittensor, Sina Adl, Alastair G. B. Simpson, and Boris Worm. 2011. "How Many Species Are There on Earth and in the Ocean?" *PLoS Biology* 9: e1001127.

Mowat, Farley. 1987. *Woman in the Mists: The Story of Dian Fossey and the Mountain Gorillas of Africa.* New York: Warner Books.

Nest, Michael. 2011. *Coltan.* Cambridge: Polity.

Newbold, Tim, Lawrence N. Hudson, Andrew P. Arnell, Sara Contu, Adriana De Palma, Simon Ferrier, Samantha L. L. Hill, et al. 2016. "Has Land Use Pushed Terrestrial Biodiversity beyond the Planetary Boundary? A Global Assessment." *Science (Washington)* 353 (6296): 288–291.

New York Times. 2013. "Hope for a Malaria Vaccine" (Editorial). October 13, www.nytimes.com.

New York Times. 2017. "China Joins the Fight to Save Elephants" (Editorial). January 3, www.nytimes.com.

Nielsen, John. 2008. "'Mother Lode' of Gorillas Found in Congo Forests." *Morning Edition*, NPR, August 5, www.npr.org.

Nixon, Ron. 2015. "Obama Administration Plans to Aggressively Target Wildlife Trafficking." *New York Times*, February 11, www.nytimes.com.

Nolan, James. 2015. "All the Reasons Why Zoos Should Be Banned." *Vice*, June 24, www.vice.com.

Novaresio, Paolo. 2006. *Great Rivers of the World*. New York: Barnes & Noble.

Oldstone, Michael B. A. 2010. *Viruses, Plagues and History*. Oxford: Oxford University Press.

Omari, Ilambu, John A. Hart, Thomas M. Butynski, N. R. Birhashirwa, Agenonga Upoki, Yuma M'Keyo, Faustin Bengana, Mugunda Bashonga, and Norbert Bagurubumwe. 1999. "The Itombwe Massif, Democratic Republic of Congo: Biological Surveys and Conservation, with an Emphasis on Grauer's Gorilla and Birds Endemic to the Albertine Rift." *Oryx* 33: 301–322.

Packard, Randall M. 2007. *The Making of a Tropical Disease: A Short History of Malaria*. Baltimore: Johns Hopkins University Press.

Patz, Jonathan A., Thaddeus K. Graczyk, Nina Geller, and Amy Y. Vittor. 2000. "Effects of Environmental Change on Emerging Parasitic Diseases." *International Journal for Parasitology* 30 (12–13): 1395–1405.

Pearson, Helen. 2003. "West Nile Virus May Have Felled Alexander the Great." *Nature, News* (blog), November 28, www.nature.com/news.

Peh, Kelvin S.-H. 2013. "Governance and Conservation in the Tropical Developing World." In *Conservation Biology: Voices from the Tropics*, edited by Navjot S. Sodhi, Luke Gibson, and Peter H. Raven, 216–225. West Sussex, UK: Wiley Blackwell.

Penner, Johannes, Gilbert B. Adum, Matthew T. McElroy, Thomas Doherty-Bone, Mareike Hirschfeld, Laura Sandberger, Ché Weldon, et al. 2013. "West Africa — A Safe Haven for Frogs? A Sub-Continental Assessment of the Chytrid Fungus (*Batrachochytrium dendrobatidis*)." *PLoS ONE* 8: e56236.

Pianka, Eric R., and Laurie J. Vitt. 2003. *Lizards: Windows to the Evolution of Diversity*. Berkeley: University of California Press.

Plumptre, Andrew J., Tim R. B. Davenport, Mathias Behangana, Robert Kityo, Gerald Eilu, Paul Ssegawa, Corneille Ewango, et al. 2007. "The Biodiversity of the Albertine Rift." *Biological Conservation* 134 (2): 178–194.

Plumptre, Andrew J., Stuart Nixon, Robert Critchlow, Ghislain Vieilledent, Radar Nishuli, Andrew Kirby, Elizabeth A. Williamson, et al. 2015. "Status of Grauer's Gorilla and Chimpanzees in Eastern Democratic Republic of the Congo: Historical and Current Distribution and Abundance." Unpublished report to Arcus Foundation, USAID, and US Fish and Wildlife Service.

Poorter, Lourens, Frans Bongers, T. Mitchell Aide, Angélica M. Almeyda

Zambrano, Patricia Balvanera, Justin M. Becknell, Vanessa Boukili, et al. 2016. "Biomass Resilience of Neotropical Secondary Forests." *Nature (London)* 530 (7589): 211–214.

Portillo, Frank, and Eli Greenbaum. 2014. "A New Species of the *Leptopelis modestus* Complex (Anura: Arthroleptidae) from the Albertine Rift of Central Africa." *Journal of Herpetology* 48 (3): 394–406.

Potapov, Peter V., Svetlana A. Turubanova, Matthew C. Hansen, Bernard Adusei, Mark Broich, Alice Alstatt, Landing Mane, et al. 2012. "Quantifying Forest Cover Loss in Democratic Republic of the Congo, 2000–2010, with Landsat ETM+ Data." *Remote Sensing of Environment* 122: 106–116.

Pough, F. Harvey, Robin A. Andrews, Martha L. Crump, Alan H. Savitzky, Kentwood D. Wells, and Matthew C. Brandley. 2016. *Herpetology*. 4th ed. Sunderland, MA: Sinauer Associates.

Pounds, J. Alan, Ana C. Carnaval, Robert Puschendorf, Célio F. B. Haddad, and Karen L. Masters. 2006. "Responding to Amphibian Loss." *Science (Washington)* 314 (5805): 1541.

Prigogine, Alexandre. 1973. "The Migratory Movements of the Pygmy Kingfisher *Ceyx picta natalensis* in the Republic of Zaire." *Bulletin of the British Ornithological Club* 93 (2): 82–89.

Prunier, Gérard. 2009. *Africa's World War: Congo, the Rwandan Genocide, and the Making of a Continental Catastrophe*. New York: Oxford University Press.

Quinn, Stephen C. 2006. *Windows on Nature: The Great Habitat Dioramas of the American Museum of Natural History*. New York: Harry N. Abrams.

Rabb, George B., and Mary S. Rabb. 1963. "On the Behavior and Breeding Biology of the African Pipid Frog *Hymenochirus boettgeri*." *Zeitschrift für Tierpsychologie* 20: 215–241.

Revkin, Andrew C. 2016. "The Future of Zoos." *New York Times*, June 21, www.nytimes.com.

Rice, Edward. 2001. *Captain Sir Richard Francis Burton: A Biography*. Cambridge, MA: Da Capo.

Roberts, E. M., N. J. Stevens, P. M. O'Connor, P. H. G. M. Dirks, M. D. Gottfried, W. C. Clyde, R. A. Armstrong, et al. 2012. "Initiation of the Western Branch of the East African Rift Coeval with the Eastern Branch." *Nature Geoscience* 5: 289–294.

Rocha, L. A., A. Aleixo, G. Allen, F. Almeda, C. C. Baldwin, M. V. L. Barclay, J. M. Bates, et al. 2014. "Specimen Collection: An Essential Tool." *Science (Washington)* 344 (6186): 814–815.

Rodriguez, D., C. G. Becker, N. C. Pupin, C. F. B. Haddad, and K. R. Zamudio.

2014. "Long-Term Endemism of Two Highly Divergent Lineages of the Amphibian-Killing Fungus in the Atlantic Forest of Brazil." *Molecular Ecology* 23 (4): 774–787.

Roelants, Kim, and Franky Bossuyt. 2005. "Archaeobatrachian Paraphyly and Pangaean Diversification of Crown-Group Frogs." *Systematic Biology* 54 (1): 111–126.

Roelke, Corey E., Eli Greenbaum, Chifundera Kusamba, Mwenebatu M. Aristote, and Eric N. Smith. 2011. "Systematics and Conservation Status of Two Distinct Albertine Rift Treefrogs, *Leptopelis karissimbensis* and *Leptopelis kivuensis* (Anura: Arthroleptidae)." *Journal of Herpetology* 45 (3): 343–351.

Roosevelt, Theodore. 1987. *African Game Trails*. Camden, SC: Briar Patch.

Root, Alan. 1991. *Heart of Brightness*. Survival Anglia Ltd. and National Geographic Society. YouTube video, posted September 24, https://www.youtube.com.

Rorison, Sean. 2008. *Congo: Democratic Republic/Republic: The Bradt Travel Guide*. Guilford, Connecticut: Globe Pequot Press.

Saad, Lydia, and Jeffrey M. Jones. 2016. "U.S. Concern about Global Warming at Eight-Year High." Gallup, March 16, www.gallup.com.

Schaller, George B. 1963. *The Mountain Gorilla: Ecology and Behavior*. Chicago: University of Chicago Press.

———. 1964. *The Year of the Gorilla*. Chicago: University of Chicago Press.

———. 2007. *A Naturalist and Other Beasts: Tales from a Life in the Field*. San Francisco: Sierra Club Books.

Schwarz, Ernst. 1927. "Paul Matschie." *Journal of Mammalogy* 8 (4): 292–295.

Seimon, Tracie, Samuel Ayebare, Robert Sekisambu, Emmanuel Muhindo, Guillain Mitamba, Eli Greenbaum, Michele Menegon, et al. 2015. "Assessing the Threat of Amphibian Chytrid Fungus in the Albertine Rift: Past, Present and Future." *PLoS ONE* 10: e0145841.

Shah, Sonia. 2010. *The Fever: How Malaria Has Ruled Humankind for 500,000 Years*. New York: Sarah Crichton Books.

Sifferlin, Alexandra. 2014. "Bill Gates Thinks Malaria Can Be Eradicated in His Lifetime." *Time*, November 3, www.time.com.

———. 2016. "What You Need to Know about Zika: How to Beat the Virus— and the Mosquitoes That Carry It." *Time* 187 (18): 32–38.

Silbergeld, E. K., J. B. Sacci Jr., and A. F. Azad. 2000. "Mercury Exposure and Murine Response to *Plasmodium yoelii* Infection and Immunization." *Immunopharmacology and Immunotoxicology* 22 (4): 685–695.

Sinclair, Ian, and Peter Ryan. 2003. *A Comprehensive Illustrated Field Guide: Birds of Africa South of the Sahara*. Cape Town: Struik.

Skerratt, Lee F., Lee Berger, Richard Speare, Scott Cashins, Keith R. McDonald, Andrea D. Phillott, Harry B. Hines, et al. 2007. "Spread of Chytridiomycosis Has Caused the Rapid Global Decline and Extinction of Frogs." *EcoHealth* 4: 125–134.

Smith, Rebecca K., and William J. Sutherland. 2014. *Amphibian Conservation: Evidence for the Effects of Interventions.* Synopses of Conservation Evidence, Vol. 4. Exeter, UK: Pelagic.

Sodhi, Navjot S., Barry W. Brook, and Corey J. A. Bradshaw. 2007. *Tropical Conservation Biology.* Malden, MA: Blackwell.

Spawls, Stephen, Kim Howell, Robert Drewes, and James Ashe. 2004. *A Field Guide to the Reptiles of East Africa: Kenya, Tanzania, Uganda, Rwanda and Burundi.* London: A & C Black.

Stauffer, Donald J., and Thomas B. Smith. 2004. "Breeding and Nest Site Characteristics of the Black-Casqued Hornbill *Ceratogymna atrata* and White-Thighed Hornbill *Ceratogymna cylindricus* in South-Central Cameroon." *Ostrich* 75 (3): 79–88.

Stearns, Jason K. 2011. *Dancing in the Glory of Monsters: The Collapse of the Congo and the Great War of Africa.* New York: PublicAffairs.

Steinhauer-Burkart, Bernd, Michael Mühlenberg, and Jolanta Slowik. 1995. "Kahuzi-Biéga National Park." Privately published pamphlet from the IZCN/GTZ Project "Integrated Nature Conservation in East-Zaire."

Streib, Lauren. 2011. "The Worst Places to Be a Woman." *Newsweek* 158: 32–33.

Sukumar, Raman. 2003. *The Living Elephants: Evolutionary Ecology, Behavior, and Conservation.* Oxford: Oxford University Press.

Tapley, Benjamin, Kay S. Bradfield, Christopher Michaels, and Mike Bungard. 2015. "Amphibians and Conservation Breeding Programmes: Do All Threatened Amphibians Belong on the Ark?" *Biodiversity and Conservation* 24 (11): 2625–2646.

Thalmann, Olaf, Daniel Wegmann, Marie Spitzner, Mimi Arandjelovic, Katerina Guschanski, Christoph Leuenberger, Richard A. Bergl, et al. 2011. "Historical Sampling Reveals Dramatic Demographic Changes in Western Gorilla Populations." *BMC Evolutionary Biology* 11: 85.

Tilbury, Colin. 2010. *Chameleons of Africa: An Atlas Including the Chameleons of Europe, the Middle East and Asia.* Frankfurt am Main: Edition Chimaira.

Tobin, Mary. 2004. *Collective Knowledge: The Value of Natural History Collections.* Washington: Natural Sciences Collections Alliance.

Tuckey, James K. 2006. *Narrative of an Expedition to Explore the River Zaire, Usually Called the Congo, in South Africa.* East Sussex, UK: Rediscovery Books.

Tullis, Tracy. 2015. "The Bronx Zoo's Loneliest Elephant." *New York Times*, June 26, www.nytimes.com.

Turnbull, Colin M. 1968. *The Forest People*. New York: Simon & Schuster.

Tuttle, Russell H. 2003. "An Introductory Perspective: Gorillas — How Important, How Many, How Long?" In *Gorilla Biology: A Multidisciplinary Perspective*, edited by Andrea B. Taylor and Michelle L. Goldsmith, 11–14. Cambridge: Cambridge University Press.

Twain, Mark. 1970. *King Leopold's Soliloquy*. New York: International.

Umutesi, Marie B. 2004. *Surviving the Slaughter: The Ordeal of a Rwandan Refugee in Zaire*. Madison: University of Wisconsin Press.

Vaidyanathan, Gayathri. 2011. "Tissues in 'Frozen Zoo' Hold Hope for Wildlife." *New York Times*, September 19, www.nytimes.com.

Vande weghe, Jean P. 2004. *Forests of Central Africa: Nature and Man*. Pretoria: Protea Book House.

Van Reybrouck, David. 2014. *Congo: The Epic History of a People*. New York: Ecco.

Van Schuylenbergh, Patricia. 2009. "Albert National Park: The Birth of Africa's First National Park (1925–1960)." In *Virunga: The Survival of Africa's First National Park*, edited by Marc Languy and Emmanuel de Merode, 64–73. Tielt, Belgium: Lannoo.

Vansina, Jan. 1990. *Paths in the Rainforests: Toward a History of Political Tradition in Equatorial Africa*. Madison: University of Wisconsin Press.

Verschuren, Jacques. 2009. "Life in Albert National Park (1925–1960)." In *Virunga: The Survival of Africa's First National Park*, edited by Marc Languy and Emmanuel de Merode, 74–83. Tielt, Belgium: Lannoo.

Vijay, Varsha, Stuart L. Pimm, Clinton N. Jenkins, and Sharon J. Smith. 2016. "The Impacts of Oil Palm on Recent Deforestation and Biodiversity Loss." *PLoS ONE* 11: e0159668.

Vittor, Amy Y., Robert H. Gilman, James Tielsch, Gregory Glass, Tim Shields, Wagner S. Lozano, Viviana Pinedo-Cancino, et al. 2006. "The Effect of Deforestation on the Human-Biting Rate of *Anopheles darlingi*, the Primary Vector of Falciparum Malaria in the Peruvian Amazon." *American Journal of Tropical Medicine and Hygiene* 74 (1): 3–11.

Wake, David B., and Vance T. Vredenburg. 2008. "Are We in the Midst of the Sixth Mass Extinction? A View from the World of Amphibians." *Proceedings of the National Academy of Sciences (USA)* 105 (Suppl. 1): 11466–11473.

Walsh, Peter D. 2006. "Ebola and Commercial Hunting: Dim Prospects for African Apes." In *Emerging Threats to Tropical Forests*, edited by William F. Laurance and Carlos A. Peres, 175–197. Chicago: University of Chicago Press.

Webb, Steve, dir. 2009. *The Real Story: The Bourne Identity*. Blink Films for Smithsonian Channel HD.

Weisman, Alan. 2013. *Countdown: Our Last, Best Hope for a Future on Earth?* New York: Back Bay Books.

White, Luise. 2000. *Speaking with Vampires: Rumor and History in Colonial Africa*. Berkeley: University of California Press.

Whittaker, Kellie, and Vance Vredenburg. 2011. "An Overview of Chytridiomycosis." Amphibiaweb, May 17, www.amphibiaweb.org.

Williams, Susan. 2016. *Spies in the Congo: America's Atomic Mission in World War II*. New York: PublicAffairs.

Wilson, Edward O. 2014. *The Meaning of Human Existence*. New York: Liveright.

———. 2016. *Half-Earth*. New York: Liveright.

Wilson, Robert A., ed. 1999. *Species: New Interdisciplinary Essays*. Cambridge, MA: MIT Press.

Wollaston, Alexander F. R. 1908. *From Ruwenzori to the Congo: A Naturalist's Journey across Africa*. New York: E. P. Dutton and Company.

Wrong, Michela. 2002. *In the Footsteps of Mr. Kurtz: Living on the Brink of Disaster in Mobutu's Congo*. New York: Perennial.

Wüster, Wolfgang, Steven Crookes, Ivan Ineich, Youssouph Mané, Catharine E. Pook, Jean-François Trape, and Donald G. Broadley. 2007. "The Phylogeny of Cobras Inferred from Mitochondrial DNA Sequences: Evolution of Venom Spitting and the Phylogeography of the African Spitting Cobras (Serpentes: Elapidae: *Naja nigricollis* Complex)." *Molecular Phylogenetics and Evolution* 45 (2): 437–453.

Yang, Qian, Xuanxuan Zhou, Meng Zhang, Linlin Bi, Shan Miao, Wei Cao, Yanhua Xie, et al. 2015. "Angel of Human Health: Current Research Updates in Toad Medicine." *American Journal of Translational Research* 7 (1): 1–14.

Zimmermann, A., M. Hatchwell, L. A. Dickie, and C. West. 2007. *Zoos in the 21st Century: Catalysts for Conservation?* Cambridge: Cambridge University Press.

INDEX

Note: Page numbers in *italics* indicate images; page numbers with "n" indicate endnotes.